CLYMER®

YAMAHA

YTM/YFM200 & YTM225 • 1983-1986

The world's finest publisher of mechanical how-to manuals

PRIMEDIA
Business Directories & Books

P.O. Box 12901, Overland Park, Kansas 66282-2901

Copyright ©1987 PRIMEDIA Business Magazines & Media Inc.

FIRST EDITION
First Printing August, 1987
Second Printing June, 1989
Third Printing January, 1991
Fourth Printing July, 1992
Fifth Printing February, 1994
Sixth Printing November, 1995
Seventh Printing December, 1996
Eighth Printing December, 1997
Ninth Printing August, 1999
Tenth Printing January, 2001
Eleventh Printing September, 2002

Printed in U.S.A.

CLYMER and colophon are registered trademarks of PRIMEDIA Business Magazines & Media Inc.

ISBN: 0-89287-438-4

TECHNICAL PHOTOGRAPHY: Ron Wright, with assistance by Action Fours, Santa Ana, California.

TECHNICAL ILLUSTRATION: Steve Amos.

TOOLS AND EQUIPMENT: K&L Supply Co.

COVER: Mark Clifford Photography, Los Angeles, California.

CONTENTS

QUICK REFERENCE DATA

MAINTENANCE SCHEDULE*

Every month or as needed	• Lubricate and adjust drive chain • Clean and re-oil air filter
Every 3 months or as needed	• Check all brake components for wear or damage • Adjust brakes
Every 6 months	• Check and adjust cam chain tension[1] • Check and adjust valve clearance • Check and adjust decompression cable free play[2] • Change engine oil and replace filter • Clean oil strainer • Change final drive oil • Check battery electrolyte level and charge • Check wheel and tire condition • Check cables for fraying and lubricate • Clean fuel tank and fuel filter • Check light operation • Check tightness of all chassis and engine fasteners • Grease throttle lever • Grease brake lever • Grease brake camshaft • Decarbonize exhast system and spark arrester • Check exhaust system for leakage; repair as necessary • Lubricate knuckle shaft[3]
Every year	• Clean carburetor • Change fork oil • Repack wheel bearings
Every 2 years	• Repack steering bearings[4]

* This maintenance schedule should be considered as a guide to general maintenance and lubrication intervals. Harder than normal use and exposure to mud, water, sand, high humidity, etc. will naturally dictate more frequent attention to most maintenance items.

1. All 1985-on models (except YFM200N) are equipped with an automatic cam chain adjuster; periodic adjustment is not required.

2. YTM200K, L and N models only.

3. YFM200 models only.

4. YTM200 and YTM225 models only.

RECOMMENDED LUBRICANTS

Engine oil	
Temperatures 40° and up	SAE 20W/40 SE/SF
Temperatures below 40°	SAE 10W/30 SE/SF
Battery refilling	Distilled water
Fork oil*	10 wt or equivalent
Final drive gear oil	SAE 80API GL-4 hypoid gear oil
Cables and pivot points	Yamaha chain and cable lube or SAE 10W/30 motor oil
Air filter	Special air filter oil
Grease	Lithium base grease

* YTM200 and YTM225 models only.

TIRE INFLATION PRESSURE

Tire size	Air pressure
YTM200 and YTM225 models	
22×11-8	
Recommended	0.15 kg/cm² (2.2 psi)
Maximum	0.7 kg/cm² (10 psi)
Minimum	0.12 kg/cm² (1.8 psi)
25×12-9	
Recommended	0.15 kg/cm² (2.2 psi)
Maximum	0.7 kg/cm² (10 psi)
Minimum	0.12 kg/cm² (1.8 psi)
YFM200 models	
YFM200N	
25×12-9 (front)	
and 22×11-8 (rear)	
Recommended	0.15 kg/cm² (2.2 psi)
Maximum	0.7 kg/cm² (10 psi)
Minimum	0.12 kg/cm² (1.8 psi)
YFM200DXS	
22×8-10 (front)	
and 22×11-8 (rear)	
Recommended	0.20 kg/cm² (2.8 psi)
Minimum	0.17 kg/cm² (2.4 psi)

TUNE-UP SPECIFICATIONS

Valve clearances	
Intake	0.05-0.09 mm (0.002-0.004 in.)
Exhaust	0.11-0.15 mm (0.0043-0.006 in.)
Compression pressure	
Standard	9 kg/cm² (128 psi)
Minimum	8 kg/cm² (114 psi)
Maximum	10 kg/cm² (142 psi)
Spark plug	
Type	NGK D7EA
	ND X22ES-U
Gap	0.6-0.7 mm (0.024-0.028 in.)
Torque specification	20 N•m (14 ft.-lb.)
Ignition timing	Fixed; see text for details
Idle speed	1,400 ±50 rpm
Cylinder head torque	
Bolt (M6)	7 (5.1)
Flange bolt (M8)	22 (16)
Bolt (M8)	20 (14)

ENGINE REFILL CAPACITIES

Engine oil	
Oil change	1,500 cc (1.6 qt.)
Engine overhaul	1,800 cc (1.9 qt.)

GENERAL TORQUE SPECIFICATIONS

Item	ft.-lb.	N·m
Bolt		
6 mm	4.5	6
8 mm	11	15
10 mm	22	30
12 mm	40	55
14 mm	61	85
16 mm	94	130
Nut		
10 mm	4.5	6
12 mm	11	15
14 mm	22	30
17 mm	40	55
19 mm	61	85
22 mm	94	130

BRAKE SPECIFICATIONS

Front drum brake	
Drum inside diameter	110 mm (4.33 in.)
Wear limit	111 mm (4.37 in.)
Lining thickness	4.0 mm (0.16 in.)
Wear limit	2.0 mm (0.08 in.)
Brake shoe spring free length	34.5 mm (1.36 in.)
Rear disc brake	
Brake disc	
Outside diameter	224 mm (8.82 in.)
Thickness	4 mm (0.16 in.)
Wear limit	3.0 mm (0.12 in.)
Brake pad thickness	8.0 mm (0.31 in.)
Wear limit	
YTM225DRS	2.0 mm (0.079 in.)
All other models	1.5 mm (0.06 in.)

CARBURETOR FUEL AND FLOAT LEVELS

Fuel level	
YFM200DXS	2.5-3.5 mm (0.10-0.14 in.)
All other models	2.0-3.0 mm (0.08-0.12 in.)
Float height	21.5 ±0.5 mm (0.85 ±0.02 in.)

STEERING SPECIFICATIONS

Toe-in	
YFM200N	0-5 mm (0-0.2 in.)
YFM200DXS	0-10 mm (0-0.4 in.)

TIGHTENING TORQUES

Item	N·m	ft.-lb.
Cylinder head		
Bolt (M6)	7	5.1
Flange bolt (M8)	22	16
Bolt (M8)	20	14
Oil galley bolt	7	5.1
Cam sprocket cover	7	5.1
Valve tappet cover	10	7.2
Rocker arm shaft stopper bolt	8	5.8
Cylinder bolt	10	7.2
Balancer shaft nut	50	36
Recoil starter pulley bolt	50	36
Valve adjuster lock nut	14	10
Sprocket cam bolt	60	43
Oil pump screw	7	5.1
Engine drain plug	43	31
Oil filter cover	10	7.2
Oil filter cover drain bolt	10	7.2
Exhaust pipe flange	10	7.2
Crankcase screws	7	5.1
Crankcase spacer		
Left-hand	7	5.1
Right-hand	7	5.1
Bearing retainer		
Left-hand	7	5.1
Right-hand	10	7.2
Shift cam segment screw	12	8.7

BATTERY STATE OF CHARGE

Specific gravity	State of charge
1.110-1.130	Discharged
1.140-1.160	Almost discharged
1.170-1.190	One-quarter charged
1.200-1.220	One-half charged
1.230-1.250	Three-quarters charged
1.260-1.280	Fully charged

ELECTRIC STARTER SPECIFICATIONS

Armature coil resistance	0.023 ohms*
Brush length	10.5 mm (0.41 in.)
Wear limit	5.0 mm (0.20 in.)
Commutator diameter	23 mm (0.901 in.)
Wear limit	22 mm (0.866 in.)
Mica undercut	
YTM200EK, EL	1.8 mm (0.071 in.)
All other models	0.55 mm (0.022 in.)
Cut-off relay resistance	75 ohms ±10% *
Starter Relay resistance	3.43 ohms*

* @ 68° F (20° C).

CLYMER®

YAMAHA
YTM/YFM200 & YTM225 • 1983-1986

INTRODUCTION

This detailed, comprehensive manual covers all 1983-1986 Yamaha YTM and YFM200 and 225. The expert text gives complete information on maintenance, tune-up, repair and overhaul. Hundreds of photos and drawings guide you through every step. The book includes all you need to know to keep your Yamaha running right.

Where repairs are practical for the owner/mechanic, complete procedures are given. Equally important, difficult jobs are pointed out. Such operations are usually more economically performed by a dealer or independent garage.

A shop manual is a reference. You want to be able to find information fast. As in all Clymer books, this one is designed with this in mind. All chapters are thumb tabbed. Important items are extensively indexed at the rear of the book. All the most frequently used specifications and capacities are summarized on the *Quick Reference Data* pages at the front of the book.

Keep the book handy in your tool box and take it with you on long trips. It will help you to better understand your Yamaha, lower repair and maintenance costs and generally improve your satisfaction with your bike.

CHAPTER ONE

GENERAL INFORMATION

Troubleshooting, tune-up, maintenance and repair are not difficult, if you know what tools and equipment to use and what to do. Anyone of average intelligence and with some mechanical ability can perform most of the procedures in this manual. This manual is written simply and clearly enough for owners who have never worked on a motorcycle, but is complete enough for use by experienced mechanics.

Some of the procedures require the use of special tools. Using an inferior substitute for a special tool is not recommended as it can be dangerous to you and may damage the part. Where possible, we have devised suitable special tools that can be fabricated in your garage or by a machinist or purchased at motorcycle or tool stores.

Metric and U.S. standards are used throughout this book. Metric to U.S. conversion is given in **Table 1**.

MANUAL ORGANIZATION

This chapter provides general information and discusses equipment and tools useful for repair, maintenance and troubleshooting.

Chapter Two provides methods and suggestions for quick and accurate diagnosis and repair of problems. Troubleshooting procedures discuss typical symptoms and logical methods to pinpoint the trouble.

Chapter Three explains all periodic lubrication and routine maintenance necessary to keep your Yamaha operating well. Chapter Three also includes recommended tune-up procedures, eliminating the need to constantly consult other chapters on the various assemblies.

Subsequent chapters describe specific systems such as the engine, clutch, transmission, fuel, exhaust, suspension, steering and brakes. Each chapter provides disassembly, repair, and assembly procedures in simple step-by-step form. If a repair is impractical for a home mechanic, it is so indicated. It is usually faster and less expensive to take such repairs to a dealer or competent repair shop. Specifications concerning a particular system are included at the end of the appropriate chapter.

NOTES, CAUTIONS AND WARNINGS

The terms NOTE, CAUTION and WARNING have specific meanings in this manual. A NOTE provides additional information to make a step or procedure easier or clearer. Disregarding a NOTE could cause inconvenience, but would not cause damage or personal injury.

A CAUTION emphasizes areas where equipment damage could occur. Disregarding a CAUTION could cause permanent mechanical damage; however, personal injury is unlikely.

A WARNING emphasizes areas where personal injury or even death could result from negligence. Mechanical damage may also occur. WARNINGS *are to be taken seriously.* In some cases, serious injury and death have resulted from disregarding similar warnings.

SAFETY FIRST

Professional mechanics can work for years and never sustain a serious injury. If you observe a few rules of common sense and safety, you can enjoy many safe hours servicing your own vehicle. If you ignore these rules you can hurt yourself or damage the equipment.

1. Never use gasoline as a cleaning solvent.
2. Never smoke or use a torch in the vicinity of flammable liquids, such as cleaning solvent, in open containers.
3. If welding or brazing is required on the machine, remove the fuel tank and rear shock to a safe distance, at least 50 feet away.
4. Use the proper sized wrenches to avoid damage to nuts and injury to yourself.
5. When loosening a tight or stuck nut, be guided by what would happen if the wrench should slip. Be careful; protect yourself accordingly.
6. When replacing a fastener, make sure to use one with the same measurements and strength as the old one. Incorrect or mismatched fasteners can result in damage to the vehicle and possible personal injury. Beware of fastener kits that are filled with cheap and poorly made nuts, bolts, washers and cotter pins. Refer to *Fasteners* in this chapter for additional information.
7. Keep all hand and power tools in good condition. Wipe grease and oil from tools after using them. They are difficult to hold and can cause injury. Replace or repair worn or damaged tools.
8. Keep your work area clean and uncluttered.
9. Wear safety goggles during all operations involving drilling, grinding, the use of a cold chisel or anytime you feel unsure about the safety of your eyes. Safety goggles should also be worn anytime compressed air is used to clean a part.
10. Keep an approved fire extinguisher nearby. Be sure it is rated for gasoline (Class B) and electrical (Class C) fires.
11. When drying bearings or other rotating parts with compressed air, never allow the air jet to rotate the bearing or part; the air jet is capable of rotating them at speeds far in excess of those for which they were designed. The bearing or rotating part is very likely to disintegrate and cause serious injury and damage.

SERVICE HINTS

Most of the service procedures covered are straightforward and can be performed by anyone reasonably handy with tools. It is suggested, however, that you consider your own capabilities carefully before attempting any operation involving major disassembly of the engine or transmission.

1. "Front," as used in this manual, refers to the front of the vehicle; the front of any component is the end closest to the front of the vehicle. The "left-" and "right-hand" sides refer to the position of the parts as viewed by a rider sitting on the seat facing forward. For example, the throttle control is on the right-hand side. These rules are simple, but confusion can cause a major inconvenience during service.
2. Whenever servicing the engine or transmission, or when removing a suspension component, the vehicle should be secured in a safe manner. Block front and rear wheels if they remain on the ground. A small hydraulic jack and a block of wood can be used to raise the chassis. If the transmission is not going to be worked on and the rear drive unit or drive chain is attached to the the rear wheel, shift the transmission into first gear.
3. If so equipped, disconnect the negative battery cable when working on or near the electrical, clutch or starter systems and before disconnecting any wires. On most batteries, the negative terminal will be marked with a minus (-) sign and the positive terminal with a plus (+) sign.
4. When disassembling a part or assembly, it is a good practice to tag the parts for location and mark all parts which mate together. Small parts, such as bolts, can be identified by placing them in plastic sandwich bags. Seal the bags and label them with masking tape and a marking pen. When reassembly will take place immediately, an accepted practice is to place nuts and bolts in a cupcake tin or egg carton in the order of disassembly.
5. Finished surfaces should be protected from physical damage or corrosion. Keep gasoline off painted surfaces.
6. Use penetrating oil on frozen or tight bolts, then strike the bolt head a few times with a hammer and punch (use a screwdriver on screws). Avoid the use of heat where possible, as it can warp, melt or affect the temper of parts. Heat also ruins finishes, especially paint and plastics.
7. Keep flames and sparks away from a charging battery or flammable fluids and do not smoke in the area. It is a good idea to have a fire extinguisher handy in the work area. Remember that many gas

appliances in home garages (water heater, clothes drier, etc.) have pilot lights.

8. No parts removed or installed (other than bushings and bearings) in the procedures given in this manual should require unusual force during disassembly or assembly. If a part is difficult to remove or install, find out why before proceeding.

9. Cover all openings after removing parts or components to prevent dirt, small tools, etc. from falling in.

10. Read each procedure *completely* while looking at the actual parts before starting a job. Make sure you *thoroughly* understand what is to be done and then carefully follow the procedure, step by step.

11. Recommendations are occasionally made to refer service or maintenance to a Yamaha dealer or a specialist in a particular field. In these cases, the work will be done more quickly and economically than if you performed the job yourself.

12. In procedural steps, the term "replace" means to discard a defective part and replace it with a new or exchange unit. "Overhaul" means to remove, disassemble, inspect, measure, repair or replace defective parts, reassemble and install major systems or parts.

13. Some operations require the use of a hydraulic press. It would be wiser to have these operations performed by a shop equipped for such work, rather than to try to do the job yourself with makeshift equipment that may damage your machine.

14. Repairs go much faster and easier if your vehicle is clean before you begin work. There are many special cleaners on the market, like Bel-Ray Degreaser, for washing the engine and related parts.

Just follow the manufacturer's directions on the container for the best results. Then rinse it away with a heavy spray of water from a garden hose. Clean all oily or greasy parts with cleaning solvent as you remove them.

WARNING
Never use gasoline as a cleaning agent. It presents an extreme fire hazard. Be sure to work in a well-ventilated area when using cleaning solvent. Keep a fire extinguisher, rated for gasoline fires, handy in any case.

15. Much of the labor charged for by dealers is to remove, disassemble, assemble, and reinstall other parts in order to reach the defective part. It is often possible to perform the preliminary operations yourself and then take the defective unit to the dealer for repair at considerable savings.

16. If special tools are required, make arrangements to get them before you start. It is frustrating and time-consuming to get partly into a job and then be unable to complete it.

17. Make diagrams (or take a Polaroid picture) wherever similar-appearing parts are found. For instance, crankcase bolts are often not the same length. You may think you can remember where everything came from—but mistakes are costly. There is also the possibility that you may be sidetracked and not return to work for days or even weeks—in which time the carefully laid out parts may have become disturbed.

18. When assembling parts, be sure all shims and washers are replaced exactly as they came out.

19. Whenever a rotating part butts against a stationary part, look for a shim or washer. Use new gaskets if there is any doubt about the condition of the old ones.

20. If it is necessary to make a gasket, and you do not have a suitable old gasket to use as a guide, apply engine oil to the gasket surface of the part. Then place the part on the new gasket material and press the part slightly. The oil will leave a very accurate outline on the gasket material that can be cut around.

21. Heavy grease can be used to hold small parts in place if they tend to fall out during assembly. However, keep grease and oil away from electrical and brake components.

22. A carburetor is best cleaned by disassembling it and soaking the parts in a commercial carburetor cleaner. Never soak gaskets and rubber parts in these cleaners. Never use wire to clean out jets and air passages, as they are easily damaged. Use compressed air to blow out the carburetor only if the float has been removed first.

23. Take your time and do the job right. Do not forget that a newly rebuilt engine must be broken in just like a new one.

TORQUE SPECIFICATIONS

Torque specifications throughout this manual are given in Newton-meters (N•m) and foot-pounds (ft.-lb.).

Table 2 lists general torque specifications for nuts and bolts that are not listed in their respective chapters. To use the table, first determine the size of the nut or bolt. **Figure 1** and **Figure 2** show how this is done.

FASTENERS

The material and design of the various fasteners used on your Yamaha are not arrived at by chance or accident. Fastener design determines the type of tool required to work the fastener. Fastener material is carefully selected to decrease the possibility of physical failure.

Threads

Nuts, bolts and screws are manufactured in a wide range of thread patterns. To join a nut and bolt, the diameter of the bolt and the diameter of the hole in the nut and the thread pitch must be the same.

The best way to tell if the threads on 2 fasteners are matched is to turn the nut on the bolt (or the bolt into the threaded hole in a piece of equipment) with fingers only. Be sure both pieces are clean. If much force is required, check the thread condition on each fastener. If the thread condition is good but the fasteners jam, the threads are not compatible. A thread pitch gauge can also be used to determine thread size.

Yamaha vehicles covered in this manual are manufactured with metric fasteners. Metric threads are designated by the letter M, followed by the thread size in millimeters and the thread pitch (number of threads per millimeter of bolt length). For example, M8 - 1.25 means the bolt shaft diameter (not the hex size) is 8mm, with 1.25 threads per millimeter of shaft length.

Most threads are cut so that the fastener must be turned clockwise to tighten it. These are called right-hand threads. Some fasteners have left-hand threads; they must be turned counterclockwise to be tightened. Left-hand threads are used in locations where normal rotation of the equipment would tend to loosen a right-hand threaded fastener.

Nuts

Nuts are manufactured in a variety of types and sizes. Most are hexagonal (6-sided) and fit on bolts, screws and studs with the same diameter and thread pitch.

Figure 3 shows several types of nuts. The common nut is generally used with a lockwasher. Self-locking nuts have a nylon insert which

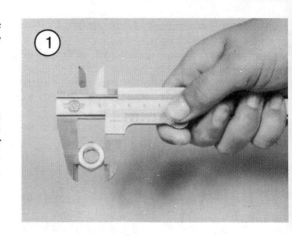

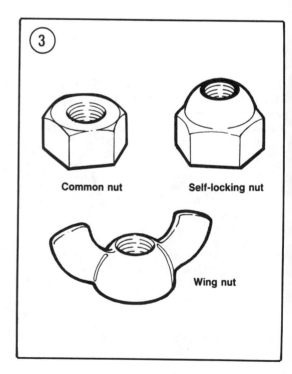

Common nut   Self-locking nut

Wing nut

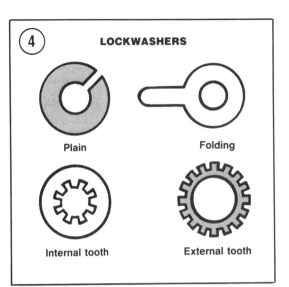

④ **LOCKWASHERS**

Plain   Folding

Internal tooth   External tooth

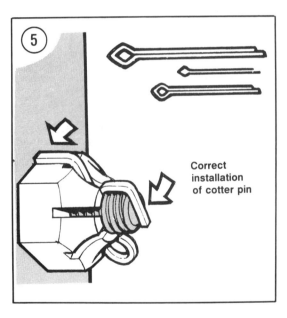

⑤

Correct
installation
of cotter pin

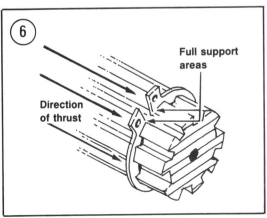

⑥

Full support
areas

Direction
of thrust

prevents the nut from loosening; no lockwasher is required. Wing nuts are designed for fast removal by hand. Wing nuts are used for convenience in non-critical locations.

To indicate the size of a metric nut, manufacturers specify the diameter of the opening and the thread pitch. This is similar to bolt specifications, but without the length dimension. The measurement of the inside bore (**Figure 2**) indicates the proper wrench size to be used.

Washers

There are 2 basic types of washers: flat washers and lockwashers. Flat washers are simple discs with a hole to fit a screw or bolt. Lockwashers are designed to prevent a fastener from working loose due to vibration, expansion and contraction. **Figure 4** shows several types of washers. Washers are also used in the following functions:

    a. As spacers.
    b. To prevent galling or damage of the equipment by the fastener.
    c. To help distribute fastener load during torquing.
    d. As seals.

Note that flat washers are often used between a lockwasher and a fastener to provide a smooth bearing surface. This allows the fastener to be turned easily with a tool.

Cotter Pins

Cotter pins (**Figure 5**) are used to secure special kinds of fasteners. The threaded stud must have a hole in it; the nut or nut lock piece has castellations around which the cotter pin ends wrap. Cotter pins should not be reused after removal.

Snap Rings

Snap rings can be internal or external design. They are used to retain items on shafts (external type) or within tubes (internal type). In some applications, snap rings of varying thicknesses are used to control the end play of parts assemblies. These are often called selective snap rings. Snap rings should be replaced during installation, as removal weakens and deforms them.

Two basic styles of snap rings are available: machined and stamped snap rings. Machined snap rings (**Figure 6**) can be installed in either direction (shaft or housing) because both faces are machined, thus creating two sharp edges. Stamped snap rings

(**Figure** 7) are manufactured with one sharp edge and one rounded edge. When installing stamped snap rings in a thrust situation (transmission shafts, fork tubes, etc.), the sharp edge must face away from the part producing the thrust. When installing snap rings, observe the following:

  a. Compress or expand snap rings only enough to install them.
  b. After the snap ring is installed, make sure it is completely seated in its groove.

LUBRICANTS

Periodic lubrication assures long life for any type of equipment. The *type* of lubricant used is just as important as the lubrication service itself, although in an emergency the wrong type of lubricant is better than none at all. The following paragraphs describe the types of lubricants most often used on motorcycle equipment. Be sure to follow the manufacturer's recommendations for lubricant types.

Generally, all liquid lubricants are called "oil." They may be mineral-based (including petroleum bases), natural-based (vegetable and animal bases), synthetic-based or emulsions (mixtures). "Grease" is an oil to which a thickening base has been added so that the end product is semi-solid. Grease is often classified by the type of thickener added; lithium soap is commonly used.

Engine Oil

Oil for motorcycle and automotive engines is classified by the American Petroleum Institute (API) and the Society of Automotive Engineers (SAE) in several categories. Oil containers display these classifications on the top or label.

API oil grade is indicated by letters; oils for gasoline engines are identified by an "S". The engines covered in this manual require SE or SF graded oil.

Viscosity is an indication of the oil's thickness. The SAE uses numbers to indicate viscosity; thin oils have low numbers while thick oils have high numbers. A "W" after the number indicates that the viscosity testing was done at low temperature to simulate cold-weather operation. Engine oils fall into the 5W-30 and 20W-50 range.

Multi-grade oils (for example 10W-40) are less viscous (thinner) at low temperatures and more viscous (thicker) at high temperatures. This allows the oil to perform efficiently across a wide range of engine operating conditions. The lower the number, the better the engine will start in cold climates. Higher numbers are usually

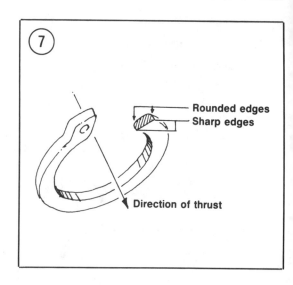

recommended for engine running in hot weather conditions.

Grease

Greases are graded by the National Lubricating Grease Institute (NLGI). Greases are graded by number according to the consistency of the grease; these range from No. 000 to No. 6, with No. 6 being the most solid. A typical multipurpose grease is NLGI No. 2. For specific applications, equipment manufacturers may require grease with an additive such as molybdenum disulfide (MOS2).

PARTS REPLACEMENT

Yamaha makes frequent changes during a model year, some minor, some relatively major. When

you order parts from the dealer or other parts distributor, always order by engine and frame number. Write the numbers down and carry them with you. Compare new parts to old before purchasing them. If they are not alike, have the parts manager explain the difference to you. The engine number is stamped on the right-hand crankcase (**Figure 8**). The chassis number is stamped on the right-hand side of the steering head (YTM200 and YTM225, **Figure 9**) or on the left-hand side of the frame (YFM200, **Figure 10**). Machine identification and model number as well as the manufacturing date are printed on a decal attached to a frame tube in an easily seen location.

Table 3 lists engine and chassis numbers with model years for all models covered in this manual.

NOTE
*When using the information in **Table 3**, note that the first 3 digits are model identification. The numbers are the unit production or serial number. The first 3 digits can be used to determine your vehicle's model year.*

BASIC HAND TOOLS

Many of the procedures in this manual can be carried out with simple hand tools and test equipment familiar to the average home mechanic. Keep your tools clean and in a tool box. Keep them orgainzed with the sockets and related drives together, the open-end and combination wrenches together, etc. After using a tool, wipe off dirt and grease with a clean cloth and return the tool to its correct place.

Top quality tools are essential; they are also more economical in the long run. If you are now starting to build your tool collection, stay away from the "advertised specials" featured at some parts houses, discount stores and chain drug stores. These are usually a poor grade tool that can be sold cheaply and that is exactly what they are—*cheap*. They are usually made of inferior material, and are thick, heavy and clumsy. Their rough finish makes them difficult to clean and they usually don't last very long. If it is ever your misfortune to use such tools, you will probably find out that the wrenches do not fit the heads of bolts and nuts correctly and damage the fastener.

Quality tools are made of alloy steel and are heat treated for greather strength. They are lighter and better balanced than cheap ones. Their surface is smooth, making them a pleasure to work with and easy to clean. The initial cost of good quality tools may be more but it is cheaper in the long run. Don't try to buy everything in all sizes in the beginning; do it a little at a time until you have the necessary tools. To sum up tool buying, "...the bitterness of poor quality lingers long after the sweetness of low price has faded."

The following tools are required to perform virtually any repair job. Each tool is described and the recomended size given for starting a tool collection. Additional tools and some duplicates may be added as you become familiar with the vehicle. Yamahas are built with metric fasteners—so if you are starting your collection now, buy metric sizes.

Screwdrivers

The screwdriver is a very basic tool, but if used improperly it will do more damage than good. The slot on a screw has a definite dimension and shape.

A screwdriver must be selected to conform with that shape. Use a small screwdriver for small screws and a large one for large screws or the screw head will be damaged.

Two basic types of screwdriver are required: common (flat-blade) screwdrivers (**Figure 11**) and Phillips screwdrivers (**Figure 12**).

Screwdrivers are available in sets which often include an assortment of common and Phillips blades. If you buy them individually, buy at least the following:

    a. Common screwdriver—5/16×6 in. blade.
    b. Common screwdriver—3/8×12 in. blade.
    c. Phillips screwdriver—size 2 tip, 6 in. blade.

Use screwdrivers only for driving screws. Never use a screwdriver for prying or chiseling metal. Do not try to remove a Phillips or Allen head screw with a common screwdriver (unless the screw has a combination head that will accept either type); you can damage the head so that the proper tool will be unable to remove it.

Keep screwdrivers in the proper condition and they will last longer and perform better. Always keep the tip of a common screwdriver in good condition. **Figure 13** shows how to grind the tip to the proper shape if it becomes damaged. Note the symmetrical sides of the tip.

Pliers

Pliers come in a wide range of types and sizes. Pliers are useful for cutting, bending and crimping. They should never be used to cut hardened objects or to turn bolts or nuts. **Figure 14** shows several pliers useful in motorcycle repairs.

Each type of pliers has a specialized function. Gas pliers are general purpose pliers and are used mainly for holding things and for bending. Locking pliers, such as vise-grips, are used as pliers or to hold objects very tight like in a vise. Needlenose pliers are used to hold or bend small objects.

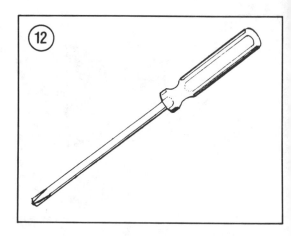

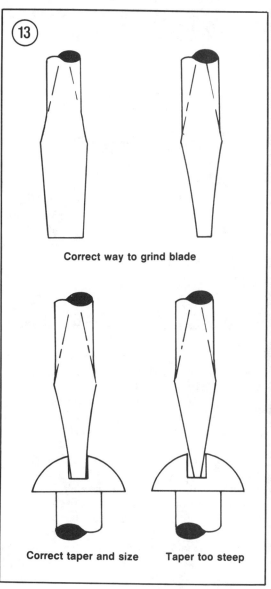

Correct way to grind blade

Correct taper and size   Taper too steep

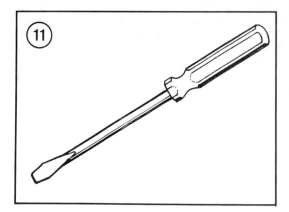

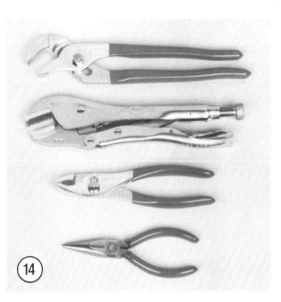

(14)

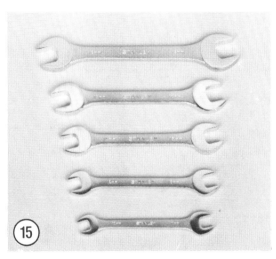

(15)

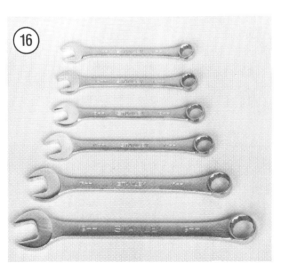

(16)

Channel lock pliers can be adjusted to hold various sizes of objects. The jaws remain parallel to grip around objects such as pipe or tubing. There are many more types of pliers.

Box and Open-end Wrenches

Box and open-end wrenches are available in sets or separately in a variety of sizes. The size number stamped near the end refers to the distance between 2 parallel flats on the hex head bolt or nut.

Box wrenches are usually superior to open-end wrenches (**Figure 15**). Open-end wrenches grip the nut on only 2 flats. Unless it fits well, it may slip and round off the points on the nut. The box wrench grips on all 6 flats. Both 6-point and 12-point openings on box wrenches are available. The 6-point gives superior holding power; the 12-point allows a shorter swing.

Combination wrenches which are open on one side and boxed on the other are also available. Both ends are the same size. See **Figure 16**.

Adjustable Wrenches

An adjustable wrench can be adjusted to fit a variety of nuts or bolt heads (**Figure 17**). However, it can loosen and slip, causing damage to the nut and injury to your knuckles. Use an adjustable wrench only when other wrenches are not available.

Adjustable wrenches come in sizes ranging from 4-18 in. overall. A 6 or 8 in. wrench is recommended as an all-purpose wrench.

Socket Wrenches

This type is undoubtedly the fastest, safest and most convenient to use. Sockets which attach to a

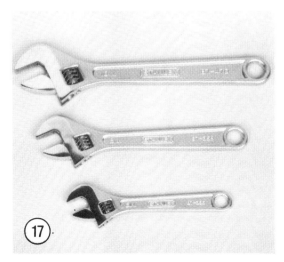

(17)

ratchet handle (**Figure 18**) are available with 6-point or 12-point openings and 1/4, 3/8, 1/2 and 3/4 inch drives. The drive size indicates the size of the square hole which mates with the ratchet handle.

Torque Wrench

A torque wrench (**Figure 19**) is used with a socket to measure how tight a nut or bolt is installed. They come in a wide price range and with either 3/8 or 1/2 in. square drive. The drive size indicates the size of the square drive which mates with the socket.

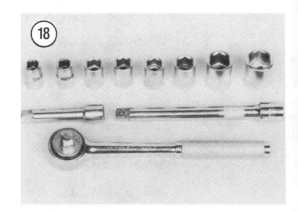

Impact Driver

This tool makes removal of tight fasteners easy and eliminates damage to bolts and screw slots. Impact drivers and interchangeable bits (**Figure 20**) are available at most large hardware and motorcycle dealers. Sockets can also be used with a hand impact driver. However, make sure the socket is designed for impact use. Do not use regular hand type sockets as they may shatter.

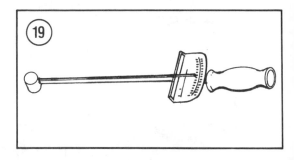

Hammers

The correct hammer is necessary for repairs. Use only a hammer with a face (or head) of rubber or plastic or the soft-faced type that is filled with buckshot. These are sometimes necessary in engine teardowns. *Never* use a metal faced hammer as severe damage will result in most cases. You can always produce the same amount of force with a soft-faced hammer.

Feeler Gauge

This tool has both flat and wire measuring gauges and is used to measure spark plug gap. See **Figure 21**. Wire gauges are used to measure spark plug gap; flat gauges are used for all other measurements.

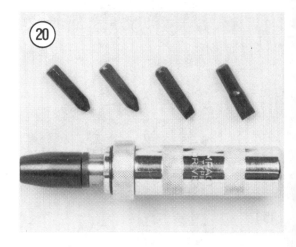

Vernier Caliper

This tool is invaluable when reading inside, outside and depth measurements to close precision. The vernier caliper can be purchased from large dealers or mail order houses. See **Figure 22**.

Other Special Tools

A few other special tools may be required for major service. These are described in the appropriate chapters and are available either from Yamaha dealers or other manufacturers as indicated.

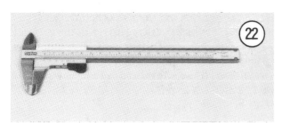

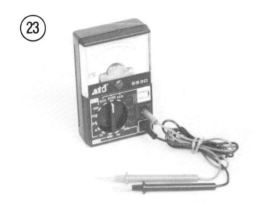

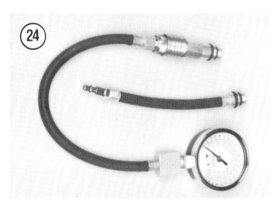

TEST EQUIPMENT

Voltmeter, Ammeter and Ohmmeter

A good voltmeter is required for testing ignition and other electrical systems. Voltmeters are available with analog meter scales or digital readouts. An instrument covering 0-20 volts is satisfactory. It should also have a 0-2 volt scale for testing points or individual contacts where voltage drops are much smaller. Accuracy should be ±1/2 volt.

An ohmmeter measures electrical resistance. This instrument is useful in checking continuity (for open and short circuits) and testing lights. A self-powered 12-volt test light can often be used in its place.

The ammeter measures electrical current. These are useful for checking battery starting and charging currents.

Some manufacturers combine the 3 instruments into 1 unit called a multimeter or VOM. See **Figure 23**.

Compression Gauge

An engine with low compression cannot be properly tuned and will not develop full power. A compression gauge measures the amount of pressure present in the engine's combustion chamber during the compression stroke. This indicates general engine condition.

The easiest type to use has screw-in adaptors that fit into the spark plug holes (**Figure 24**). Press-in rubber-tipped types (**Figure 25**) are also available.

Dial Indicator

Dial indicators (**Figure 26**) are precision tools used to check dimension variations on machined

parts such as transmission shafts and axles and to check crankshaft and axle shaft end play. Dial indicators are available with various dial types for different measuring requirements.

Strobe Timing Light

This instrument is necessary for checking ignition timing. By flashing a light at the precise instant the spark plug fires, the position of the timing mark can be seen. The flashing light makes a moving mark appear to stand still opposite a stationary mark.

Suitable lights range from inexpensive neon bulb types to powerful xenon strobe lights. See **Figure 27**. A light with an inductive pickup is recommended to eliminate any possible damage to ignition wiring.

Portable Tachometer

A portable tachometer is necessary for tuning. See **Figure 28**. Ignition timing and carburetor adjustments must be performed at the specified idle speed. The best instrument for this purpose is one with a low range of 0-1,000 or 0-2,000 rpm range and a high range of 0-4,000 rpm. Extended range (0-6,000 or 0-8,000 rpm) instruments lack accuracy at lower speeds. The instrument should be capable of detecting changes of 25 rpm on the low range.

Expendable Supplies

Certain expendable supplies are also required. These include grease, oil, gasket cement, shop rags, and cleaning solvent. Ask your dealer for the special locking compounds, silicone lubricants and lube products which make vehicle maintenance simpler and easier. Cleaning solvent is available at some service stations.

MECHANIC'S TIPS

Removing Frozen Nuts and Screws

When a fastener rusts and cannot be removed, several methods may be used to loosen it. First, apply penetrating oil such as Liquid Wrench or WD-40 (available at hardware or auto supply stores). Apply it liberally and let it penetrate for 10-15 minutes. Rap the fastener several times with a small hammer; do not hit it hard enough to cause damage. Reapply the penetrating oil if necessary.

For frozen screws, apply penetrating oil as described, then insert a screwdriver in the slot and rap the top of the screwdriver with a hammer. This loosens the rust so the screw can be removed in the normal way. If the screw head is too chewed up to use this method, grip the head with Vise Grips and twist the screw out.

Avoid applying heat unless specifically instructed, as it may melt, warp or remove the temper from parts.

Remedying Stripped Threads

Occasionally, threads are stripped through carelessness or impact damage. Often the threads

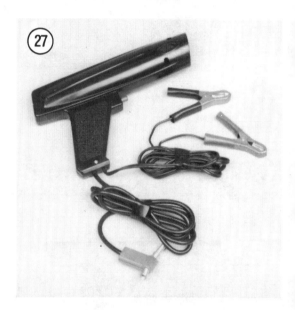

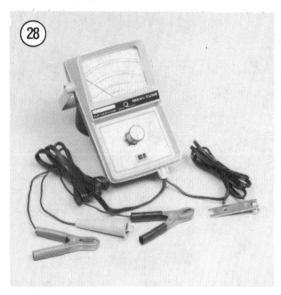

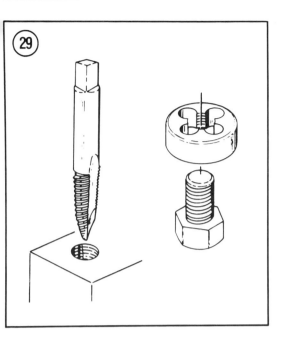

can be cleaned up by running a tap (for internal threads on nuts) or die (for external threads on bolts) through the threads. See **Figure 29**. To clean or repair spark plug threads, a spark plug tap can be used.

Removing Broken Screws or Bolts

When the head breaks off a screw or bolt, several methods are available for removing the remaining portion.

If a large portion of the remainder projects out, try gripping it with Vise Grips. If the projecting portion is too small, file it to fit a wrench or cut a slot in it to fit a screwdriver. See **Figure 30**.

If the head breaks off flush, use a screw extractor. To do this, centerpunch the exact center of the remaining portion of the screw or bolt. Drill a small hole in the screw and tap the extractor into the hole. Back the screw out with a wrench on the extractor. See **Figure 31**.

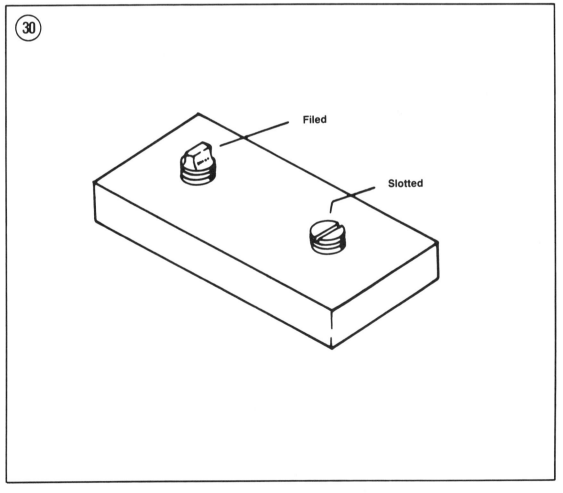

Filed

Slotted

(31)

REMOVING BROKEN SCREWS AND BOLTS

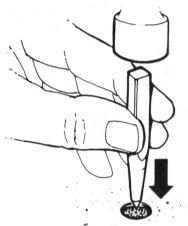

1. Center punch broken stud

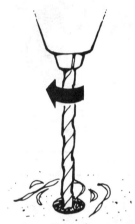

2. Drill hole in stud

3. Tap in screw extractor

4. Remove broken stud

Table 1 DECIMAL AND METRIC EQUIVALENTS

Fractions	Decimal in.	Metric mm	Fractions	Decimal in.	Metric mm
1/64	0.015625	0.39688	33/64	0.515625	13.09687
1/32	0.03125	0.79375	17/32	0.53125	13.49375
3/64	0.046875	1.19062	35/64	0.546875	13.89062
1/16	0.0625	1.58750	9/16	0.5625	14.28750
5/64	0.078125	1.98437	37/64	0.578125	14.68437
3/32	0.09375	2.38125	19/32	0.59375	15.08125
7/64	0.109375	2.77812	39/64	0.609375	15.47812
1/8	0.125	3.1750	5/8	0.625	15.87500
9/64	0.140625	3.57187	41/64	0.640625	16.27187
5/32	0.15625	3.96875	21/32	0.65625	16.66875
11/64	0.171875	4.36562	43/64	0.671875	17.06562
3/16	0.1875	4.76250	11/16	0.6875	17.46250
13/64	0.203125	5.15937	45/64	0.703125	17.85937
7/32	0.21875	5.55625	23/32	0.71875	18.25625
15/64	0.234375	5.95312	47/64	0.734375	18.65312
1/4	0.250	6.35000	3/4	0.750	19.05000
17/64	0.265625	6.74687	49/64	0.765625	19.44687
9/32	0.28125	7.14375	25/32	0.78125	19.84375
19/64	0.296875	7.54062	51/64	0.796875	20.24062
5/16	0.3125	7.93750	13/16	0.8125	20.63750
21/64	0.328125	8.33437	53/64	0.828125	21.03437
11/32	0.34375	8.73125	27/32	0.84375	21.43125
23/64	0.359375	9.12812	55/64	0.859375	21.82812
3/8	0.375	9.52500	7/8	0.875	22.22500
25/64	0.390625	9.92187	57/64	0.890625	22.62187
13/32	0.40625	10.31875	29/32	0.90625	23.01875
27/64	0.421875	10.71562	59/64	0.921875	23.41562
7/16	0.4375	11.11250	15/16	0.9375	23.81250
29/64	0.453125	11.50937	61/64	0.953125	24.20937
15/32	0.46875	11.90625	31/32	0.96875	24.60625
31/64	0.484375	12.30312	63/64	0.984375	25.00312
1/2	0.500	12.70000	1	1.00	25.40000

Table 2 GENERAL TORQUE SPECIFICATIONS

Item	ft.-lb.	N•m
Bolt		
6 mm	4.5	6
8 mm	11	15
10 mm	22	30
12 mm	40	55
14 mm	61	85
16 mm	94	130
Nut		
10 mm	4.5	6
12 mm	11	15
14 mm	22	30
17 mm	40	55
19 mm	61	85
22 mm	94	130

Table 3 ENGINE NUMBERS

Model	Number
YTM200K	21V-000101-100100
YTM200L	21V-100101-160100
YTM200N	21V-160101-on
YTM200EK	24W-000101-100100
YTM200EL	24W-100101-on
YTM225DXK	29U-000101-060100
YTM225DXL	29U-060101-on
YTM225DXN	29U-100101-on
YTM200ERN	52G-000101-on
YTM225DRN	1EV-000101-on
YTM225DRS	1NV-000101-on
YFM200N	52H-000101-on
YFM200DXS	1NU-000101-ON

CHAPTER TWO

TROUBLESHOOTING

Every motorcycle engine requires an uninterrupted supply of fuel and air, proper ignition and adequate compression (**Figure 1**). If any of these are lacking, the engine will not run.

Diagnosing mechanical problems is relatively simple if you use orderly procedures and keep a few basic principles in mind.

The troubleshooting procedures in this chapter analyze typical symptoms and show logical methods of isolating causes. These are not the only methods. There may be several ways to solve a problem, but only a systematic approach can guarantee success.

Never assume anything. Do not overlook the obvious. If you are riding along and the vehicle suddenly quits, check the easiest, most accessible problem spots first. Is there gasoline in the tank? Has the spark plug wire fallen off?

If nothing obvious turns up in a quick check, look a little further. Learning to recognize and describe symptoms will make repairs easier for you or a mechanic at the shop. Describe problems accurately and fully. Saying that "it won't run" isn't the same thing as saying "it quit at high speed and won't start," or that "it sat in my garage for 3 months and then wouldn't start."

Gather as many symptoms as possible to aid in diagnosis. Note whether the engine lost power gradually or all at once. Remember that the more complicated a machine is, the easier it is to troubleshoot because symptoms point to specific problems.

After the symptoms are defined, areas which could cause problems are tested and analyzed. Guessing at the cause of a problem may provide the solution, but it can easily lead to frustration, wasted time and a series of expensive, unnecessary parts replacements.

You do not need fancy equipment or complicated test gear to determine whether repairs can be attempted at home. A few simple checks could save a large repair bill and lost time while the bike sits in a dealer's service department. On the other hand, be realistic and don't attempt repairs beyond your abilities. Service departments tend to charge heavily for putting together a disassembled engine that may have been abused. Some won't even take on such a job—so use common sense, don't get in over your head.

OPERATING REQUIREMENTS

An engine needs 3 basics to run properly: correct fuel/air mixture, compression and a spark at the correct time (**Figure 1**). If one or more are missing, the engine will not run. Four-stroke engine operating principles are described in Chapter Four under *Engine Principles*. The electrical system is the weakest link of the 3 basics. More problems result from electrical breakdowns than from any other source. Keep that in mind before you begin tampering with carburetor adjustments and the like.

If the machine has been sitting for any length of time and refuses to start, check and clean the spark plugs and then look to the gasoline delivery system. This includes the fuel tank, fuel shutoff valve and fuel line to the carburetor. Gasoline deposits may have formed and gummed up the carburetor jets and air passages. Gasoline tends to lose its potency after standing for long periods. Condensation may contaminate the fuel with water. Drain the old fuel (fuel tank, fuel lines and carburetor) and try starting with a fresh tankful.

TROUBLESHOOTING INSTRUMENTS

Chapter One lists the instruments needed and gives instruction on their use.

EMERGENCY TROUBLESHOOTING

When the vehicle is difficult to start, or won't start at all, it doesn't help to wear down the battery (if so equipped) or your arm by using the starter. Check for obvious problems even before getting out your tools. Go down the following list step by step. Do each one; you may be embarrassed to find the kill switch off, but that is better than wearing down the battery. If the bike still will not start, refer to the appropriate troubleshooting procedures which follow in this chapter.

1. Is there fuel in the tank? Open the filler cap and rock the bike. Listen for fuel sloshing around.

> *WARNING*
> *Do not use an open flame to check in the tank. A serious explosion is certain to result.*

2. Is the fuel supply valve in the ON position? Turn the valve to the reserve position to be sure you get the last remaining gas.

3. Make sure the kill switch is not stuck in the OFF position and that the wire is not broken and shorting out.

4. Is the spark plug wire on tight? Push the spark plug cap on and slightly rotate it to clean the electrical connection between the plug and the connector.

5. Is the choke in the right position?

ENGINE STARTING

An engine that refuses to start or is difficult to start is very frustrating. More often than not, the problem is very minor and can be found with a simple and logical troubleshooting approach.

The following items show a beginning point from which to isolate engine starting problems.

Engine Fails to Start

Perform the following spark test to determine if the ignition system is operating properly.

1. Remove the spark plug.

2. Connect the spark plug wire and connector to the spark plug and touch the spark plug base to a

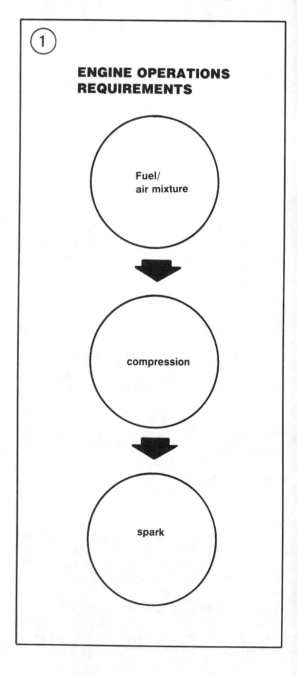

good ground like the engine cylinder head. Position the spark plug so you can see the electrodes. See **Figure 2**.

> *WARNING*
> *In the next step, do not hold the spark plug, wire or connector or a serious electrical shock may result. If necessary, use a pair of insulated pliers to hold the spark plug or wire. The high voltage generated by the ignition system could produce serious or fatal shocks.*

3. Crank the engine over with the recoil starter. A fat blue spark should be evident across the spark plug electrodes.

4. If the spark is good, check for one or more of the following possible malfunctions:
  a. Obstructed fuel line or fuel filter.
  b. Leaking head gasket.
  c. Low compression.
5. If the spark is not good, check for one or more of the following:
  a. Loose electrical connections.
  b. Dirty electrical connections.
  c. Loose or broken ignition coil ground wire (A, **Figure 3**).
  d. Broken or shorted high tension lead to the spark plug (B, **Figure 3**).
  e. Discharged battery (if used).
  f. Disconnected or damaged battery connection.
  g. Defective starting circuit cut-off relay (electric start models only).

Engine is Difficult to Start

Check for one or more of the following possible malfunctions:
  a. Fouled spark plug.
  b. Improperly operating choke.
  c. Intake manifold air leak.
  d. Contaminated fuel system.
  e. Improperly adjusted carburetor.
  f. Weak CDI unit.
  h. Weak ignition coil.
  i. Poor compression.
  j. Engine and transmission oil too heavy.

Engine Will Not Crank

Check for one or more of the following possible malfunctions:
  a. Blown fuse.
  b. Discharged battery.
  c. Defective recoil starter assembly.
  d. Defective starter motor (if used).
  e. Seized piston.
  f. Seized crankshaft bearings.
  g. Broken connecting rod.
  h. Locked-up transmission or clutch assembly.

ENGINE PERFORMANCE

In the following check list, it is assumed that the engine runs, but is not operating at peak performance. This will serve as a starting point from which to isolate a performance malfunction.

The possible causes for each malfunction are listed in a logical sequence and in order of probability.

Engine Will Not Idle

a. Carburetor incorrectly adjusted.
b. Fouled or improperly gapped spark plug.
c. Leaking head gasket.
d. Obstructed fuel line or fuel shutoff valve.
e. Obstructed fuel filter.
f. Ignition timing incorrect due to defective ignition component(s).
g. Valve clearance incorrect.
h. Incorrect decompression cable adjustment (YTM200K, L and N).

Engine Misses at High Speed

a. Fouled or improperly gapped spark plug.
b. Improper carburetor main jet selection.
c. Ignition timing incorrect due to defective ignition component(s).
d. Obstructed fuel line or fuel shutoff valve.
e. Obstructed fuel filter.
f. Clogged or loose carburetor jets.

Engine Overheating

a. Incorrect carburetor adjustment or jet selection.
b. Ignition timing retarded due to defective ignition component(s).
c. Obstructed cooling fins on cylinder head and cylinder.
d. Improper spark plug heat range.
e. Oil level low.
f. Oil not circulating properly.
g. Valves leaking.
h. Heavy engine carbon deposit.
i. Dragging brake(s).

Smoky Exhaust and Engine Runs Roughly

a. Clogged air filter element.
b. Carburetor adjustment incorrect—mixture too rich.
c. Choke not operating correctly.
d. Water or other contaminants in fuel.
e. Clogged fuel line.
f. Spark plug fouled.
g. Ignition coil defective.
h. Defective ignition component(s).
i. Loose or defective ignition circuit wire.
j. Short circuit from damaged wire insulation.
k. Loose battery cable connection.
l. Valve timing incorrect.
m. Intake manifold or air cleaner air leak.

Engine Loses Power

a. Carburetor incorrectly adjusted.
b. Engine overheating.
c. Ignition timing incorrect due to faulty ignition component(s).
d. Incorrectly gapped spark plug.
e. Obstructed muffler.
f. Dragging brake(s).

Engine Lacks Acceleration

a. Carburetor mixture too lean.
b. Clogged fuel line.
c. Ignition timing incorrect due to faulty ignition component(s).
d. Dragging brake(s).

ENGINE NOISES

Often the first evidence of an internal engine problem is a strange noise. That knocking, clicking or tapping sound which you never heard before may be warning you of impending trouble.

While engine noises can indicate problems, they are difficult to interpret correctly; inexperienced mechanics can be seriously misled by them.

Professional mechanics often use a special stethoscope (which looks like a doctor's stethoscope) for isolating engine noises. You can do nearly as well with a "sounding stick" which can be an ordinary piece of doweling, a length of broom handle or a section of small hose. By placing one end in contact with the area to which you want to listen and the other end near your ear, you can hear sounds emanating from that area. The first time you do this, you may be horrified at the strange sounds comming from even a normal engine. If you can, have an experienced friend or mechanic help you sort out the noises.

Consider the following when troubleshooting engine noises:

1. *Knocking or pinging during acceleration*—Caused by using a lower octane fuel than recommended. May also be caused by poor fuel. Pinging can also be caused by a spark plug of the wrong heat range. Refer to *Correct Spark Plug Heat Range* in Chapter Three.

2. *Slapping or rattling noises at low speed or during acceleration*—May be caused by piston slap, i.e., excessive piston-cylinder wall clearance.

3. *Knocking or rapping while decelerating*—Usually caused by excessive rod bearing clearance.

4. *Persistent knocking and vibration*—Usually caused by worn main bearing(s).

5. *Rapid on-off squeal*—Compression leak around cylinder head gasket or spark plug.

6. *Valve train noise*—Check for the following:
   a. Worn or damaged cam chain.
   b. Worn or damaged cam chain guides.
   c. Valve sticking in guide.
   d. Low oil pressure—probably caused by obstructed oil screen or oil passages. Also check oil pump.
   e. Damaged rocker arm or shaft. Rocker arm may be binding on shaft.
   f. Incorrect valve adjustment.
   g. Loose valve adjuster nut.

ENGINE LUBRICATION

An improperly operating engine lubrication system will quickly lead to engine seizure. The engine oil level should be checked weekly and refilled, as described in Chapter Three. Oil pump service is described in Chapter Four.

Oil Consumption High or Engine Smokes Excessivly

   a. Worn valve guides.
   b. Worn or damaged piston rings.

Excessive Engine Oil Leaks

   a. Clogged air cleaner breather hose.
   b. Loose engine parts.
   c. Damaged gasket sealing surfaces.

CLUTCH

The three basic clutch troubles are:
   a. Clutch noise.
   b. Clutch slipping.
   c. Improper clutch disengagement or dragging.

All clutch troubles, except adjustments, require partial clutch disassembly to identify and cure the problem. The troubleshooting chart in **Figure 4** lists clutch troubles and checks to make. Refer to Chapter Five for clutch service procedures.

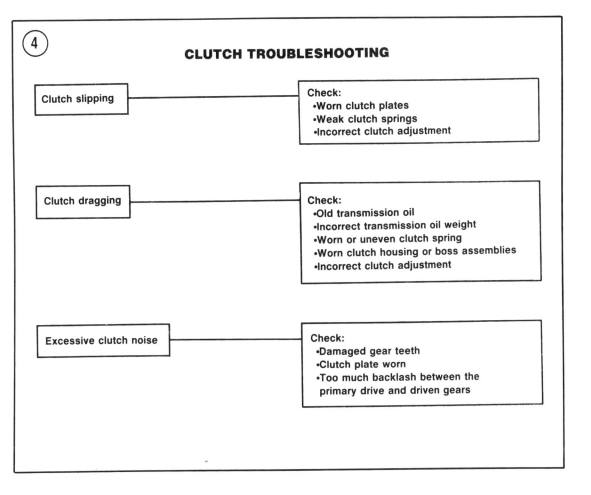

(4) CLUTCH TROUBLESHOOTING

| Clutch slipping | Check:
 •Worn clutch plates
 •Weak clutch springs
 •Incorrect clutch adjustment |

| Clutch dragging | Check:
 •Old transmission oil
 •Incorrect transmission oil weight
 •Worn or uneven clutch spring
 •Worn clutch housing or boss assemblies
 •Incorrect clutch adjustment |

| Excessive clutch noise | Check:
 •Damaged gear teeth
 •Clutch plate worn
 •Too much backlash between the primary drive and driven gears |

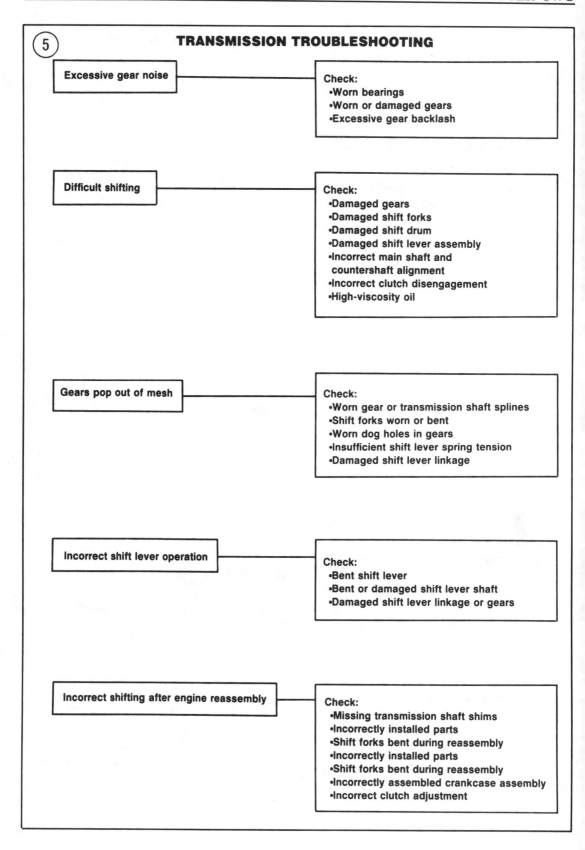

⑤ **TRANSMISSION TROUBLESHOOTING**

Excessive gear noise

Check:
- Worn bearings
- Worn or damaged gears
- Excessive gear backlash

Difficult shifting

Check:
- Damaged gears
- Damaged shift forks
- Damaged shift drum
- Damaged shift lever assembly
- Incorrect main shaft and
  countershaft alignment
- Incorrect clutch disengagement
- High-viscosity oil

Gears pop out of mesh

Check:
- Worn gear or transmission shaft splines
- Shift forks worn or bent
- Worn dog holes in gears
- Insufficient shift lever spring tension
- Damaged shift lever linkage

Incorrect shift lever operation

Check:
- Bent shift lever
- Bent or damaged shift lever shaft
- Damaged shift lever linkage or gears

Incorrect shifting after engine reassembly

Check:
- Missing transmission shaft shims
- Incorrectly installed parts
- Shift forks bent during reassembly
- Incorrectly installed parts
- Shift forks bent during reassembly
- Incorrectly assembled crankcase assembly
- Incorrect clutch adjustment

TRANSMISSION

The basic transmission troubles are:

a. Excessive gear noise.
b. Difficult shifting.
c. Gears pop out of mesh.
d. Incorrect shift lever operation.

Transmission symptoms are sometimes hard to distinguish from clutch symptoms. The troubleshooting chart in **Figure 5** lists transmission troubles and checks to make. Refer to Chapter Five for transmission service procedures. Be sure that the clutch is not causing the trouble before working on the transmission.

CARBURETOR

The carburetor mixes the air and fuel in correct proportions for an air/fuel mixture. To work properly, the carburetor must be adjusted and serviced correctly. This includes proper throttle cable adjustment and air filter maintenance. (Both of these services are covered in Chapter Three).

Carburetor problems result usually from dust and dirt, worn parts, incorrect adjustments or improper fuel level. The stock Mikuni carburetors installed on all models covered in this manual are designed so that individual components can be adjusted to best suit various throttle openings. When troubleshooting a carburetor, first check whether the air/fuel mixture is lean or rich, and then determine at what throttle opening the carburetor is working incorrectly. If the mixture does not have enough gasoline vapor in proportion to air, the mixture is "lean" or if the mixture has too much gasoline vapor, the mixture is "rich."

Fuel Mixture is too Rich

When making the following checks, it is assumed that the engine troubles have been traced to the carburetor. The following engine conditions and signs indicate a rich carburetor condition:

a. Engine performance worsens after the engine has warmed up.
b. The spark plug firing tip is covered with soot. See Chapter Three.

CAUTION
Step "c" describes a check procedure only. Do not ride the vehicle with the air filter removed.

c. The engine runs smoother when the air filter is removed.
d. There is visible black exhaust smoke.

e. Throttle response is very sluggish.
f. The engine starts more easily with the choke off than when on.
g. Excessive fuel consumption.

Fuel Mixture is too Lean

When making the following checks, it is assumed that the engine troubles have been traced to the carburetor. The following engine conditions and signs indicate a lean carburetor condition:

a. The engine is difficult to start.
b. Engine overheats.
c. When the choke is on, the engine runs more smoothly.
d. Engine idle is very erratic or will idle only with the choke on.
e. Erratic acceleration.
f. Spark plug tip very white.

CAUTION
Step "g" describes a check procedure only. Do not ride the vehicle with the air filter removed.

g. Engine idle worse when the air filter is removed.

Troubleshooting

The troubleshooting chart in **Figure 6** lists carburetor troubles and checks to make. Refer to Chapter Six for carburetor service procedures.

CHARGING SYSTEM

Charging system testing procedures are described in Chapter Seven.

ELECTRIC STARTING SYSTEM

The basic starter related troubles are:

a. The starter does not crank.
b. The starter cranks, but the engine does not start.

Testing

Starting system problems are relatively easy to find. In most cases, the trouble is a loose or dirty electrical connection. Use the troubleshooting chart in **Figure 7** with the following tests.

Starter does not crank

1. Turn on the headlight and push the starter button. Check for one of the following conditions.

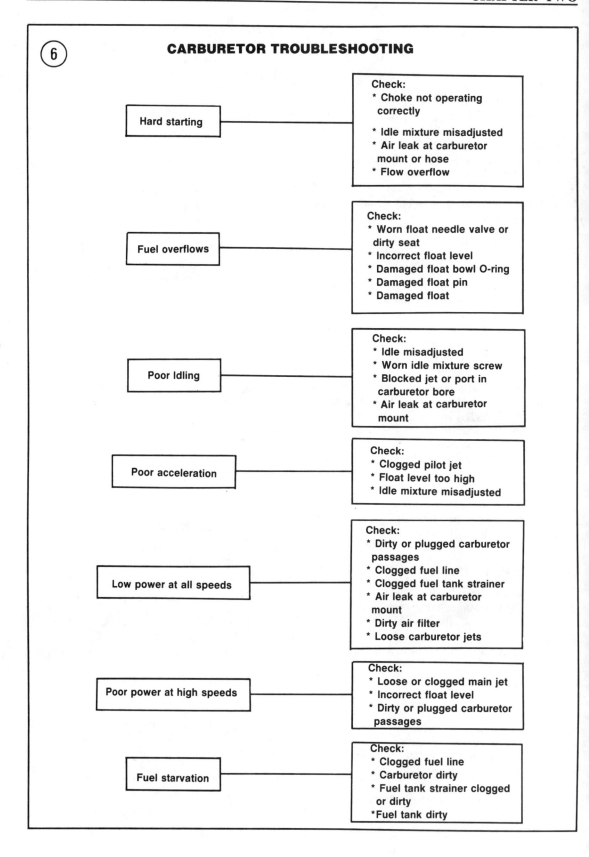

CARBURETOR TROUBLESHOOTING

⑥

Hard starting

Check:
* Choke not operating correctly
* Idle mixture misadjusted
* Air leak at carburetor mount or hose
* Flow overflow

Fuel overflows

Check:
* Worn float needle valve or dirty seat
* Incorrect float level
* Damaged float bowl O-ring
* Damaged float pin
* Damaged float

Poor Idling

Check:
* Idle misadjusted
* Worn idle mixture screw
* Blocked jet or port in carburetor bore
* Air leak at carburetor mount

Poor acceleration

Check:
* Clogged pilot jet
* Float level too high
* Idle mixture misadjusted

Low power at all speeds

Check:
* Dirty or plugged carburetor passages
* Clogged fuel line
* Clogged fuel tank strainer
* Air leak at carburetor mount
* Dirty air filter
* Loose carburetor jets

Poor power at high speeds

Check:
* Loose or clogged main jet
* Incorrect float level
* Dirty or plugged carburetor passages

Fuel starvation

Check:
* Clogged fuel line
* Carburetor dirty
* Fuel tank strainer clogged or dirty
*Fuel tank dirty

2. *Starter does not crank and headlight does not come on*: The battery is dead or there is a loose battery connection. Check the battery charge as described in Chapter Three. If the battery is okay, check the starter connections at the battery, solenoid and at the starter switch.

3. *Headlight comes on, but goes out when the starter button is pushed*: There may be a bad connection at the battery. Wiggle the battery terminals and recheck. If the starter cranks, you've found the problem. Remove and clean the battery terminal clamps. Clean the battery posts also. Reinstall the clamps and tighten securely.

4. *Headlight comes on, but dims slightly when the starter button is pushed*: The problem is probably in the starter. Remove and test the starter as described in Chapter Seven.

5. *Headlight comes on, but dims severely when the starter button is pushed*: Either the battery is run down severely or the starter or engine is partially seized. Check the battery as described in Chapter Three. Check the starter as described in Chapter Seven before checking for partial engine seizure.

6. *Headlight comes on and stays bright when the starter button is pushed*: The problem is in the starter button-to-solenoid wiring or in the starter itself. Check the starter switch, kill switch, starter relay and the solenoid switch. Check each switch by bypassing it with a jumper wire. Check the starter as described in Chapter Seven.

Starter spins but engine does not crank

If the starter spins at normal or high speed but the engine fails to crank, the starter system is working correctly. The problem is in the starter drive mechanism. Refer to Chapter Seven.

NOTE
Depending upon battery condition, the battery will eventually run down as the starter button is continually pressed. Remember that if the starter cranks normally, but the engine fails to start, the starter is working properly. It's time to start checking other engine systems. Don't wear the battery down.

ELECTRICAL PROBLEMS

If bulbs burn out frequently, the cause may be excessive vibration, loose connections that permit sudden current surges, or the installation of the wrong type of bulb.

Most light and ignition problems are caused by loose or corroded ground connections. Check these first prior to replacing a bulb or electrical component.

⑦

Table 2 STARTER TROUBLESHOOTING

Symptom	Probable Cause	Remedy
Starter does not work	Low battery	Recharge battery
	Worn brushes	Replace brushes
	Defective solenoid	Replace solenoid
	Defective clutch switch, NEUTRAL switch or sidestand switch	Replace switches
	Defective wiring or connection	Repair wire or clean connection
	Defective cut-off relay	Replace relay
Starter action is weak	Low battery	Recharge battery
	Pitted solenoid contacts	Replace solenoid
	Worn brushes	Replace brushes
	Defective connection	Clean and tighten
	Short circuit in commutator	Replace armature
Starter runs continuously	Stuck solenoid	Replace solenoid
Starter turns; engine does not	Defective starter clutch	Replace starter clutch

IGNITION SYSTEM

All models are equipped with a capacitor discharge ignition (CDI) system. Problems with the CDI are usually limited to the production of a weak spark or no spark at all.

Test procedures for troubleshooting the ignition system are found in **Figure 8**. A volt/ohm/ammeter, described in Chapter One, is required to perform the test procedures. When using the procedures in **Figure 7** to troubleshoot the ignition system, keep in mind that the procedures cannot accurately determine ignition problems due to vibration or detect marginal units that malfunction only when the engine is under load or hot.

Before beginning actual troubleshooting, read the entire test procedure (**Figure 8**). The diagnostic chart will refer you to a certain chapter and procedure for service information when required. Basic ignition system and spark plug service information can be found in Chapter Three.

Note the following symptoms:
a. Engine misses.
b. Stumbles on acceleration (misfiring).
c. Loss of power at high speed (misfiring).
d. Hard starting (if at all).
e. Rough idle.

Most of the symptoms can also be caused by a carburetor that is worn or improperly adjusted. But considering the law of averages, the odds are far better that the source of the problem will be found in the ignition system rather than the fuel system.

EXCESSIVE VIBRATION

Usually this is caused by loose engine mounting hardware. High speed vibration may be due to a bent axle shaft or loose or faulty suspension components. Vibration can also be caused by the following conditions:
a. Broken frame.
b. Damaged engine balancer shaft or gears.
c. Defective or damaged wheels.
d. Defective or damaged tires.
e. Internal engine wear or damage.

FRONT SUSPENSION AND STEERING

Poor handling may be caused by improper tire pressure, a damaged or bent frame or front steering components, worn wheel bearings, dragging brakes or incorrect toe-in adjustment on YFM200 models.

Possible causes for suspension and steering malfunctions are listed below.

Irregular or Wobbly Steering

a. Loose wheel axle nuts.
b. *YTM200 and YFM225:* Loose or worn steering head bearings.
c. *YFM200:* Loose or worn steering shaft, tie-rods or knuckle shaft.
d. Excessive wheel hub bearing play.
e. Damaged wheel.
f. Worn hub bearings.
g. *YFM200:* Incorrect toe-in alignment.
h. Bent or damaged steering stem or frame (at steering neck).
i. Tire incorrectly seated on rim.
j. Excessive front end loading from non-standard equipment.

Stiff Steering

a. Low front tire air pressure.
b. Bent or damged steering stem or frame (at steering neck).
c. Loose or worn steering bearings or bushings.

Stiff or Heavy Fork Operation (YTM200 and YTM225)

a. Incorrect fork springs.
b. Incorrect fork oil viscosity.
c. Excessive amount of fork oil.
d. Bent fork tubes.

Poor Fork Operation (YTM200 and YTM225)

a. Worn or damaged fork tubes.
b. Fork oil capacity low due to leaking fork seals.
c. Bent or damaged fork tubes.
d. Contaminated fork oil.
e. Incorrect fork springs.
f. Heavy front end loading from non-standard equipment.

Poor Front Shock Absorber Operation (YFM200)

a. Damaged shock absorbers.
b. Weark or worn springs.
c. Damper unit leaking.
d. Shock shaft worn or bent.
e. Front shock adjusted incorrectly.
f. Loose or damaged shock mounting bolts.
g. Heavy front end loading from non-standard equipment.

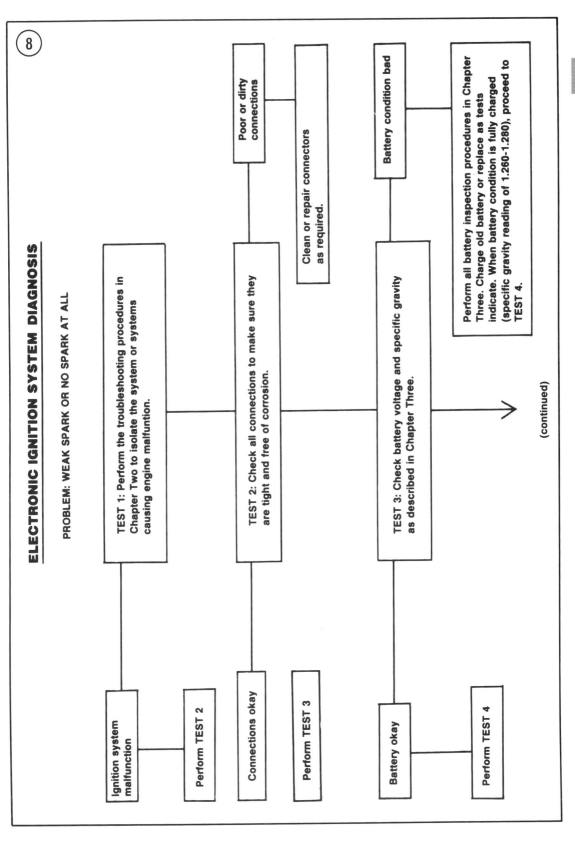

⑧

ELECTRONIC IGNITION SYSTEM DIAGNOSIS

PROBLEM: WEAK SPARK OR NO SPARK AT ALL

TEST 1: Perform the troubleshooting procedures in Chapter Two to isolate the system or systems causing engine malfuntion.

Ignition system malfunction

Perform TEST 2

TEST 2: Check all connections to make sure they are tight and free of corrosion.

Poor or dirty connections

Clean or repair connectors as required.

Connections okay

Perform TEST 3

TEST 3: Check battery voltage and specific gravity as described in Chapter Three.

Battery condition bad

Perform all battery inspection procedures in Chapter Three. Charge old battery or replace as tests indicate. When battery condition is fully charged (specific gravity reading of 1.260-1.280), proceed to TEST 4.

Battery okay

Perform TEST 4

(continued)

2

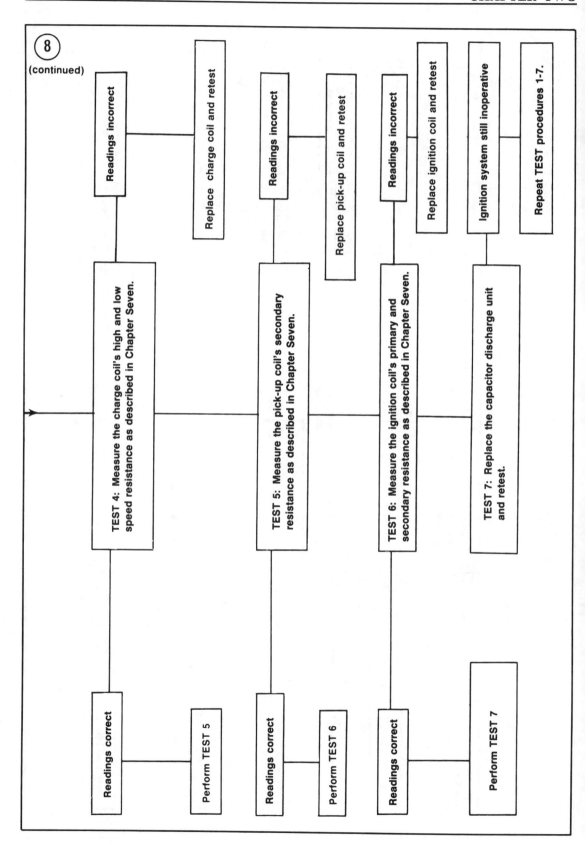

⑧ (continued)

Readings correct — Perform TEST 5

TEST 4: Measure the charge coil's high and low speed resistance as described in Chapter Seven.

Readings incorrect — Replace charge coil and retest

Readings correct — Perform TEST 6

TEST 5: Measure the pick-up coil's secondary resistance as described in Chapter Seven.

Readings incorrect — Replace pick-up coil and retest

Readings correct — Perform TEST 7

TEST 6: Measure the ignition coil's primary and secondary resistance as described in Chapter Seven.

Readings incorrect — Replace ignition coil and retest

TEST 7: Replace the capacitor discharge unit and retest.

Ignition system still inoperative — Repeat TEST procedures 1-7.

Poor Rear Shock Absorber Operation

a. Weak or worn springs.

b. Damper unit leaking.

c. Shock shaft worn or bent.

d. Incorrect rear shock springs.

e. Rear shocks adjusted incorrectly.

f. Heavy rear end loading from non-standard equipment.

g. Incorrect loading.

BRAKE PROBLEMS

A sticking front drum brake may be caused by worn or weak return springs, dry pivot and cam bushings or improper adjustment. Grabbing brakes may be caused by greasy linings, which must be replaced.

Brake grab may also be due to an out-of-round drum. Glazed linings will cause loss of stopping power.

Sticking rear disc brakes may be caused by a stuck caliper, sluggish caliper operation or improper rear brake adjustment.

CHAPTER THREE

LUBRICATION, MAINTENANCE, AND TUNE-UP

Because an off-road vehicle is subjected to tremendous heat, stress and vibration, preventive maintenance prevents costly and untimely corrective maintenance. By maintaining a routine service schedule as described in this chapter, costly mechanical problems and unexpected breakdowns can be prevented. The last thing you want is to have a weekend ride cut short because your vehicle broke down in the boonies. Unless the cause is minor, you may be forced to trailer your vehicle home.

The more you get involved with your Yamaha the more you will want to work on it. Start out by doing simple tune-up, lubrication and maintenance. Tackle more involved jobs as you gain experience.

This chapter explains lubrication, maintenance and tune-up procedures required for the Yamaha models covered in this manual. **Table 1** is a suggested factory maintenance schedule. **Tables 1-8** are located at the end of this chapter.

ROUTINE CHECKS

The following checks should be performed prior to the first ride of the day.

1. Inspect all fuel lines and fittings for wetness (**Figure 1**).
2. Make sure the fuel tank is full of fresh gasoline.
3. Make sure the engine oil level is correct.
4. Make sure the air cleaner element is clean.
5. Check the throttle and brake levers. Make sure they operate properly with no binding.
6. Check the clutch operation; adjust if necessary.
7. Inspect the front and rear suspension (if so equipped); make sure it has a good solid feel with no looseness.
8. *Chain drive:* Check the drive chain for wear and correct tension.
9. *Shaft drive:* Check the final drive oil level.
10. Check tire pressure. See **Table 2**.
11. Check the exhaust system for damage.
12. Check the tightness of all fasteners, especially engine mounting hardware.
13. Make sure the headlight and taillight work.

SERVICE INTERVALS

The services and intervals shown in **Table 1** are recommended by the factory. Strict adherence to these recommendations will ensure long service from your Yamaha. However, if the vehicle is run in an area of high humidity the lubrication and services must be done more frequently to prevent possible rust damage. This is especially true if you have run the vehicle through water (particularly salt water).

For convenience when maintaining your vehicle, most of the services shown in **Table 1** are described in this chapter. However, some procedures which require more than minor disassembly or adjustment are covered elsewhere in the appropriate chapter. The index at the end of this book can be used to locate specific items quickly.

TIRES AND WHEELS

Tire pressure should be checked and adjusted to maintain tire shape, good traction and handling and to get the maximum life out of the tire. A simple, accurate gauge can be purchased for a few dollars and should be carried in your tool box in the tow vehicle. The appropriate tire pressures are shown in **Table 2**.

> *WARNING*
> *Always inflate both rear tires to the same pressure. If the tires are run with unequal air pressures, the vehicle will run toward one side and handle poorly.*

> *CAUTION*
> *Do not overinflate the stock tires, as they will be permanently distorted and damaged. If overinflated, they will bulge out similar to an inner tube that is not within the constraints of a tire. If this happens, the tire will not return to its original contour.*

Tire Inspection

The tires take a lot of punishment due to the variety of terrain they are subjected to. Inspect them periodically for excessive wear, cuts, abrasions, etc. If you find a nail or other object in the tire, mark its location with a light crayon before removing it. This will help locate the hole for repair. Refer to Chapter Eight for tire changing and repair information.

Rim Inspection

Frequently inspect the wheel rims, especially the outer side (A, **Figure 2**). If the wheel has hit a tree or large rock, rim damage may be sufficient to cause an air leak or knock it out of alignment. Improper wheel alignment can cause severe vibration and result in an unsafe riding condition.

Make sure that the cotter pins are securely in place on the rear wheels (B, **Figure 2**). If they are lost and the castellated nut works loose, it's good-bye wheel. On some models, special nuts with a nylon insert are used together with a cotter pin to secure each rear wheel. While a Nyloc nut is a self-locking device, the nylon insert loses its locking effectiveness as the nut is continually removed and installed. When servicing your Yamaha, never depend solely on a nut to keep the rear wheel secure. Always install a new cotter pin after installing and torquing the nut. It's a good idea to purchase dozen or so new cotter pins and keep them in your tool box.

BATTERY

All models, except 1983-1985 YTM200, are equipped with 12-volt batteries.

CAUTION
If it becomes necessary to remove the battery breather tube when performing any of the following procedures, make sure to route the tube correctly during installation to prevent acid spillage on parts that would cause permanent damage.

Checking Electrolyte Level

The battery is the heart of the electrical system. It should be checked and serviced as indicated. Most electrical system troubles can be attributed to neglect of this vital component.

In order to correctly service the electrolyte level it is necessary to remove the battery from the frame. The electrolyte level should be maintained between the two marks on the battery case (**Figure 3**). If the electrolyte level is low, it's a good idea to completely remove the battery so that it can be thoroughly cleaned, serviced, and checked.

Removal/Installation

1. Remove the seat and fender assembly.
2. Disconnect the negative cable from the battery.
3. Disconnect the positive cable from the battery.
4. Remove the battery hold-down strap and pull the battery (**Figure 4**) out slightly to provide access to the vent tube and disconnect it.
5. Lift the battery out of the box.
6. Service the battery as described later in this section.
7. Installation is the reverse of these steps.

Cleaning

After the battery has been removed from the vehicle, check it for corrosion or excessive dirt. The top of the battery in particular should be kept clean. Acid film and dirt will permit current to flow between the terminals, causing the battery to slowly discharge.

For best results when cleaning, first rinse off the top of the battery with plenty of clean water (avoid letting water enter the cells). Then carefully wash the case, both terminals and the battery box with a solution of baking soda and tap water. Keep the cells sealed tight with the filler plugs so that none of the cleaning solution enters a cell, as this would neutralize the cell's electrolyte and seriously damage the battery. Brush the solution on liberally with a stiff bristle parts cleaning brush. Using a

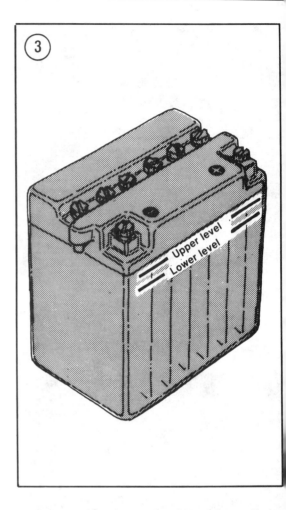

strong spray from a garden hose, clean all the residue from the solution off the battery and all painted surfaces.

Service

CAUTION
Be careful not to spill battery electrolyte on painted or polished surfaces. The liquid is highly corrosive and will damage the finish. If it is spilled, wash it off immediately with soapy water and thoroughly rinse with clean water.

1. Remove the caps from the battery cells and add distilled water to correct the level. Never add tap water or electrolyte (acid) to correct the level.

NOTE
Distilled water is available at most supermarkets.

2. After the level has been corrected and the battery allowed to stand for a few minutes, check the specific gravity of the electrolyte in each cell

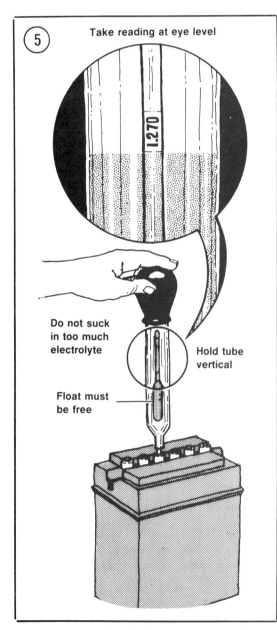

Take reading at eye level

1.270

Do not suck
in too much
electrolyte

Hold tube
vertical

Float must
be free

with a hydrometer (**Figure 5**). See *Testing* in this chapter. Follow the manufacturer's instructions for reading the instrument.

Testing

Hydrometer testing is the best way to check battery condition. Use a hydrometer with numbered graduations from 1.100 to 1.300 rather than one with color-coded bands. To use the hydrometer, squeeze the rubber ball, insert the tip into the cell and release the ball. Draw enough electrolyte to float the weighted float inside the hydrometer. Note the number in line with the electrolyte surface; this is the specific gravity for this cell. Return the electrolyte to the cell from which it came.

The specific gravity of the electrolyte in each battery cell is an excellent indication of that cell's condition. A fully charged cell will read 1.260-1.280 while a cell in good condition reads from 1.230-1.250 and anything below 1.140 is practically dead.

> *NOTE*
> *Specific gravity varies with temperature. For each 10° that electrolyte temperature exceeds 80° F, add 0.004 to reading indicated on hydrometer. Subtract 0.004 for each 10° below 80° F.*

If the cells test in the poor range, the battery requires recharging. The hydrometer is useful for checking the progress of the charging operation. **Table 3** shows approximate state of charge.

Charging

> *CAUTION*
> *Always remove the battery from the vehicle before connecting charging equipment. Never recharge a battery in the vehicle's frame due to the corrosive mist that is emitted during the charging process. If this mist settles on the frame it will corrode the surface.*

> *WARNING*
> *During charging, highly explosive hydrogen gas is released from the battery. The battery should be charged only in a well-ventilated area, and open flames and cigarettes should be kept away. Never check the charge of the battery by arcing across the terminals; the resulting spark can ignite the hydrogen gas.*

1. Connect the positive (+) charger lead to the positive battery terminal and the negative (–)charger lead to the negative battery terminal.

2. Remove all vent caps from the battery, set the charger at 12 volts, and switch it on or plug it into the wall. If the output of the charger is variable, it is best to select a low setting—1 1/2 to 2 amps.

3. After the battery has been charged for about 8 hours, turn the charger off, disconnect the leads and check the specific gravity. It should be within the limits specified in **Table 3**. If it is, and remains stable for one hour, the battery is charged.

4. To ensure good electrical contact, cables must be clean and tight on the battery's terminals. If the cable terminals are badly corroded, even after performing the above cleaning procedures, the cables should be disconnected, removed from the vehicle and cleaned separately with a wire brush and a baking soda solution. After cleaning, apply a very thin coating of petroleum jelly (Vaseline) to the battery terminals before reattaching the cables. After connecting the cables, apply a light coating to the connections also—this will delay future corrosion.

New Battery Installation

When replacing the old battery with a new one, be sure to charge it completely (specific gravity, 1.260-1.280) before installing it in the bike.

Failure to do so, or using the battery with a low electrolyte level will permanently damage the battery.

PERIODIC LUBRICATION

Oil

Oil is graded according to its viscosity, which is an indication of how thick it is. The Society of Automotive Engineers (SAE) system distinguishes oil viscosity by numbers. Thick (heavy) oils have higher viscosity numbers than thin (light) oils. For example, an SAE 5 oil is a thin oil while SAE 90 oil is relatively thick.

Grease

A good quality grease (preferably waterproof) should be used. Water does not wash grease off parts as easily as it washes oil off. In addition, grease maintains its lubricating qualities better than oil on long and strenuous rides.

Cleaning Solvent

A number of solvents can be used to remove old dirt, grease and oil. Kerosene is readily available and comparatively inexpensive. Another inexpensive solvent similar to kerosene is ordinary diesel fuel. Both of these solvents have a very high flash point (they have to be very hot in order to

ignite and catch fire) and can be used safely in any adequately ventilated area away from open flames. This includes pilot lights on home water heaters and clothes dryers that are sometimes located in the garage.

> *WARNING*
> *Never use gasoline to clean parts. Gasoline is extremely volatile and contains tremendously destructive potential energy. The slightest spark from metal parts accidently hitting or a tool slipping could cause a fatal explosion.*

Engine Oil Level Check

Proper operation and long service for the engine, clutch and transmission require clean oil. Check the oil level frequently and add fresh oil as necessary to maintain the correct level. Oil should be changed at the intervals specified in **Table 1**. Refer to **Table 5** for oil capacity.

Try to always use the same brand of oil; do not mix 2 brands at the same time as they all vary slightly in their composition. *Do not* use a 2-stroke engine oil. Use of oil additives is not recommended as it may cause clutch slippage.

Engine Oil Level Check

Engine oil level is checked with the dipstick located at the center of the clutch cover (**Figure 6**).
1. Park the vehicle on level ground and set the parking brake.
2. Start the engine and let it warm up approximately 2-3 minutes.
3. Shut off the engine.
4. Unscrew the dipstick and wipe it clean. Reinsert the dipstick so that the dipstick cap rests on the threads in the hole; *do not* screw it in.
5. Remove the dipstick and check the oil level.

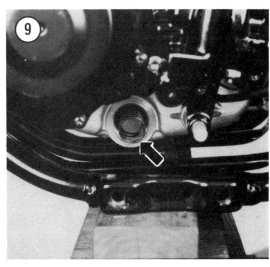

6. The level should be between the 2 lines and not above the upper one. If the level is below the lower line, add the recommended type engine oil (**Table 4**) to correct the level.

> *NOTE*
> *If the engine oil level is too high, remove the excess oil with a syringe or a fork oil level gauge tool.*

Engine Oil and Filter Change

The factory-recommended oil and filter change interval is listed in **Table 1**. This assumes that the vehicle is operated in moderate climates. In extreme climates, oil should changed every 3 months or less, depending upon use. The time interval is more important than the mileage interval because acids formed by combustion blow-by will contaminate the oil even if the vehicle is not run for several months.

Use only a high-quality detergent motor oil with an API classification of SE or SF. The classification is stamped or printed on top of the can or on the label (**Figure 7**). Try to use the same brand of oil at each change.

Use of oil additives is not recommended as it may cause clutch slippage. Refer to **Table 4** for correct oil viscosity to use under anticipated ambient temperatures (not engine oil temperature).

> *NOTE*
> *Never dispose of motor oil in the trash, on the ground, or down a storm drain. Many service stations accept used motor oil and waste haulers provide curbside used motor oil collection. Do not combine other fluids with motor oil to be recycled. To locate a recycler, contact the American Petroleum Institute (API) at www.recycleoil.org.*

To change the clutch/transmission oil you will need the following:
a. Drain pan.
b. Funnel.
c. Can opener or pour spout.
d. 2 quarts of oil.
e. New oil filter.

There are a number of ways to discard the old oil safely. The easiest way is to pour it from the drain pan into a gallon plastic bleach or milk container. Some service stations and oil retailers will accept your used oil for recycling. Check local regulations before discarding the oil in your household trash. Never drain the oil onto the ground.
1. Start the engine and let it reach operating temperature.

2. Park the vehicle on level ground and set the parking brake.

3. Shut the engine off and place a drain pan under it.

4. Remove the drain plug (**Figure 8**) from the left-hand side of the engine. When the drain plug is removed, also remove the compression spring and oil strainer (**Figure 9**).

5. Remove the oil filter cover drain screw (A, **Figure 10**). Then remove the 2 remaining cover screws (B, **Figure 10**).

6. Remove the oil filter cover (C, **Figure 10**) and oil filter (A, **Figure 11**).

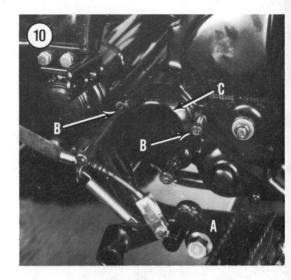

> *NOTE*
> *If you do not plan on replacing the oil filter, remove only the lower oil filter cover bolt as shown in **Figure 12**. This will allow complete draining of the oil filter cavity.*

7. Let the oil drain for at least 15-20 minutes.

8. Clean the oil drain bolt cavity (**Figure 13**) of all sludge or other debris.

9. Inspect the sealing washers on all plugs and bolts. Replace if damaged.

10. Clean the oil strainer screen spring (**Figure 14**) and drain plug in solvent and thoroughly dry. Inspect the strainer screen for holes or defects; replace if necessary.

11. Install the spring onto the filter screen (**Figure 15**). Then insert the screen into the engine cavity (**Figure 9**). Install the drain plug and tighten to 43 N•m (31 ft.-lb.).

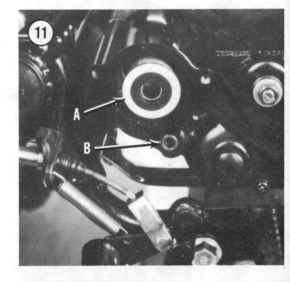

> *NOTE*
> *Make sure the O-ring is installed onto the oil filter cover (**Figure 16**) and onto the crankcase (B, **Figure 11**) before installing the filter cover in Step 12.*

12. Install a new oil filter. See **Figure 17** and A, **Figure 11**. Install the oil filter cover (C, **Figure 10**) and tighten the bolts securely.

13. Wipe the end of a funnel off and insert it into the oil fill hole and fill the engine with the correct type (**Table 4**) and quantity (**Table 5**) of oil.

14. Screw in the oil filter cap securely.

15. Start the engine, let it run at moderate speed and check for leaks.

16. Turn the engine off and check for correct oil level as described in this chapter; adjust as necessary.

> *NOTE*
> *If the engine oil level is too high, remove the excess oil with a syringe or a fork oil level gauge tool.*

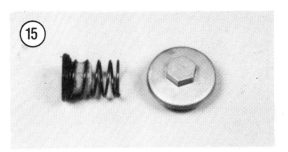

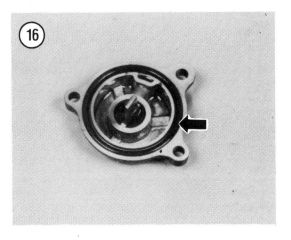

17. After changing the engine oil, check the oil flow as follows:
   a. Remove the oil check bolt in the cylinder head (**Figure 18**).
   b. Start the engine and allow it to idle. Do not increase engine rpm.
   c. Oil should start to seep out of the oil check bolt hole (**Figure 18**) within one minute. If not, immediately stop the engine and find and correct the cause.
   d. When the oil flow is correct, install the check bolt and tighten it to 7 N•m (5.1 ft.-lb.).
18. Reinstall all parts.

Front Fork Oil Change
(YTM200 and YTM225)

NOTE
*All models use a wire ring to secure the fork cap and spring. See **Figure 19**. It will be easier to remove the wire ring with the front fork and front tire installed on the vehicle.*

1. Jack up the vehicle and remove the front wheel as described in Chapter Eight.
2. Remove the fork rubber cap (**Figure 20**).

> *WARNING*
> *The fork is assembled with spring preload. Keep your face away from the fork end. The fork cap may spring out.*

> *NOTE*
> *An assistant will be required to help remove the fork caps.*

3. Remove the fork cap (**Figure 21**) by pushing the cap in and prying out the wire ring. See **Figure 22**.

> *NOTE*
> *A small screwdriver or probe will be necessary to pry out the wire ring. See* **Figure 23**.

4. Repeat Step 2 and Step 3 for the opposite fork cap.

> *NOTE*
> *Because the front forks are not equipped with drain screws, the forks must be removed to drain the oil.*

5. Remove the fork tube as follows:
   a. Disconnect the brake cable from the left side fork tube (**Figure 24**).
   b. Pull the fork boot breather hose from the steering stem (**Figure 25**).
   c. Loosen the front fork bolts (**Figure 26**) and slide the fork tube out of the steering stem.
6. Remove the fork spring (**Figure 27**). Wipe the spring clean of all oil and lay it on clean newspapers.
7. Turn the fork over and pour the fork oil out and discard it. Pump the fork several times by hand to expel most of the remaining oil.

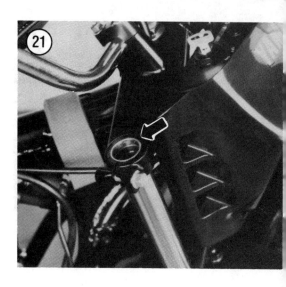

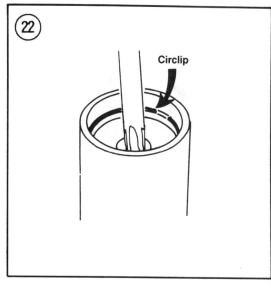

Circlip

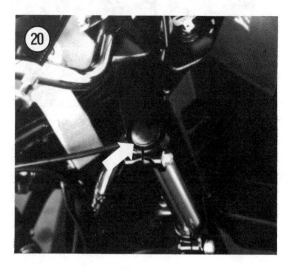

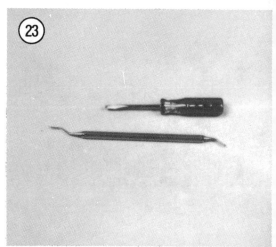

8. Reverse Step 4 to install the fork tube. Tighten the fork bolt to 20 N•m (14 ft.-lb.) and the lower bolts to (30 N•m (22 ft.-lb.).

9. Fill each fork with the specified viscosity and quantity of fork oil. Refer to **Table 6**.

NOTE
*The viscosity of the oil can be varied according to your own preference and to the type of riding terrain (lower viscosity for less damping and higher viscosity for more damping action). Always use the specified **amount** of oil.*

NOTE
To measure the correct amount of fluid, use a plastic baby bottle. These have measurements in fluid ounces (oz.) and cubic centimeters (cc) on the side.

WARNING
Be sure the baby bottle is inaccessible to children after using it to measure oil. A poisonous residue will remain.

NOTE
Steps 10-13 describe front fork oil level check.

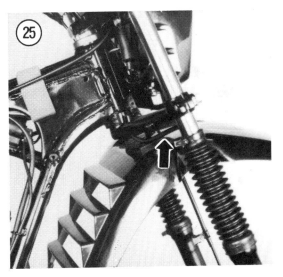

10. Allow the oil to settle for a few minutes. Then push the front fork up and down to remove all air bubbles from the fork oil.

11. Install the front wheel as described in Chapter Eight.

12. With an assistant's help, position the vehicle so that the forks are placed in a vertical position.

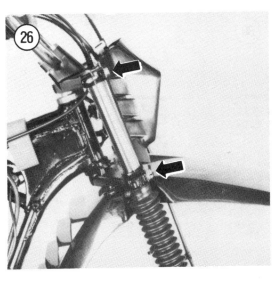

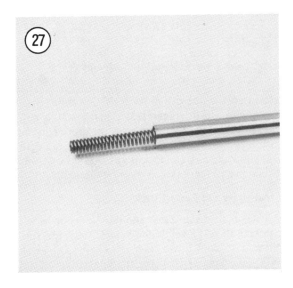

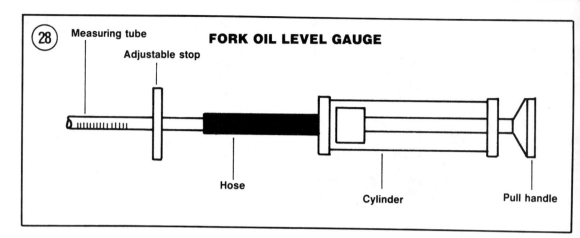

FORK OIL LEVEL GAUGE

28 Measuring tube — Adjustable stop — Hose — Cylinder — Pull handle

13. Using a fork oil level gauge (**Figure 28**) measure the distance from the top of the fork tube to the top of the oil (**Figure 29**). Refer to **Table 6** for the correct specifications. Repeat for the opposite fork.

> *NOTE*
> *A tape measure can be used to perform Step 13. However, to assure a precise oil level, you may want to invest in a fork oil level gauge offered by Yamaha or one of the numerous companies dealing in suspension accessories.*

14. Position the vehicle so that the front wheel clears the ground. Push down on the front wheel so that the forks are completely extended.

15. Check the O-ring in the fork cap (**Figure 30**); replace it if worn or damaged.

16. Install the fork spring (**Figure 27**) so that the small spring end faces down.

> *NOTE*
> *An assistant will be required in Step 17.*

> *WARNING*
> *If the wire ring installed in Step 17 is not engaged completely in the fork tube groove, the fork cap may fly out of the tube and injure your face.*

17. Insert the fork cap in the fork tube and push it down with a drift (**Figure 22**). Then install a new wire ring, making sure it engages the groove in the fork tube. Slowly release tension against the drift and allow the fork cap to seat against the wire ring.

18. Reinstall the fork cap cover (**Figure 20**).

Final Drive Oil Level Check

The final drive case should be cool when checking the oil level. If the vehicle has been run, allow it to cool down, then check the oil level. When checking or changing the final drive oil, do

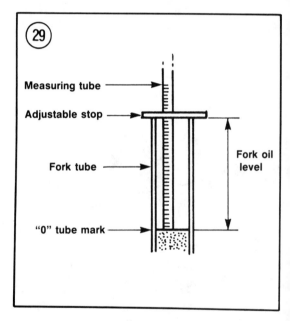

29 Measuring tube — Adjustable stop — Fork tube — "0" tube mark — Fork oil level

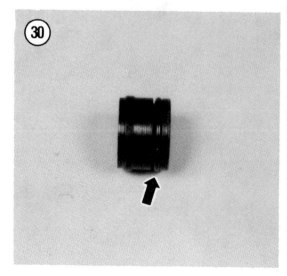

30

not allow any dirt or foreign matter to enter the case opening.

1. Park the vehicle on a level surface. Set the parking brake.

2. Wipe the area around the oil filler cap clean and unscrew the oil filler cap (**Figure 31**).

3. The oil level is correct if the oil is up to the lower edge of the filler cap hole. If the oil level is low, add the correct type gear oil (**Table 4**) until the oil level is correct.

4. Install the oil filler cap.

Final Drive Oil Change

The factory-recommended oil change interval is listed in **Table 1**.

To drain the oil you will need the following:

   a. Drain pan.

   b. Funnel.

   c. Approximately 0.13 liter (0.14 qt.) of hypoid gear oil.

Discard oil as outlined under *Engine Oil and Filter Change* in this chapter.

1. Ride the vehicle until normal operating temperature is obtained.

2. Park the vehicle on level ground and set the parking brake.

3. Place a drain pan under the drain plug.

4. Remove the oil filler cap (**Figure 31**) and the drain plug (**Figure 32**).

5. Let the oil drain for at least 10 minutes to ensure that most of the oil has drained out.

6. Inspect the sealing washer on the drain plug; replace the sealing washer if necessary.

7. Install the drain plug and tighten it securely.

8. Add recommended type (**Table 4**) and amount (**Table 7**) hypoid gear oil. Remove the funnel and make sure the oil level is correct.

NOTE
In order to measure the correct amount of fluid, use a discarded baby bottle. These have measurements in cubic centimeters (cc) and fluid ounces (oz.) on the side.

9. Install the oil filler cap (**Figure 31**).

10. Test ride the vehicle and check for oil leaks. After the test ride, recheck the oil level as described in this chapter and readjust if necessary.

**Drive Chain Lubrication
(YTM200K, L, N)**

Lubricate the drive chain throughout the riding day.

1. Remove the rubber inspection cap (**Figure 33**) from the chain guard.

2. The drive chain has small rubber O-rings fitted between the side plates (**Figure 34**). The chain should be lubricated only with SAE 20W-50 motor oil. Do not use any other type of lubricant as it may damage the O-rings.

> *CAUTION*
> *Special care must be observed when servicing and cleaning a drive chain on all YTM200K, L and N models. The drive chain should be cleaned with kerosene (do not use any other solvent) and wiped dry. Lubricate it with SAE 20W-50 motor oil.*

3. Shift the transmission into NEUTRAL. Push the vehicle forward while lubricating the drive chain through the inspection hole (**Figure 35**).

> *NOTE*
> *When using motor oil to lubricate the chain, it is easier to first pour the oil into an oil can with a long spout.*

4. Reinstall the inspection cap (**Figure 33**).

Control Cables

The control cables should be lubricated at the intervals specified in **Table 1**. They should also be inspected at this time for fraying and the cable sheath should be checked for chafing. The cables are relatively inexpensive and should be replaced when found to be faulty.

The control cables can be lubricated either with oil or any of the popular cable lubricants and a cable lubricator.

> *NOTE*
> *Inadequate lubrication is the main cause of cable breakage or cable stiffness. Maintaining the cables as described in this section will assure long service.*

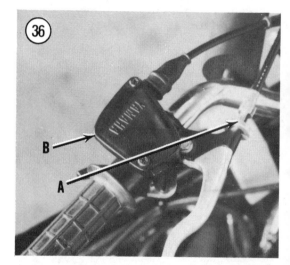

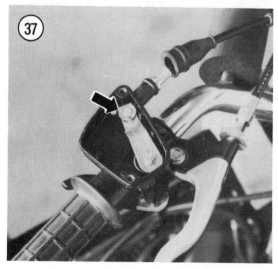

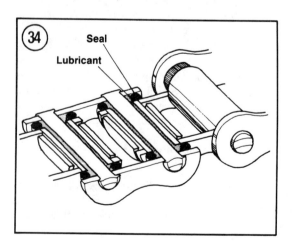

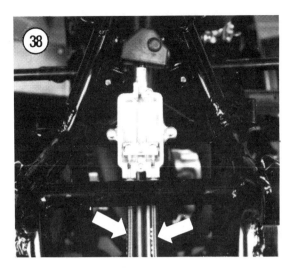

1. Disconnect the brake cables from the handlebar levers (A, **Figure 36**).
2. Remove the throttle housing cover (B, **Figure 36**) and disconnect the cable (**Figure 37**).

NOTE

*On YFM200 models, disconnect the left- and right-hand brake cables at the junction block and lubricate them separately. See **Figure 38**.*

3. Loosen the rear brake cable adjuster and disconnect the cable at the brake pedal (**Figure 39**).
4. Attach a lubricator to the end of the cable following the manufacturer's instructions.
5. Insert the nozzle of the lubricant can in the lubricator, press the button on the can and hold it down until the lubricant begins to flow out of the other end of the cable. See **Figure 40**. Repeat for each cable.

NOTE

*Place a shop cloth at the end of the brake cable(s) to catch all excess lubricant that will flow out. When servicing the throttle cable, remove the throttle slide (**Figure 41**) and clean it of excess lubricant.*

6. Remove the lubricator, reconnect the cable(s) and adjust the cable(s) as described in this chapter.

Steering Head Bearings
(YTM200 and YTM225)

Lubricate the steering head bearings at the intervals specified in **Table 1**. The steering head must be removed and the bearings disassembled to perform this procedure. See Chapter Eight.

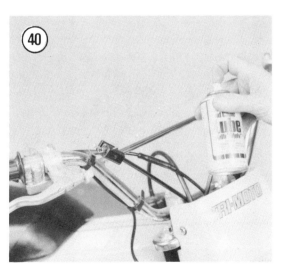

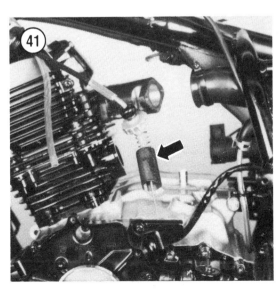

Knuckle and Steering Shaft Lubrication (YFM200)

The steering knuckle and shaft are equipped with grease fittings. See **Figure 42** and **Figure 43**. At the intervals specified in **Table 1**, lubricate the steering knuckle and shaft with a lithium soap base grease.

Swing Arm Bushing Lubrication

On models equipped with swingarms, lubricate the swing arm bushings at the intervals specified in **Table 1**. The swing arm must be removed on all models to perform this procedure. See Chapter Ten.

Brake Cam Lubrication

Lubricate the front brake cam at the specified intervals (**Table 1**), or whenever the front wheel is removed.

1. Remove the front wheel as described in Chapter Eight or Chapter Nine.
2. Remove the brake panel assembly from the wheel hub.
3. Remove the brake shoes from the backing plate by pulling up on the center of each shoe. See **Figure 44**.

> *NOTE*
> *Place a clean shop rag on the linings to protect them from oil and grease during removal.*

4. Wipe away old grease from the camshaft and pivot pins on the backing plate (**Figure 45**). Also clean the pivot hole and camshaft contact area of each shoe. Be careful not to get any grease on the linings.

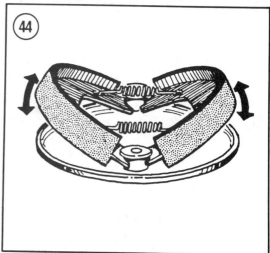

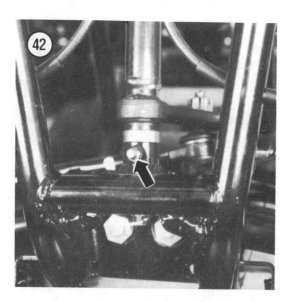

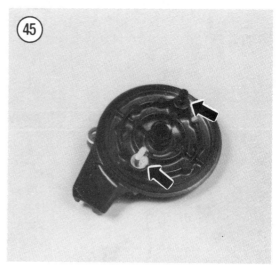

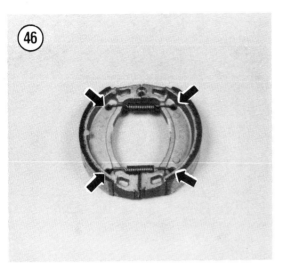

5. Lightly apply a high-temperature grease to all brake pivot shoe points (**Figure 45**) and to the brake return spring ends (**Figure 46**).

6. Reassemble the brake assembly.

7. Reinstall the brake panel assembly as described in Chapter Eleven.

8. Reinstall the wheel as described in Chapter Eight or Chapter Nine.

9. Adjust the front brake as described in this chapter.

Miscellaneous Lubrication Points

Lubricate the front brake lever, rear brake lever and rear brake pedal pivot points with lightweight machine oil.

PERIODIC MAINTENANCE

Drive Chain Adjustment
(YTM200K, L, N)

The drive chain tension should be checked throughout the riding day and adjusted as needed.

1. Park the vehicle on level ground and set the parking brake.

2. Shift the transmission into NEUTRAL.

3. Remove the rubber inspection cover.

4. Through the inspection hole, push up on the drive chain and then let it fall back down. The correct amount of free play is 10-15 mm (7/16-5/8 in.). Refer to **Figure 47**.

5. If the free play is excessive, perform the following.

6. Loosen the rear wheel hub bolts (**Figure 48**).

7. Referring to **Figure 49**, turn the chain adjuster in or out as required to obtain the free play specified in Step 4.

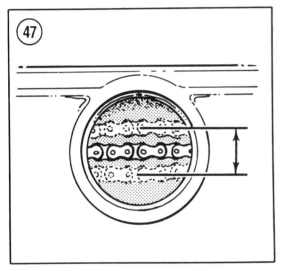

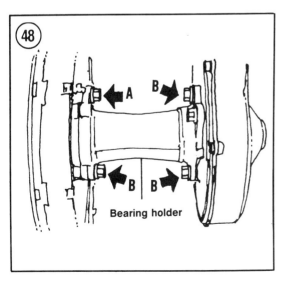

Bearing holder

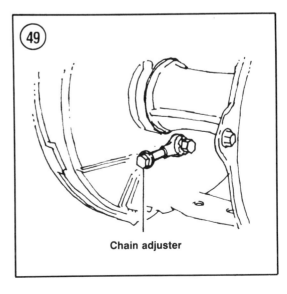

Chain adjuster

8. Release the parking brake and push the vehicle forward to move the chain to another position. Recheck the adjustment. Chains rarely wear or stretch evenly and, as a result, the free play will not remain constant over the entire chain.

9. If the chain cannot be adjusted within the limits specified in Step 4, it is excessively worn and stretched and should be replaced. Refer to Chapter Ten. Always replace both sprockets when replacing the drive chain; never install a new chain over worn sprockets.

10. Tighten the rear wheel hub bolts as follows:
   a. Upper left hub bolt (A, **Figure 48**): 60 N•m (43 ft.-lb.).
   b. All other bolts (B, **Figure 48**): 45 N•m (32 ft.-lb.).

Front Brake Lining Inspection

The front brake pads can be checked by depressing the brake pedal and observing the position of the wear indicator. See **Figure 50**. If the indicator reaches the limit line, the brake shoes must be replaced as described in Chapter Eleven.

Rear Brake Pad Inspection

Rear brake pad wear is checked by observing the position of the brake caliper adjusting bolt (**Figure 51**). If the bolt head is close to the locknut, the brake pads are worn and should be replaced as described in Chapter Eleven.

> *NOTE*
> *Always replace both pads at the same time.*

Brake Adjustment

Periodic brake adjustment is required to compensate for brake drum and shoe lining wear and brake cable stretch. However, brake adjustment cannot compensate for excessive wear. Check the front and rear brake linings as described in this chapter before adjusting the front or rear brake.

Front Brake Lever Adjustment (YTM200 and YTM225)

The front brake lever free play should be checked before each ride and adjusted as necessary. The brake lever should travel 5-8 mm (1/4-5/16 in.) before the brake shoes come in contact with the brake drum, but it must not be adjusted so closely that the brake shoes contact the brake drum with the lever at rest. If adjustment is necessary, perform the following.

1. Loosen the locknut and turn the adjuster at the hand lever in or out to achieve the correct amount of free play (A, **Figure 36**). If the correct amount of free play cannot be obtained at the hand lever, proceed to Step 2.

2. Turn the hand lever adjuster all the way in. Then turn the wheel adjustment nut at the brake arm (**Figure 52**) in or out to achieve the correct amount of free play. Tighten the hand lever adjuster locknut.

3. Make final adjustments, as required, with the hand lever adjuster (A, **Figure 36**).

NOTE
Make sure the cutout relief in the wheel adjustment nut is properly seated on the brake arm pivot pin.

Front Brake Lever Adjustment (YFM200)

The front brake lever free play should be checked before each ride and adjusted as necessary. The brake levers should travel 5-8 mm (1/4-5/16 in.) before the brake shoes come in contact with the brake drum, but it must not be adjusted so closely that the brake shoes contact the brake drum with the lever at rest. If adjustment is necessary, perform the following.

1. Loosen the locknut and turn the adjuster at the hand lever in or out to achieve the correct amount of free play (A, **Figure 36**). If the correct amount of free play cannot be obtained at the hand lever, proceed to Step 2.

2. Turn the hand lever adjuster all the way in. Then turn the wheel adjustment nut at the left and right brake arms (**Figure 53**) in or out to achieve the correct amount of free play. Tighten the hand lever adjuster locknut.

NOTE
*Make sure the brake cable joint is level as shown in **Figure 54** when adjusting the front brake.*

3. Make final adjustments, as required, with the hand lever adjuster (A, **Figure 36**).

Rear Brake Adjustment

The rear brake pedal free play should be checked before each ride and adjusted if necessary. Free play is the distance the pedal travels from the at-rest position to the applied position when the pedal is lightly depressed. If the rear brake pedal is adjusted, the parking brake must also be adjusted.

1. The rear brake pedal should be adjusted when the free play exceeds 50 mm (2 in.). Adjust as follows:

    a. Park the vehicle on a level surface.

    b. Loosen the locknut (**Figure 55**) and turn the adjuster bolt until the free play is approximately 5 mm (3/16 in.).

    c. Tighten the locknut and recheck the adjustment.

2. Pump the brake pedal 2 or 3 times.

3. Loosen the rear brake handlebar cable adjuster and loosen the adjuster all the way (**Figure 56**).

4. Refer to **Figure 57**. At the brake caliper, loosen the rear brake pedal cable (A) and brake lever cable (B) adjusters.

5. Loosen the brake caliper adjusting bolt locknut and loosen the adjusting bolt (C, **Figure 57**).

6. Turn the rear brake lever cable adjuster (B, **Figure 57**) in so that the brake caliper brake arm can be adjusted as shown in **Figure 58**.

7. Slowly turn the brake caliper adjusting bolt (C, **Figure 57**) in (clockwise) until it becomes tight, then back it out (counterclockwise) 1/4 turn. Tighten the locknut.

> *NOTE*
> *When tightening the adjusting bolt locknut in Step 7, make sure to hold the adjusting bolt with a wrench to prevent the bolt from turning.*

8. Tighten the brake pedal cable adjuster (A, **Figure 57**) to obtain a gap of 0-1 mm (1/32 in.) between the brake caliper lever and the pin as shown in **Figure 59**.

9. Block the rear end of the vehicle so that the rear wheels clear the ground. Shift the transmission to NEUTRAL and spin the rear wheels. There should be *no noticeable* brake drag. If there is, repeat Steps 2-8.

10. Remove the wood blocks from the vehicle and lower it to the ground. Check the free play at the brake pedal (**Figure 55**) and at the hand brake lever (**Figure 56**). The free play should be:

   a. Rear brake pedal: 50 mm or less (2 in. or less).
   b. Hand brake lever: 10 mm or less (7/16 in. or less).

If these dimensions are incorrect, the brake is adjusted improperly. Repeat Steps 1-9 and recheck.

Clutch Adjustment

The clutch should be adjusted at the intervals specified in **Table 1**.

1. Loosen the clutch adjuster locknut (**Figure 60**).

2. Using a screwdriver, turn the clutch adjuster counterclockwise until resistance is felt. Then turn the adjuster 1/8 turn clockwise.

3. Tighten the clutch adjuster locknut to 15 N•m (11 ft.-lb.).

Cam Chain Adjustment
(All Models Except YFM200DXS)

In time the camshaft chain and guide will wear and develop slack. This will cause engine noise and if neglected too long will cause engine damage. The cam chain tension should be adjusted at the

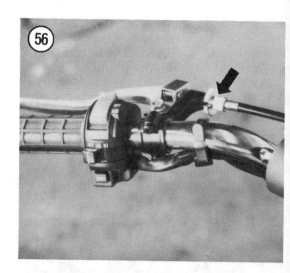

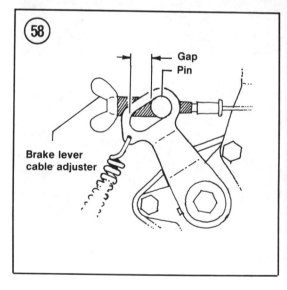

Gap
Pin

Brake lever
cable adjuster

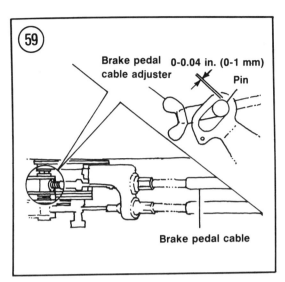

Brake pedal cable adjuster   0-0.04 in. (0-1 mm)   Pin

Brake pedal cable

specified intervals (**Table 1**) or whenever it becomes noisy. Refer to *Tune-Up* in this chapter for adjustment procedures.

Throttle Lever Adjustment

The throttle lever should have 3-5 mm (1/8-3/16 in.) free play measured at the tip of the throttle lever (**Figure 61**). If adjustment is necessary, perform the following.

1. Slide the cable adjuster cover away from the adjuster (**Figure 62**).
2. Loosen the cable locknut and turn the adjuster (**Figure 62**) to obtain the correct amount of free play. Tighten the locknut and recheck the adjustment.
3. Slide the cable adjuster cover over the adjuster.
4. Check the throttle cable from lever to carburetor. Make sure it is not kinked or chafed. Replace as necessary.

> *NOTE*
> *If the throttle operation feels tight and the throttle cable is not kinked or damaged, the cable is probably dry and requires lubrication. Refer to **Control Cables** in this chapter.*

Decompression Lever Adjustment (YTM200K, L, N)

The decompression lever on these models must be adjusted after adjusting the valves. Refer to *Tune-Up* in this chapter.

Air Cleaner

The air cleaner element should be removed and cleaned after each day's ride and replaced whenever it is damaged or starts to deteriorate.

The air cleaner removes dust and abrasive particles from the air before the air enters the

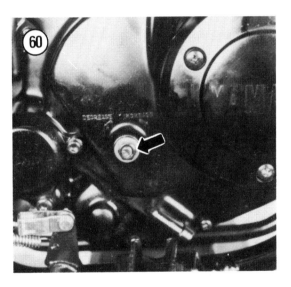

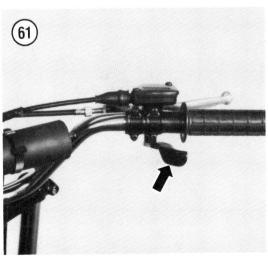

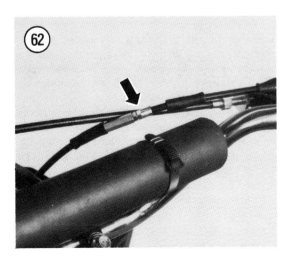

carburetor and engine. Without the air cleaner or
with improper air cleaner service, dirt and dust will
enter the engine and cause rapid wear to the
cylinder, piston, rings, bearings, etc. In addition,
dust particles can clog small passages in the
carburetor. Never run the vehicle without the air
cleaner properly cleaned and installed.

1. Remove the seat and fender assembly.

2. Remove the screws securing the air cleaner case
cover (**Figure 63**) and remove the cover. On some
models, the air cleaner case cover is installed at the
top of the frame directly underneath the seat.

3. Remove the air filter (**Figure 64**).

4. Remove the wingbolt from the back of the guide
(**Figure 65**) and pull the element (A, **Figure 66**) off
of the guide (B, **Figure 66**).

5. Clean the element gently in cleaning solvent or
soap and water until all dirt is removed.
Thoroughly dry in a clean shop cloth until all
solvent residue is removed. Let it dry for about one
hour.

> *CAUTION*
> *Do not clean the element in solvent that
> has been used to clean engine parts.
> Small metal particles in the solvent can
> become lodged in the air filter element
> and enter the engine, resulting in
> abnormal engine wear.*

> *CAUTION*
> *Inspect the element; if it is torn or
> broken in any area it should be
> replaced. Do not run with a damaged
> element as it may allow dirt to enter the
> engine.*

6. Pour a small amount of foam air filter oil or
SAE 10W/30 motor oil into the element and work
it into the porous foam material. Do not
oversaturate the element as too much oil will
restrict air flow. The element will be discolored by
the oil and should have an even color indicating
that the oil is distributed evenly.

7. Install the element into the guide and secure
with the wingbolt (**Figure 65**). Then apply a band
of waterproof grease to the bottom of the air filter
where it seats in the air box (C, **Figure 66**). The
grease provides a leak-proof seal between the air
filter and air cleaner housing.

8. Wipe out the interior of the air cleaner case with
a shop rag and cleaning solvent. Remove any
foreign matter that may have passed through a
broken element.

9. Install the assembly into the air cleaner case. If your air filter guide is marked with UPPER, that end should face up.

CAUTION
An improperly installed air cleaner element will allow dirt and grit to enter the carburetor and engine, causing expensive engine damage.

10. Install the case cover (**Figure 63**). If your case cover is marked with UPPER, that end should face up.

11. Install the seat and fender assembly.

Fuel Shutoff Valve and Filter

The integral fuel filter in the fuel shutoff valve removes particles in the fuel which would otherwise enter the carburetor. This could cause

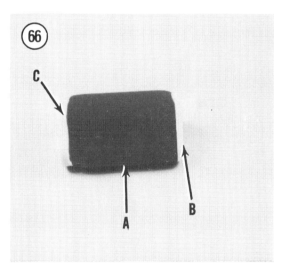

the float needle to stay in the open position or clog one of the jets. Refer to Chapter Six for service procedures.

Fuel Line Inspection

Inspect all fuel lines from the fuel tank to the carburetor. If any line is cracked or starting to deteriorate it must be replaced. Make sure the small hose clamps are in place and holding securely.

WARNING
A damaged or deteriorated fuel line presents a very dangerous fire hazard to both the rider and the vehicle if fuel should spill onto a hot engine or exhaust pipe.

Steering Head Adjustment Check (YTM200 and YFM225)

The steering head is fitted with loose ball bearings. It should be checked and repacked with grease at the intervals specified in **Table 1**.

Jack up the front end so that the front wheel is off the ground. Hold onto the front fork tubes and gently rock the fork assembly back and forth. If you can feel looseness, refer to Chapter Eight.

Steering Inspection (YFM200)

The front steering assembly should be checked for looseness, wear and damage at the intervals specified in **Table 1** or whenever a serious spill or collision is experienced.

1. Stand beside the vehicle and grasp the handlebar. Gently pull the handlebar up and down and then from side to side. If you can feel excessive looseness or play, replace the steering shaft bushings as described in Chapter Nine.

2. Turn the handlebar to the left until it stops. Then gently move the handlebar from the right to left a few times. While shaking the handlebar in this manner, check the tie-rod ends (**Figure 67**) for excessive movement or play. If any vertical play is detected, replace the tie-rod ends as described in Chapter Nine.

3. Repeat Step 2 for the opposite side.

4. Place the vehicle on wood blocks so that the front wheels clear the ground. Move each wheel back and forth and from side to side to check for excessive looseness in the knuckles or wheel bearings. Replace worn or damaged parts as described in Chapter Nine.

Wheel Bearings

The wheel bearings should be checked for looseness or damage at the specified intervals in **Table 1**. The wheel bearings can be checked by raising the vehicle's front or rear end and rotating the wheels. Check for excessive wheel bearing noise. Then grasp the wheels and try to move the wheel from side to side. If you can feel looseness or the bearings emit a loud grinding sound when the wheel is turned, replace them as described in Chapter Eight or Chapter Nine.

The wheel bearings should be repacked at the intervals specified in **Table 1**. Refer to Chapter Eight or Chapter Nine.

Front Toe-in Adjustment (YFM200)

Complete procedures are described in Chapter Nine.

Spark Arrester Cleaning

The spark arrester should be cleaned every 30 days. Refer to *Carbon Removal* in Chapter Six.

Nuts, Bolts and Other Fasteners

Constant vibration from off-road riding can loosen many of the fasteners. Check the tightness of all fasteners, especially those on:

a. Engine mounting hardware.
b. Engine crankcase covers.
c. Handlebar and front forks.
d. Brake pedal and lever.
e. Exhaust system.
f. Suspension system.

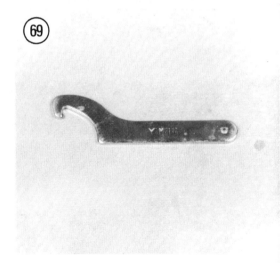

> *NOTE*
> *If any fasteners are loose, refer to the appropriate chapter for torque specifications.*

SUSPENSION ADJUSTMENT

Suspension adjustments should be performed to best suit varying riding conditions.

Front Shock Absorber Adjustment (YFM200DXS)

Spring adjustment on this model can be adjusted by rotating the cam ring at the base of the spring—clockwise to increase preload and counterclockwise to decrease it. See **Figure 68**. Both cams must be indexed on the same detent.

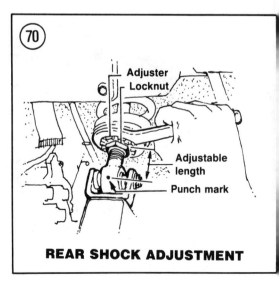

REAR SHOCK ADJUSTMENT

Monoshock Spring Pre-load Adjustment

Spring adjustment can be performed with the 32 mm wrench in the owner's tool kit (**Figure 69**).
1. Using the 32 mm wrench, loosen the locknut and turn the adjuster. Tighten the spring to increase spring preload or loosen it to decrease it. See **Figure 70**.

> *NOTE*
> *Adjustments should be made in increments of 10 mm each time; test ride the vehicle after each adjustment.*

2A. *YTM200 and YTM225:* The installed adjustment length (A, **Figure 71**) must be within the following range:
  a. Standard length: 57.8 mm (2.3 in.).
  b. Minimum length: 57.8 mm (2.3 in.).
  c. Maximum length: 67.8 mm (2.7 in.).
2B. *YFM200DXS:* The installed adjustment length (B, **Figure 71**) must be within the following range:
  a. Standard length: 74.3 mm (2.9 in.).

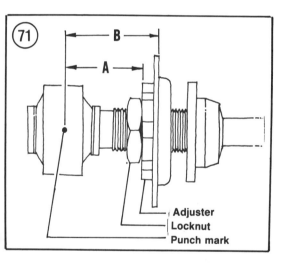

71

Adjuster
Locknut
Punch mark

72

A

B

  b. Minimum length: 67.3 mm (2.6 in.).
  c. Maximum length: 77.3 mm (3.0 in.).
3. After the adjustment is set, tighten the locknut to 42 N•m (30 ft.-lb.).

TUNE-UP

A complete tune-up should be performed at the intervals specified in **Table 1**. The purpose of the tune-up is to restore the performance lost due to normal wear and deterioration of parts.

Table 8 summarizes tune-up specifications.

Before starting a tune-up procedure, make sure to first have all new parts on hand.

Because different systems in an engine interact, the procedures should be done in the following order:
  a. Clean or replace the air cleaner element.
  b. Tighten cylinder head bolts.
  c. Adjust valve clearances.
  d. Adjust decompression lever (YTM200K, L, N).
  e. Adjust camshaft chain tension.
  f. Check engine compression.
  g. Check or replace spark plug.
  h. Check ignition timing.
  i. Adjust carburetor idle speed.

Tools

To perform a tune-up on your Yamaha, you will need the following tools:
  a. Spark plug wrench.
  b. Socket wrench and assorted sockets.
  c. Flat feeler gauge.
  d. Compression gauge.
  e. Spark plug feeler gauge and gap adjusting tool.
  f. Ignition timing light.
  g. Portable tachometer.
  h. Torque wrench.

Air Filter Element

The air filter element should be cleaned or replaced before doing other tune-up procedures. Refer to *Air Filter Servicing* in this chapter.

Cylinder Head Bolts

The engine must be at room temperature for this procedure (80° F/26° C or cooler).
1. Park the vehicle on level ground. Set the parking brake.
2. Remove the fuel tank. See Chapter Six.
3. Tighten the 4 cylinder head bolts (A, **Figure 72**) to 22 N•m (16 ft.-lb.) in a criss-cross pattern.

4. The fender and seat should be left off at this time for the following procedures.

Valve Adjustment

Valve clearance measurement must be made with the engine cool, at room temperature.

1. Park the vehicle on level ground. Set the parking brake.

2. Remove the fuel tank. See Chapter Six.

3. Remove the fender and seat assembly.

4. Remove the spark plug (this makes it easier to turn over the engine by hand).

5. Remove both valve adjustment covers (B, **Figure 72**).

6. Unscrew the timing plug from the left-hand crankcase cover (**Figure 73**).

7. Rotate the engine by turning the recoil starter handle.

8. Turn the engine until the piston is at top dead center (TDC) on the compression stroke and the "T" mark on the flywheel is aligned with the stationary pointer on the crankcase (**Figure 74**).

> *NOTE*
> *A piston at TDC on its compression stroke will have free play in both of its rocker arms, indicating that both the intake and exhaust valves are closed.*

9. If the engine timing mark is aligned with the "T" mark, but both rocker arms are not loose, rotate the engine 360° until both valves have free play.

10. Check the intake and exhaust valve clearance by inserting a flat feeler gauge between the rocker arm pad and the camshaft lobe (**Figure 75**). When the clearance is correct, there will be a slight resistance on the feeler gauge when it is inserted and withdrawn. Refer to **Table 8** for the correct valve clearance specification.

> *NOTE*
> *Step 11 describes valve adjustment. The valve adjusting wrench used in the following procedures may be purchased from Yamaha (Part No. YM-08035).*

11. To correct the clearance, loosen the valve locknut (**Figure 76**). Then turn the adjuster in or out so there is a slight resistance felt on the feeler gauge. Hold the adjuster to prevent it from turning further and tighten the locknut securely. Then recheck the clearance to make sure the adjuster did not slip when the locknut was tightened. Readjust if necessary.

12. Rotate the engine 360° and repeat Step 9 to make sure the adjustment is correct. If the

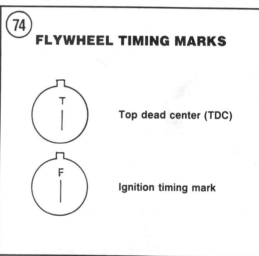

FLYWHEEL TIMING MARKS

T — Top dead center (TDC)

F — Ignition timing mark

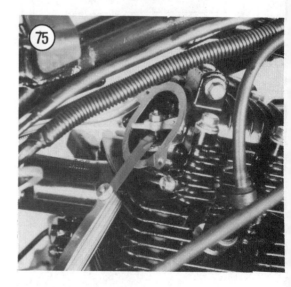

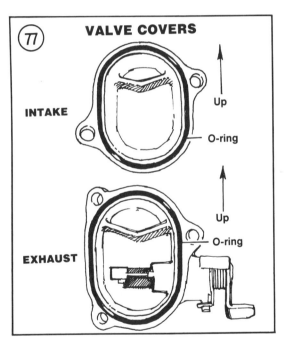

VALVE COVERS

INTAKE

Up

O-ring

Up

O-ring

EXHAUST

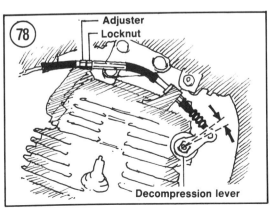

Adjuster

Locknut

Decompression lever

clearance is still not correct, repeat Step No. 11 until it is correct.

13. Inspect the rubber O-ring on each valve adjusting cover. Replace if they are starting to deteriorate or harden. Install both covers and tighten securely. **Figure 77** identifies the valve covers.

14. Install the spark plug and timing hole plug.

Decompression Lever Adjustment (YTM200K, L, N)

1. Park the vehicle on level ground.
2. Remove the fuel tank. See Chapter Six.
3. Remove the fender and seat assembly.
4. Remove the spark plug (this makes it easier to turn over the engine by hand).
5. Remove both valve adjustment covers (B, **Figure 72**).
6. Unscrew the timing plug from the left-hand crankcase cover (**Figure 73**).
7. Rotate the engine by turning the recoil starter handle.
8. Turn the engine until the piston is at top dead center (TDC) on the compression stroke and the "T" mark on the flywheel is aligned with the stationary pointer on the crankcase (**Figure 74**).

NOTE
A piston at TDC on its compression stroke will have free play in both of its rocker arms, indicating that both the intake and exhaust valves are closed.

9. If the engine timing mark is aligned with the "T" mark, but both rocker arms are not loose, rotate the engine 360° until both valves have free play.

10. Refer to **Figure 78**. Perform the following:
   a. Loosen the decompression cable adjuster locknut.
   b. Turn the adjuster to obtain 2-3 mm (3/32-1/8 in.) free play at the end of the decompression lever.
   c. Tighten the locknut and recheck the adjustment.

11. Reinstall all parts previously removed. Refer to **Figure 77** for valve cover identification.

Camshaft Chain Tensioner Adjustment (All Models Except YFM200DXS)

In time the camshaft chain and guide will wear and develop slack. This will cause engine noise and if neglected too long will cause engine damage. The cam chain tension should be adjusted at the specified intervals (**Table 1**) or whenever it becomes noisy.

1. Park the vehicle on a level surface.

2. Remove the seat and fender assembly.

3. Remove both valve covers (B, **Figure 72**).

4. Remove the timing plug from the left-hand crankcase cover (**Figure 73**).

5. Rotate the engine by turning the recoil starter handle.

6. Turn the engine until the piston is at top dead center (TDC) on the compression stroke and the "T" mark on the flywheel is aligned with the stationary pointer on the crankcase (**Figure 74**).

> *NOTE*
> *A piston at TDC on its compression stroke will have free play in both of its rocker arms, indicating that both the intake and exhaust valves are closed.*

7. Grasp and attempt to move both rocker arms. If both rocker arms are not loose, rotate the engine 360° until both valves have free play. Reinstall the valve adjustment covers. See **Figure 77**.

8. Remove the cam chain adjuster cover (**Figure 79**).

9. Loosen the adjuster locknut (A, **Figure 80**) and turn the adjuster (B, **Figure 80**) until the pushrod (inside the adjuster) is flush with the end of the adjuster. Do not tighten the locknut or install the cover at this point; continue with Step 10.

10. Start the engine and allow it to idle. Check the movement of the pushrod. If it moves slightly, the adjustment is correct. If the push rod does not move, the adjuster is too tight. Loosen the adjuster so that the pushrod moves slightly when the engine is running.

11. When Step 10 is correct, turn the engine off and tighten the adjuster locknut (A, **Figure 80**).

12. Install all parts previously removed.

Compression Test

At every tune-up check cylinder compression. Record the results and compare them at the next check. A running record will show trends in deterioration so that corrective action can be taken before complete failure.

The results, when properly interpreted can indicate general cylinder, piston ring, and valve condition.

1. Park the vehicle on level ground.

2. Start the engine and let it warm to normal operating temperature. Shut the engine off.

> *NOTE*
> *Make sure the ON/OFF switch is turned OFF.*

3. Remove the spark plug. Install the spark plug back into the plug cap to ground the wire (**Figure 81**).

4. Connect the compression tester to the cylinder following manufacturer's instructions.

5. Push the throttle all the way open.

6. Operate the recoil starter several times while watching the gauge. Stop turning the engine over when the pressure reading stops climbing.

7. Remove the tester and record the reading.

8. When interpreting the results, actual readings are not as important as the difference between the readings. Compare readings to specifications in **Table 8**. If a reading is higher than normal, there may be a buildup of carbon deposits in the combustion chamber or on the piston crown.

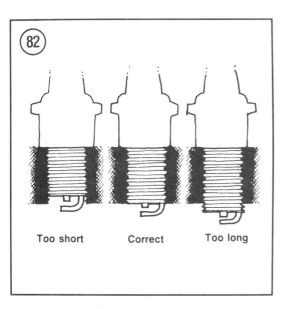

Too short   Correct   Too long

If a low reading (10% or more) is obtained it can be caused by one or more of the following faulty items:

a. A leaking cylinder head gasket.

b. Incorrect valve clearance.

c. Valve leakage (burned valve face).

d. Worn or broken piston ring.

e. Misadjusted starter decompressor lever free play (YTM200, L, N) or a damaged decompressor lever (all other models).

If the head gasket is okay, perform a "wet" test to determine which other component is faulty. Pour a teaspoon of engine oil through the spark plug hole onto the top of the piston. Turn the engine over once to clear some of the excess oil, then take another compression test and record the reading. If the compression returns to normal, the valves are good but the rings are defective. If compression does not increase, the valves require servicing (providing the starter decompressor lever is adjusted correctly on YTM200K, L and N models. A valve could be hanging open or burned or a piece of carbon could be on a valve seat.

Install the spark plug and connect the spark plug lead.

Correct Spark Plug Heat Range

Spark plugs are available in various heat ranges that are hotter or colder than the spark plugs originally installed at the factory.

Select a plug in a heat range designed for the loads and temperature conditions under which the engine will operate. Use of incorrect heat ranges can cause a seized piston, scored cylinder wall or damaged piston crown.

In general, use a hot plug for low speeds, low loads and low temperatures. Use a cold plug for high speeds, high engine loads and high temperatures. The plug should operate hot enough to burn off unwanted deposits, but not so hot that it is damaged or causes preignition. A spark plug of the correct heat range will show a light tan color on the portion of the insulator within the cylinder after the plug has been in service.

The reach (length) of a plug is also important. A longer than normal plug could interfere with the valves and pistons causing permanent and severe damage; refer to **Figure 82**. The standard heat range spark plugs are found in **Table 8**.

Spark Plug Cleaning/Replacement

1. Grasp the spark plug lead (**Figure 83**) as near to the plug as possible and pull it off the plug.

2. Blow away any dirt that has accumulated in the spark plug well.

> *CAUTION*
> *The dirt could fall into the cylinder when the plug is removed, causing serious engine damage.*

3. Remove the spark plug with a spark plug wrench.

> *NOTE*
> *If the plug is difficult to remove, apply penetrating oil, such as WD-40 or Liquid Wrench, around base of plug and let it soak in about 10-20 minutes.*

4. Inspect spark plug carefully. Look for a broken center porcelain, excessively eroded electrodes, and excessive carbon or oil fouling. If any problems are found, replace the plug. If deposits are light, the plug may be cleaned with a wire brush. Regap the plug as described in this chapter.

Gapping and Installing the Plug

A spark plug should be carefully gapped to ensure a reliable, consistent spark. You must use a special spark plug gapping tool with a round gauge.

1 Remove the new spark plug from the box. *Do not* screw on the small cap that is loose in the box; it is not used.

2. Insert a round gauge between the spark plug's center and side electrodes (**Figure 84**). The correct gap is found in **Table 8**. If the gap is correct, you will feel a slight drag as you pull the gauge through. If there is no drag, or the gauge won't pass through, bend the side electrode *with the gapping tool* (**Figure 85**) to set the proper gap (**Table 8**).

3. Put a small drop of oil on the threads of the spark plug.

4. Screw the spark plug in by hand until it seats. Very little effort is required. If force is necessary, you have the plug cross-threaded; unscrew it and try again.

5. Tighten the spark plug to 20 N•m (14 ft.-lb.). If you don't have a torque wrench, an additional 1/4 to 1/2 turn is sufficient after the gasket has made contact with the head. If you are reinstalling the old, regapped plug and are reusing the old gasket, tighten only an additional 1/4 turn.

> *NOTE*
> *Do not overtighen. This will only squash the gasket and destroy its sealing ability.*

6. Install the spark plug wire. Make sure it is on tight.

Reading Spark Plugs

Much information about engine and spark plug performance can be determined by careful examination of the spark plug. This information is valid only after performing the following steps. See **Figure 86**.

1. Ride the vehicle a short distance at full throttle in any gear.

2. Turn kill switch to off before closing throttle, then coast to a stop. Do *not* downshift transmission in stopping.

3. Remove the spark plug and examine it. Compare to **Figure 86**.

   a. If the insulator is white or burned, the plug is too hot and should be replaced with a colder one.

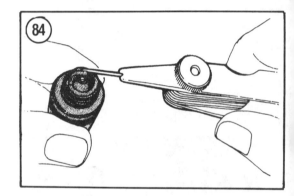

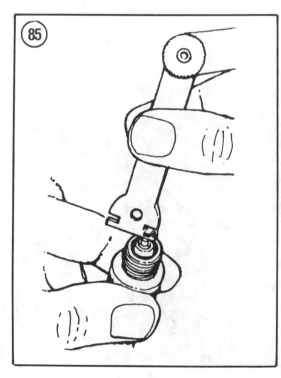

SPARK PLUG CONDITION

NORMAL
• Identified by light tan or gray deposits on the firing tip.
• Can be cleaned.

GAP BRIDGED
• Identified by deposit buildup closing gap between electrodes.
• Caused by oil or carbon fouling. If deposits are not excessive, the plug can be cleaned.

OIL FOULED
• Identified by wet black deposits on the insulator shell bore and electrodes.
• Caused by excessive oil entering combustion chamber through worn rings and pistons, excessive clearance between valve guides and stems, or worn or loose bearings. Can be cleaned. If engine is not repaired, use a hotter plug.

CARBON FOULED
• Identified by black, dry fluffy carbon deposits on insulator tips, exposed shell surfaces and electrodes.
• Caused by too cold a plug, weak ignition, dirty air cleaner, too rich a fuel mixture or excessive idling. Can be cleaned.

LEAD FOULED
• Identified by dark gray, black, yellow or tan deposits or a fused glazed coating on the insulator tip.
• Caused by highly leaded gasoline. Can be cleaned.

WORN
• Identified by severely eroded or worn electrodes.
• Caused by normal wear. Should be replaced.

FUSED SPOT DEPOSIT
• Identified by melted or spotty deposits resembling bubbles or blisters.
• Caused by sudden acceleration. Can be cleaned.

OVERHEATING
• Identified by a white or light gray insulator with small black or gray brown spots and with bluish-burnt appearance of electrodes.
• Caused by engine overheating, wrong type of fuel, loose spark plugs, too hot a plug or incorrect ignition timing. Replace the plug.

PREIGNITION
• Identified by melted electrodes and possibly blistered insulator. Metallic deposits on insulator indicate engine damage.
• Caused by wrong type of fuel, incorrect ignition timing or advance, too hot a plug, burned valves or engine overheating. Replace the plug.

b. A too-cold plug will have sooty deposits ranging in color from dark brown to black. Replace with a hotter plug and check for too-rich carburetion or evidence of oil blow-by at the piston rings.

c. If the plug has a light tan or gray colored deposit and no abnormal gap wear or electrode erosion is evident, the plug and the engine are running properly.

d. If the plug exhibits a black insulator tip, a damp and oily film over the firing end or a carbon layer over the entire nose, it is oil or gas fouled. An oil or gas fouled plug can be cleaned, but it is better to replace it.

Ignition Timing

All models are equipped with a capacitor discharge ignition system (CDI). Timing is set on all models and is not adjustable (the base plate screws have no slots for adjustment). The following procedure can be used to check ignition timing only.

> *NOTE*
> *Before starting this procedure, check all electrical connections related to the ignition system. Make sure all connections are tight and free of corrosion and that all ground connections are tight.*

1. Park the vehicle on level ground. Set the parking brake.
2. Start the engine and let it reach normal operating temperature. Turn the engine off.
3. Connect a portable tachometer following the manufacturer's instructions.
4. Unscrew the timing window plug (**Figure 73**).
5. Connect a timing light following the manufacturer's instructions.
6. Restart the engine and let it idle at the specified rpm. See **Table 8**.
7. Adjust the idle speed if necessary as described in this chapter.
8. Aim the timing light toward the timing marks and pull the trigger. The timing is correct if the crankcase stationary pointer is aligned with the "F" mark on the flywheel (**Figure 74**).
9. If the ignition timing is incorrect, proceed as follows:

a. Check all ignition components for tightness. Remove the alternator cover (Chapter Seven) and check the tightness of the coils in the cover (**Figure 87**).

b. Check all electrical connectors for loose connections or damage.

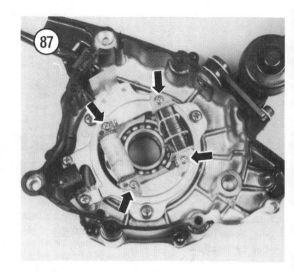

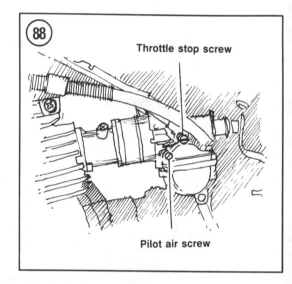

Throttle stop screw

Pilot air screw

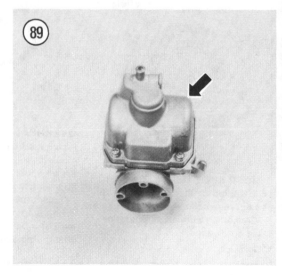

c. If these conditions are okay, refer to Chapter Two for ignition system troubleshooting. Ignition timing cannot be adjusted on these models.

Pilot Screw and Idle Speed Adjustment

Before starting this procedure the air cleaner must be clean, otherwise this procedure cannot be done properly.

1A. *Chain drive:* Turn the pilot air screw (**Figure 88**) in until it lightly seats. Back the screw out the correct number of turns for your model (**Table 8**). (**Table 8**).

1B. *Shaft drive:* The pilot screw on these models is only accessible by removing the carburetor from the vehicle and removing the float bowl. Perform the following:

 a. Remove the carburetor from the vehicle as described in Chapter Six. It is not necessary to disconnect the throttle valve or choke assemblies.

> *WARNING*
> *Fuel will flow out of the carburetor when performing the next step. Take precautions to prevent the fuel from contacting the engine and exhaust pipes (if hot) and work away from all open flames.*

 b. Remove the float bowl (**Figure 89**).
 c. Turn the pilot air screw (**Figure 90**) in until it lightly seats. Then back it out the specified number of turns (**Table 8**).
 d. Reinstall the float bowl and install the carburetor as described in Chapter Six.

2. Start the engine and let it reach normal operating temperature.

3. Turn the idle stop screw in or out to achieve the desired idle speed. See **Figure 91** and **Figure 92**. **Table 8** lists the correct idle speed for all models.

> *WARNING*
> *With the engine idling, move the handlebar from side to side. If idle speed increases during this movement, the throttle cable needs adjusting or it may be incorrectly routed through the frame. Correct this problem immediately. Do not ride the vehicle in this unsafe condition.*

Table 1 MAINTENANCE SCHEDULE*

Every month **or as needed**	• Lubricate and adjust drive chain • Clean and re-oil air filter
Every 3 months or as needed	• Check all brake components for wear or damage • Adjust brakes
Every 6 months	• Check and adjust cam chain tension[1] • Check and adjust valve clearance • Check and adjust decompression cable free play[2] • Change engine oil and replace filter • Clean oil strainer • Change final drive oil • Check battery electrolyte level and charge • Check wheel and tire condition • Check cables for fraying and lubricate • Clean fuel tank and fuel filter • Check light operation • Check tightness of all chassis and engine fasteners • Grease throttle lever • Grease brake lever • Grease brake camshaft • Decarbonize exhast system and spark arrester • Check exhaust system for leakage; repair as necessary • Lubricate knuckle shaft[3]
Every year	• Clean carburetor • Change fork oil • Repack wheel bearings
Every 2 years	• Repack steering bearings[4]

*This Yamaha factory maintenance schedule should be considered as a guide to general maintenance and lubrication intervals. Harder than normal use and exposure to mud, water, sand, high humidity, etc. will naturally dictate more frequent attention to most maintenance items.

1. All 1985-on models (except YFM200N) are equipped with an automatic cam chain adjuster; periodic adjustment is not required.
2. YTM200K, L and N models only.
3. YFM200 models only.
4. YTM200 and YTM225 models only.

Table 2 TIRE INFLATION PRESSURE

Tire size	Air pressure
YTM200 and YTM225 models	
22×11-8	
Recommended	0.15 kg/cm² (2.2 psi)
Maximum	0.7 kg/cm² (10 psi)
Minimum	0.12 kg/cm² (1.8 psi)
25×12-9	
Recommended	0.15 kg/cm² (2.2 psi)
Maximum	0.7 kg/cm² (10 psi)
Minimum	0.12 kg/cm² (1.8 psi)
YFM200 models	
YFM200N	
25×12-9 (front)	
and 22×11-8 (rear)	
Recommended	0.15 kg/cm² (2.2 psi)
Maximum	0.7 kg/cm² (10 psi)
Minimum	0.12 kg/cm² (1.8 psi)
YFM200DXS	
22×8-10 (front)	
and 22×11-8 (rear)	
Recommended	0.20 kg/cm² (2.8 psi)
Minimum	0.17 kg/cm² (2.4 psi)

Table 3 BATTERY STATE OF CHARGE

Specific gravity	State of charge
1.110-1.130	Discharged
1.140-1.160	Almost discharged
1.170-1.190	One-quarter charged
1.200-1.220	One-half charged
1.230-1.250	Three-quarters charged
1.260-1.280	Fully charged

Table 4 RECOMMENDED LUBRICANTS

Engine oil	
Temperatures 40° and up	SAE 20W/40 SE/SF
Temperatures below 40°	SAE 10W/30 SE/SF
Battery refilling	Distilled water
Fork oil*	10 wt or equivalent
Final drive gear oil	SAE 80API GL-4 hypoid gear oil
Cables and pivot points	Yamaha chain and cable lube or SAE 10W/30 motor oil
Air filter	Special air filter oil
Grease	Lithium base grease

* YTM200 and YTM225 models only.

Table 5 ENGINE REFILL CAPACITIES

Engine oil	
Oil change	1,500 cc (1.6 qt.)
Engine overhaul	1,800 cc (1.9 qt.)

Table 6 FRONT FORK OIL CAPACITY AND LEVEL—YTM200 AND YTM225

Model	Oil capacity cc (oz.)	Oil level mm (in.)
YTM200K, L, N	193 (6.53)	311 (12.2)
YTM200EK, EL	194 (6.56)	311 (12.2)
YTM200ERN	194 (6.56)	311 (12.2)
YTM225DXK, DXL, DXN, DRN	117 (3.96)	419.6 (16.5)
YTM225DRS	203 (6.86)	383.5 (15.1)

Table 7 FINAL DRIVE GEAR OIL CAPACITY

All shaft drive models	0.13 liters (0.14 qt.

Table 8 TUNE-UP SPECIFICATIONS

Valve clearances	
Intake	0.05-0.09 mm (0.002-0.004 in.)
Exhaust	0.11-0.15 mm (0.0043-0.006 in.)
Compression pressure	
Standard	9 kg/cm² (128 psi)
Minimum	8 kg/cm² (114 psi)
Maximum	10 kg/cm² (142 psi)
Spark plug	
Type	NGK D7EA
	ND X22ES-U
Gap	0.6-0.7 mm (0.024-0.028 in.)
Torque specification	20 N•m (14 ft.-lb.)
Ignition timing	Fixed; see text for details
Idle speed	1,400 ±50 rpm
Cylinder head torque	
Bolt (M6)	7 (5.1)
Flange bolt (M8)	22 (16)
Bolt (M8)	20 (14)

ENGINE

All models covered in this book are equipped with an air-cooled, 4-stroke single cylinder engine with a single overhead camshaft. The crankshaft is supported by 2 main ball bearings. The camshaft is chain driven from the timing sprocket on the left-hand side of the crankshaft and operates rocker arms that are individually adjustable.

The engine used in the various models is the same basic unit with different compression ratios and different bore and stroke dimensions to achieve varying displacements.

This chapter contains information for removal, inspection, service and reassembly of the engine. **Table 1** (YTM200 and YFM200) and **Table 2** (YTM225) provide complete specifications for the engines. **Table 3** lists the major engine torque specifications. **Tables 1-5** are located at the end of this chapter.

Although the clutch and transmission are located within the engine, they are covered in Chapter Five to simplify this material.

ENGINE PRINCIPLES

Figure 1 explains how the engine works. This will be helpful when troubleshooting or repairing the engine.

ENGINE COOLING

Cooling is provided by air passing over the cooling fins on the engine cylinder head and cylinder. It is very important to keep these fins free from buildup of dirt, oil, grease and other foreign matter. Brush out the fins with a whisk broom or small stiff paint brush.

CAUTION
Remember, these fins are thin in order to dissipate heat and may be damaged if struck too hard. The loss of cooling fins will cause engine overheating.

SERVICING ENGINE IN FRAME

The following components can be serviced while the engine is mounted in the frame (the vehicle's frame is a great holding fixture for breaking loose stubborn bolts and nuts):

a. Cylinder head.
b. Cylinder and piston assembly.
c. Carburetor.
d. Alternator.
e. Clutch assembly.
f. External shift mechanism.
g. Starting systems.

①

4-STROKE OPERATING PRINCIPLES

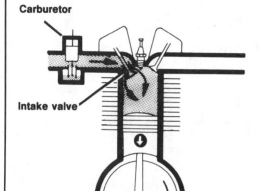

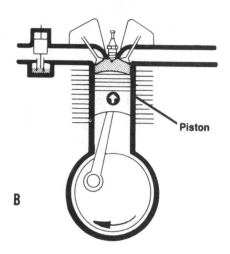

A

B

As the piston travels downward, the exhaust valve is closed and the intake valve opens, allowing the new air-fuel mixture from the carburetor to be drawn into the cylinder. When the piston reaches the bottom of its travel (BDC), the intake valve closes and remains closed for the next 1 1/2 revolutions of the crankshaft.

While the crankshaft continues to rotate, the piston moves upward, compressing the air-fuel mixture.

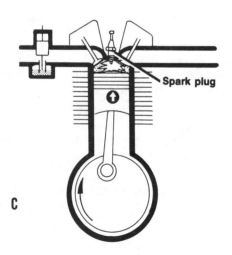

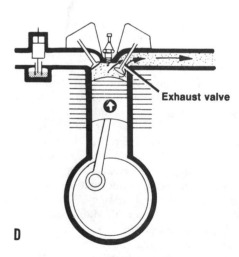

C

D

As the piston almost reaches the top of its travel, the spark plug fires, igniting the compressed air-fuel mixture. The piston continues to top dead center (TDC) and is pushed downward by the expanding gases.

When the piston almost reaches BDC, the exhaust valve opens and remains open until the piston is near TDC. The upward travel of the piston forces the exhaust gases out of the cylinder. After the piston has reached TDC, the exhaust valve closes and the cycle starts all over again.

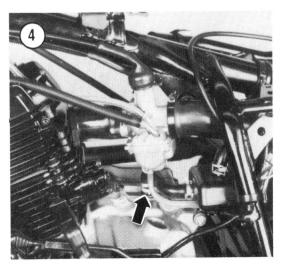

ENGINE

Removal/Installation

1. Drain the engine oil as described in Chapter Three.
2. Remove the seat and fender assembly.
3. Remove the exhaust system as described in Chapter Six.
4. *YFM200 models:* Perform the following:
   a. Remove the front carrier bolts and remove the carrier.
   b. Remove the front panel.
   c. Remove the left and right fuel tank cover bolts (**Figure 2**). Then pull the covers foward and remove them.
5. Disconnect the negative battery cable.
6. Remove the fuel tank as described in Chapter Six.
7. Disconnect the spark plug lead and tie it up out of the way.
8. Disconnect the CDI electrical connector (**Figure 3**).

> *NOTE*
> **Figure 3** *shows the CDI connector for all drive shaft models. The connector on YTM200K, L and N models is located underneath the ignition coil above the cylinder head.*

Position the CDI connector so that it cannot become tangled or damaged when the engine is removed.

9. *YTM200K, L and N:* Disconnect the decompression wire cable at the cylinder head and remove the wire cable and brackets.
10. Disconnect the engine breather hose (**Figure 4**) from the crankcase.
11. Remove the carburetor as described in Chapter Six.
12. Remove the intake manifold (**Figure 5**).

13. Remove the electric starter as described in Chapter Seven, if so equipped.

NOTE
It is not necessary to loosen the reverse lever rod adjuster when removing it in Step 14.

14. On models with reverse, disconnect the reverse lever rod at the engine (**Figure 6**) and reverse housing (**Figure 7**).

15. Remove the shift lever clamp bolt and slide the shift lever off of the shift shaft.

NOTE
If the shift lever is is difficult to remove, insert the tip of a screwdriver into the open slot in the end of the shift lever and gently pry it open so that the shift lever can be removed.

16. Remove the recoil starter as described in this chapter.

NOTE
*Do not remove the recoil starter pulley (**Figure 8**) at this time. The pulley will be used for camshaft positioning during cylinder head removal.*

17. Remove the cylinder head as described in this chapter.

18. Remove the cylinder as described in this chapter.

19. Remove the recoil starter pulley (**Figure 8**) as described under *Recoil Starter* in this chapter.

20. Remove the alternator as described in Chapter Seven.

21. *YTM200K, L, N:* Remove the drive chain (**Figure 9**) as described in Chapter Ten.

22. Remove the clutch assembly as described in Chapter Five.

23. *Drive shaft models without reverse:* Perform the following:

   a. Remove the rear wheels as described in Chapter Ten.

   b. Disconnect the brake cables at the brake caliper (**Figure 10**).

   c. Remove the rear hitch bracket bolts and remove the bracket (**Figure 11**).

   d. Disconnect the final gear breather hose from the final gear housing.

   e. Remove the 2 bolts securing the final gear housing to the chassis (**Figure 12**).

   f. Remove the 4 nuts securing the final gear housing to the coupling housing (**Figure 12**).

NOTE
It will take 2 people to remove the rear wheel housing assembly in Step g.

   g. Remove the rear wheel housing attaching bolts (**Figure 13**) and carefully lower the rear wheel housing assembly to the ground. Then remove the rear wheel housing assembly (**Figure 14**).

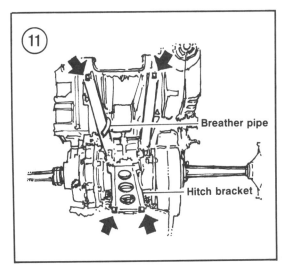

Breather pipe

Hitch bracket

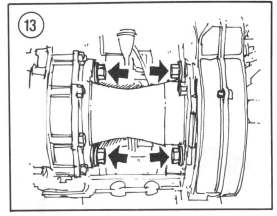

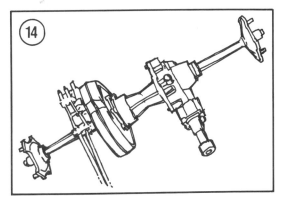

24. *Drive shaft models with reverse:* Loosen the middle/reverse gear housing rubber boot clamp (**Figure 15**). Then push the rubber boot away from the middle/reverse gear housing.

25. Take a final look all over the engine to make sure everything has been disconnected.

26A. *YTM200K, L, N:* Remove the lower front engine mount bolts and brackets.

26B. *All other models:* Remove the front engine mount bolt (**Figure 16**).

27. Remove the upper and lower rear engine mount bolts (**Figure 17**).

28A. *Models without reverse:* Lift the engine up and remove it from the left-hand side.

28B. *Models with reverse:* Lift the front of the engine up. Then move it forward to disengage the universal joint (**Figure 18**) from the drive shaft (**Figure 19**). Remove the engine from the left-hand side (**Figure 20**).

29. While the engine is removed, check all frame-to-engine mount areas for cracks or other damage (**Figure 21**).

30. Install by reversing these removal steps, noting the following.

31. Tighten the engine mounting bolts to the specifications in **Table 4**.

32. Tighten the drive shaft mounting bolts to the specifications in **Table 5**.

33. Fill the engine with the recommended type and quantity of oil; refer to Chapter Three.

34. Adjust the clutch and brakes as described in Chapter Three.

35. *YTM200K, L, N:* Adjust the following as described in Chapter Three:

   a. Drive chain.

   b. Decompression cable.

36. Start the engine and check for leaks.

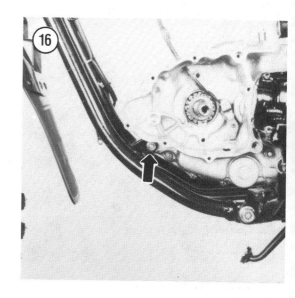

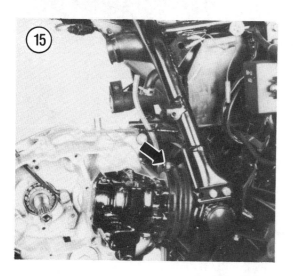

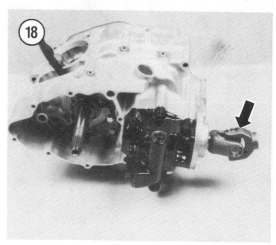

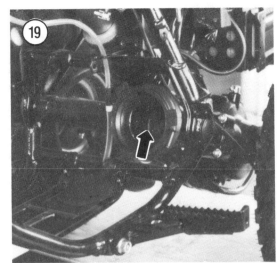

CYLINDER HEAD

The cylinder head carries the rocker arm assemblies, valves and camshaft. This procedure describes all service procedures for cylinder head removal, inspection and installation. While the camshaft and rocker assemblies, and valves are also carried in the cylinder head, their related service and inspection procedures are found in a separate section.

Cylinder Head Removal

> *CAUTION*
> *To prevent any warpage and damage, remove the cylinder head cover and cam only when the engine is at room temperature.*

1. Perform Steps 1-6 under *Engine Removal* in this chapter.
2. *YTM200K, L, and N:* Disconnect the decompression cable at the cylinder head.
3. Remove the carburetor as described in Chapter Six.
4. Remove the top engine-to-chassis brace (**Figure 22**).

> *NOTE*
> *It is not necessary to disconnect the reverse lever at the middle/reverse gear housing in Step 5.*

5. *Drive shaft models with reverse:* Remove the front reverse lever bracket at the recoil starter housing (**Figure 6**) and lay it to one side.

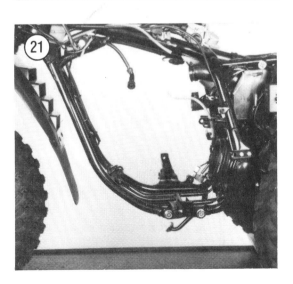

6. Remove the screws securing the recoil starter housing to the left-hand crankcase and remove the starter (**Figure 23**) housing.

7. Remove the exhaust pipe as described in Chapter Six.

8A. *Models with adjustable chain tensioner:* Referring to **Figure 24**, perform the following:

   a. Remove the chain tensioner cap (**Figure 25**).

   b. Loosen the chain tensioner lock nut (**Figure 26**) and remove the chain tensioner assembly (**Figure 27**).

8B. *Models with automatic chain tensioner:* Remove the 2 camshaft chain tensioner Allen bolts and remove the tensioner assembly (**Figure 28**).

9. Remove the camshaft sprocket cover (**Figure 29**) from the left-hand side.

10. Remove the spark plug (**Figure 30**). This allows the engine to be turned easily by hand.

11. Refer to **Figure 31**. Hold the recoil starter pulley with a universal type holding tool and loosen the camshaft sprocket bolt.

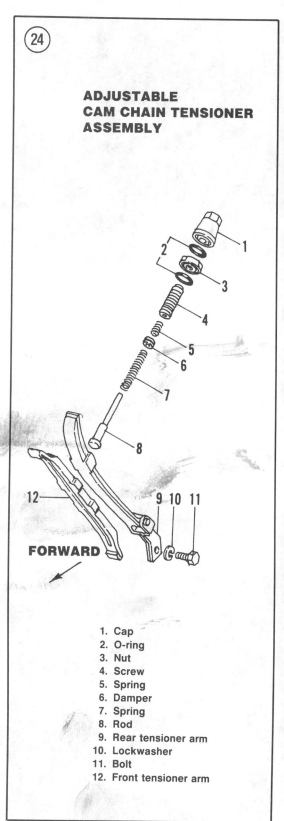

**ADJUSTABLE
CAM CHAIN TENSIONER
ASSEMBLY**

FORWARD

1. Cap
2. O-ring
3. Nut
4. Screw
5. Spring
6. Damper
7. Spring
8. Rod
9. Rear tensioner arm
10. Lockwasher
11. Bolt
12. Front tensioner arm

12. Unscrew the cam sprocket bolt (**Figure 32**) and remove it.

> *NOTE*
> *If removal of the cam sprocket (Step 13) is as far as you plan to go on this procedure, attach a piece of wire to the cam chain to prevent it from falling into the lower crankcase.*

13. Slide the cam sprocket (**Figure 33**) off the camshaft and drop it down slightly. Then detach it from the cam chain and remove it. Drop the cam chain down and remove it from the crankshaft sprocket.

14. Loosen the cylinder head bolts in the following order:

   a. Loosen the 2 left side cylinder head Allen bolts (**Figure 34**).
   b. Loosen the 4 top cylinder head bolts in a criss-cross pattern (**Figure 35**).
   c. Remove all bolts and their washers.

15. Loosen the head by tapping around the perimeter with a rubber or plastic mallet.

> *CAUTION*
> *Remember, the cooling fins are fragile and may be damaged if tapped or pried on too hard. Never use a metal hammer.*

16. Remove the cylinder head (**Figure 36**) by pulling it straight up and off the cylinder.

17. Remove the cylinder head gasket and discard it.

18. From the cylinder, remove the 2 dowel pins from the left-hand side and the right rear dowel pin with O-ring. See **Figure 37**.

Inspection

1. Remove all traces of gasket material from the cylinder head mating surface (A, **Figure 38**).

2. *Without removing the valves*, remove all carbon deposits from the combustion chamber (B, **Figure 38**) and valve ports with a wire brush. A blunt screwdriver or a piece of hardwood can be used if care is taken not to damage the head, valves and spark plug threads.

> *NOTE*
> *Carbon build-up in the combustion chamber increases the engine's compression ratio and reduces heat dissipation. These conditions may result in overheating, preignition or detonation. It is critical to engine performance to remove all carbon build-up as described in Step 2.*

3. After the carbon is removed from the combustion chamber and the valve intake and exhaust ports, clean the entire head in cleaning solvent. Blow dry with compressed air.

4. Rotate the engine so that the piston is at top dead center. Clean away all carbon from the piston crown (A, **Figure 39**). Do not remove the carbon ridge at the top of the cylinder bore.

5. Check for cracks in the combustion chamber and exhaust port. A cracked head must be replaced.

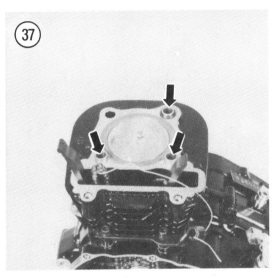

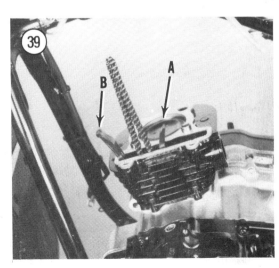

6. Check the cylinder head spark plug threads for carbon build-up. Remove carbon build-up with a 12 mm spark plug tap (**Figure 40**).

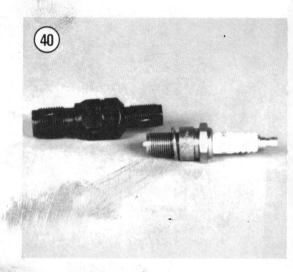

> *NOTE*
> *When using a tap to clean up the spark plug threads, it will be helpful to coat the tap with an aluminum thread tap fluid or kerosene.*

7. After the head has been thoroughly cleaned, place a straightedge across the cylinder head/cylinder gasket surface (**Figure 41**) at several points. Measure the warp by inserting a flat feeler gauge between the straightedge and the cylinder head at each location. The allowable warpage is 0.03 mm (0.0012 in.) or less; if the warpage exceeds this limit, the cylinder head should be taken to a Yamaha dealer to determine if it is possible to resurface the head.

8. Check the camshaft and rocker arm components as described under *Camshaft* in this chapter.

9. Check the valves and valve guides as described under *Valve and Valve Components*.

10. Check the cylinder head bolts (**Figure 42**) for thread damage or twisting. Check the copper washers to make sure they are not crushed or cracked. Replace worn or damaged parts if necessary.

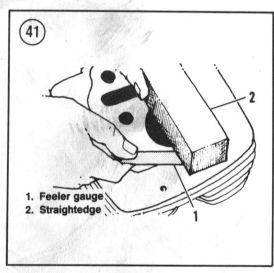

1. Feeler gauge
2. Straightedge

> *NOTE*
> *If replacement of the cylinder head bolt washers is required, make sure to use factory replacement copper washers. These washers will help assure accurate and even torquing of the cylinder head bolts and prevent galling.*

Cylinder Head Installation

1. Clean the mating surfaces of the head and cylinder block of all gasket residue.

2. Install 2 locating dowels on the left-hand side. On the right-hand rear hole, install a locating dowel and a new O-ring. See **Figure 37**.

3. Tie a piece of wire to the cam chain (**Figure 39**).

4. Install a new cylinder head gasket.

5. Loosen all valve adjusters fully. This relieves strain on the rocker arms and cylinder head during installation.

6. Align the cylinder head over the cylinder. Then guide the cam chain (by the wire) up through the

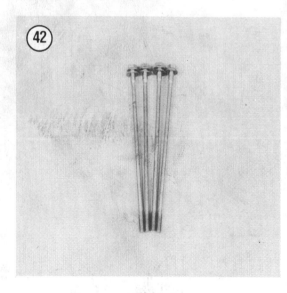

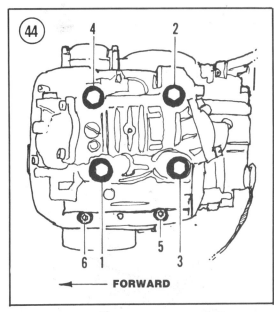

FORWARD

cylinder head. Lower the cylinder head onto the cylinder.

NOTE
After installing the cylinder head, make sure the front chain guide (B, Figure 39) engages the cam chain guide slot in the cylinder head (Figure 43).

NOTE
Apply engine oil to the 4 cylinder head copper washers before installation.

7. Install the 4 cylinder head long stud bolts (**Figure 35**) and the 2 shorter bolts (**Figure 34**). Tighten all cylinder head bolts in the sequence shown in **Figure 44** to specifications listed in **Table 3**.

8. Remove the timing plug from the alternator cover (**Figure 45**).

CAUTION
When rotating the crankshaft in Step 9, always pull the camshaft chain taut at the same time to prevent the chain from kinking on the lower crankshaft sprocket. This could damage both the chain and the sprocket.

9. Rotate the crankshaft counterclockwise and align the "T" mark on the flywheel with the stationary pointer on the alternator cover (**Figure 46**).

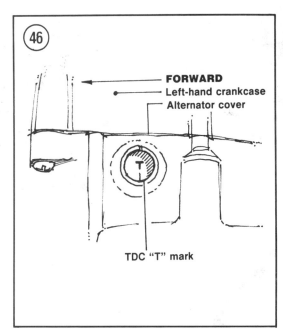

FORWARD
Left-hand crankcase
Alternator cover

TDC "T" mark

10. Turn the camshaft in the cylinder head until the cam drive sprocket locating pin (A, **Figure 47**) is pointing up at the fixed pointer on the cylinder head housing (B, **Figure 47**).

11. Pull up on the cam chain and remove the wire from it. Then continue to pull up on the cam chain and make sure the chain is meshed properly with the drive sprocket on the crankshaft.

12. With the timing slot in the cam chain sprocket facing up at 12 o'clock, slide the sprocket into the cam chain and install the sprocket onto the end of the camshaft. The alignment mark on the sprocket must be aligned with the fixed pointer on the cylinder head housing as shown in **Figure 48**.

> *CAUTION*
> *Very expensive damage could result from improper cam and chain alignment. Recheck your work several times to be sure alignment is correct.*

13. When alignment is correct, install the cam sprocket bolt (**Figure 32**) and tighten to specifications in **Table 3**. Use the same tool to hold the recoil starter pulley (**Figure 31**) as during removal.

14. Make one final check to make sure alignment is correct. The alignment mark on the top sprocket must be aligned with the fixed pointer on the cylinder head housing (**Figure 48**).

15A. *Models with adjustable chain tensioner:* Perform the following:

   a. Insert the cam chain tensioner into the cylinder. Do not tighten it at this time.

   b. Adjust the valves and cam chain tension as described in Chapter Three.

15B. *Models with automatic chain tensioner:* Install the chain tensioner as described under *Cam Chain Tensioner (Automatic Type)* in this chapter.

16. Reverse Steps 1-6 under *Disassembly.*

CAMSHAFT/ROCKER ARMS

Disassembly

When performing this procedure, label and package each part in individual plastic bags.

1. Remove the cylinder head as described in this chapter.

2. Remove the intake and exhaust valve covers.

3. Flatten the bearing retainer lockwasher and remove the bolts (**Figure 49**) and lockwasher (**Figure 50**).

4. Thread a 6 mm screw into the end of one rocker arm shaft and remove the shaft (**Figure 51**) and rocker arm (**Figure 52**). If the shaft is difficult to remove, use a special knock puller as shown in **Figure 53**. Repeat for the opposite rocker arm shaft.

NOTE
*The knock puller used in Step 4 (**Figure 54**) can be fabricated by obtaining a long bolt with M6×1 threads and drilling a guide hole through a heavy piece of metal stock.*

5. Thread a 10 mm bolt into the end of the camshaft (**Figure 55**) and remove it and the bushing carefully through the cylinder head.

CAUTION
Use care when removing the camshaft to prevent damaging the journals.

Camshaft Inspection

1. Slide the camshaft bushing (**Figure 56**) off of the camshaft.

2. Check the cam bearing journals for wear and scoring (**Figure 57**). Next check the camshaft bushing (**Figure 58**) inner and outer surfaces for pitting or any other signs of wear or damage. If any abnormal conditions are detected, replace the worn part.

3. Even though the cam journals may appear to be satisfactory, the bearing journals should be measured with a micrometer. Compare to dimensions given in **Table 1** or **Table 2**. If worn to the service limit, the cam must be replaced.

4. Check the cam lobes for wear (**Figure 59**). The lobes should show no signs of scoring and the edges should be square. Slight damage may be removed with a silicon carbide oilstone. Use a No. 100-120 grit stone initially, then polish with a No. 280-320 grit stone.

5. Even though the cam lobe surface appears to be satisfactory, with no visible signs of wear, the cam lobes must be measured with a micrometer as shown in **Figure 60**. Compare to dimensions given in **Table 1** or **Table 2**.

> *NOTE*
> *Measuring the cam lobes with a micrometer is important in maintaining engine performance. If the cam lobe wear exceeds factory wear limits, valve lift and timing will be affected.*

6. The right-hand camshaft bearing journal rides in an integral bearing bore in the cylinder head. Check the bearing bore by hand. If the surface is damaged, the cylinder head must be replaced.

7. Check the left-hand side camshaft bushing surface in the cylinder head. This surface should not be scored or excessively worn. Replace the cylinder head if wear is evident.

8. Inspect the cam sprocket (**Figure 61**) for wear; replace if necessary.

> *NOTE*
> *If the sprocket is worn, inspect the camshaft chain as described in this chapter.*

Rocker Arm and Shaft Inspection

1. Remove the O-rings (**Figure 62**) from the rocker arm shafts and discard them.

2. Wash all parts in cleaning solvent and thoroughly dry.

3. Inspect the rocker arm pad (**Figure 63**) where it rides on the cam lobe and where the adjuster rides

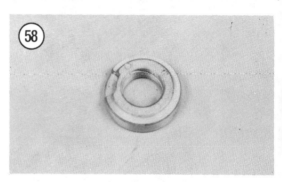

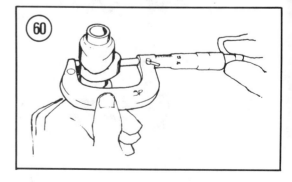

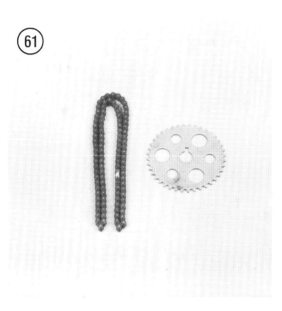

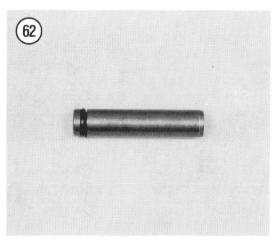

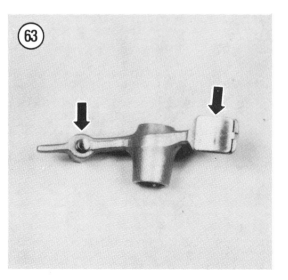

on the valve stem. If the pad is scratched or unevenly worn, inspect the cam lobe for scoring, chipping or flat spots. Replace the rocker arm if defective.

4. Measure the inside diameter of the rocker arm bore (A, **Figure 64**) with an inside micrometer and check against dimensions in **Table 1** or **Table 2**. Replace if worn to the service limit or greater.

5. Inspect the rocker arm shaft for signs of wear or scoring. Measure the outside diameter (B, **Figure 64**) with a micrometer and check against dimensions in **Table 1** or **Table 2**. Replace if worn to the service limit or less.

Assembly

1. Coat the camshaft and bore and the rocker arm shafts and rocker arm bore with assembly oil.

2. Install a new O-ring (**Figure 62**) on each rocker arm shaft.

CAUTION
If the rocker arm shaft is installed in the wrong direction, it will be difficult or impossible to remove later.

3. Install the rocker arm shaft with the threaded hole facing *out*. Partially insert the rocker arm shaft into the cover (**Figure 65**) and position the rocker arm into the cylinder head cover.

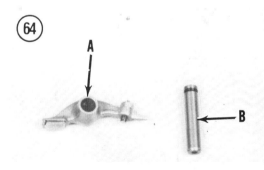

4. Make sure the locking relief in the rocker arm shaft (if so equipped) is aligned with the hole in the cylinder head to allow the cylinder head stud to pass by it during installation.

5. Repeat Step 2 and Step 3 for the opposite rocker arm and shaft.

6. Install the bushing (**Figure 56**) onto the left-hand side of the camshaft.

7. Insert the camshaft and bushing into the cylinder head so that the recessed portion of the bushing faces toward the intake valve as shown in **Figure 66**.

8. Install the bearing retainer (**Figure 50**), lockwashers and bolts (**Figure 49**). Tighten the bolts securely. Bend the lockwasher tabs over the bolts to lock them.

CAMSHAFT CHAIN

Removal/Installaion

1. Remove the cylinder head as described in this chapter.

2. Remove the alternator rotor as described in Chapter Seven.

3. Remove the front cam chain guide (A, **Figure 67**) and the cam chain (B, **Figure 67**).

> *NOTE*
> *Before removing the rear cam chain guide, place a shop rag in the left-hand crankcase cavity opening as shown in* **Figure 68**. *The cavity opening is large enough to allow a washer or bolt to fall into the lower crankcase.*

4. Remove the 2 rear cam chain guide bolts and remove the chain guide (**Figure 69**).

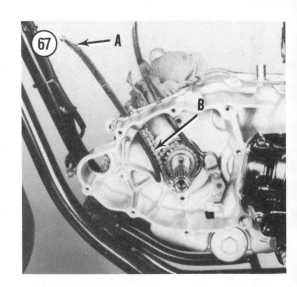

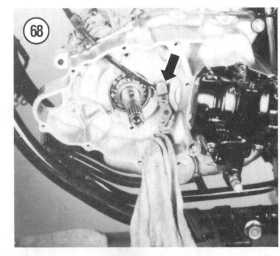

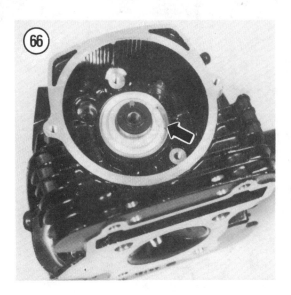

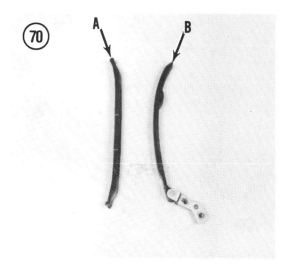

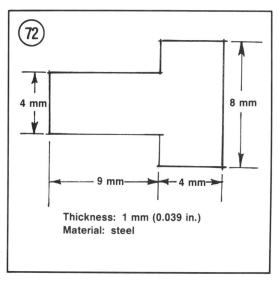

Thickness: 1 mm (0.039 in.)
Material: steel

5. Installation is the reverse of these steps, noting the following.

6. When installing the front cam chain guide, make sure it faces in the direction shown in A, **Figure 67** and that the lower end of the guide seats in the crankcase cam chain guide slot (**Figure 69**).

7. Tighten the rear cam chain guide bolts to 8 N•m (5.8 ft.-lb.).

Inspection

Referring to **Figure 70**, inspect the surface of the front (A) and rear (B) chain guides. If either is worn or disintegrating it must be replaced. This may indicate a worn cam chain or improper cam chain adjustment. On automatic chain tensioner models, the tensioner assembly may be damaged or defective.

Inspect the cam chain (**Figure 61**) for wear and damage. If the chain needs replacing, also replace the cam sprocket (**Figure 61**) and the crankshaft drive sprocket (**Figure 71**). Intermixing new and worn parts will cause premature failure of the new part.

CAM CHAIN TENSIONER (AUTOMATIC TYPE)

Removal

Remove the cam chain tensioner as described under *Cylinder Head Removal* in this chapter.

Installation

Whenever the cam chain tensioner is removed, install it as follows.

1. From a sheet of steel 1 mm (0.039 in.) thick, cut a plate to the dimensions in **Figure 72**. This plate is necessary to correctly install the automatic cam chain tensioner.

2. Remove the plug from the end of the tensioner body.

3. Hold the tensioner in your hand as shown in **Figure 73** and insert a small screwdriver into the

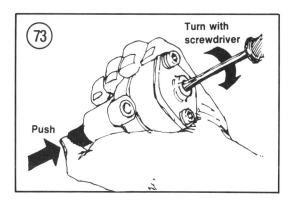

Turn with screwdriver

Push

end of the tensioner body. Turn the screwdriver counterclockwise while at the same time pushing the tension rod into the tensioner housing.

4. Turn the screwdriver until it stops. Still holding the tension rod, remove the screwdriver and install the steel plate (fabricated in Step 1) into the slot in the end of the tensioner body (**Figure 74**).

5. Install the cam chain tensioner (**Figure 75**) into the cylinder using a new gasket. Install the tensioner bolts and tighten to 12 N•m (8.7 ft.-lb.).

6. Remove the tensioner plate and reinstall the rubber plug.

7. Store the tensioner plate for reuse.

CAM CHAIN TENSIONER (ADJUSTABLE TYPE)

Removal/Installation

Remove the cam chain tensioner as described under *Cylinder Head Removal* in this chapter. Install the camshaft tensioner as described under *Camshaft Installation*. During installation, adjust the cam chain tensioner as described in Chapter Three.

Inspection

Disassemble the cam chain tensioner as shown in **Figure 76**. Replace any parts that appear worn or damaged. Check the O-ring in the tensioner cap and replace it if worn.

VALVES AND VALVE COMPONENTS

Refer to **Figure 77** for this procedure.

1. Remove the cylinder head as described in this chapter.

2. Remove the rocker arms and camshaft as described in this chapter.

3. Install a valve spring compressor squarely over valve retainer with other end of tool placed against valve head (**Figure 78**).

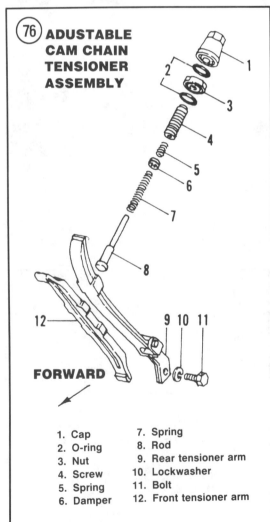

76 ADUSTABLE CAM CHAIN TENSIONER ASSEMBLY

FORWARD

1. Cap	7. Spring
2. O-ring	8. Rod
3. Nut	9. Rear tensioner arm
4. Screw	10. Lockwasher
5. Spring	11. Bolt
6. Damper	12. Front tensioner arm

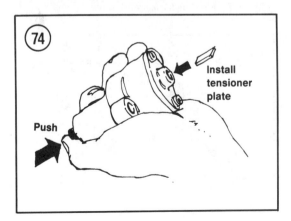

74 Install tensioner plate

Push

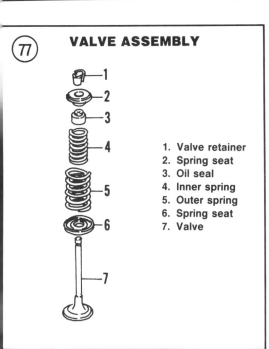

VALVE ASSEMBLY

1. Valve retainer
2. Spring seat
3. Oil seal
4. Inner spring
5. Outer spring
6. Spring seat
7. Valve

4. Tighten the valve spring compressor until the split valve keepers separate. Lift out split keepers with needle nose pliers.

5. Gradually loosen the valve spring compressor and remove from head. Lift off the valve retainer.

CAUTION
*Remove any burrs from the valve stem grooves before removing the valve (**Figure 79**). Otherwise the valve guides will be damaged.*

6. Remove inner and outer springs and valve (**Figure 80**).

7. Remove the seal (**Figure 81**).

CAUTION
All component parts of each valve assembly must be kept together; do not mix with like components from the opposite valve or excessive wear may result.

8. Repeat Steps 3-7 and remove opposite valve.

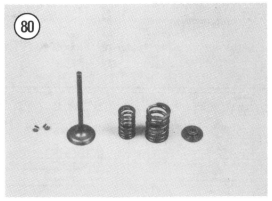

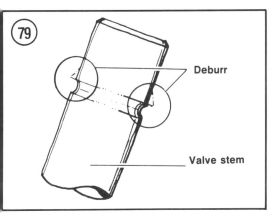

Deburr

Valve stem

Inspection

1. Clean valves with a wire brush and solvent.

2. Inspect the contact surface of each valve for burning (**Figure 82**). Minor roughness and pitting can be removed by lapping the valve as described under *Valve Lapping* in this chapter. Excessive unevenness to the contact surface is an indication that the valve is not serviceable. The contact surface of the valve may be ground on a valve grinding machine, but it is best to replace a burned or damaged valve with a new one.

3. Inspect the valve stems for wear and roughness and measure the vertical runout of the valve stem as shown in **Figure 83**. The runout should not exceed 0.03 mm (0.0012 in.).

4. Measure valve stems for wear using a micrometer (**Figure 84**). Compare with specifications in **Figure 85**.

5. Remove all carbon and varnish from the valve guides with a stiff spiral wire brush.

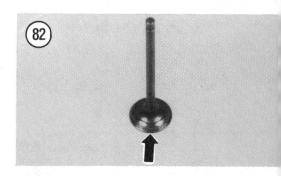

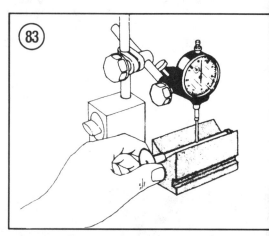

> *NOTE*
> *Step 6 requires special measuring equipment to measure the diameter of the valve guides. If you do not have the required measuring devices, proceed to Step 8.*

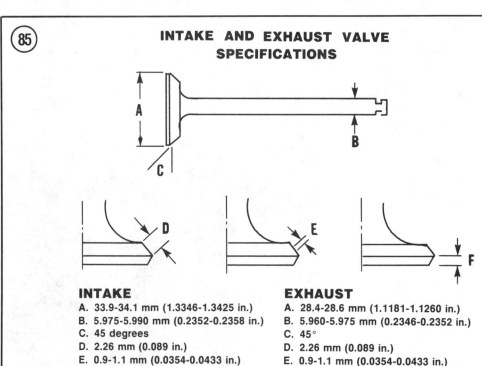

INTAKE AND EXHAUST VALVE SPECIFICATIONS

INTAKE
A. 33.9-34.1 mm (1.3346-1.3425 in.)
B. 5.975-5.990 mm (0.2352-0.2358 in.)
C. 45 degrees
D. 2.26 mm (0.089 in.)
E. 0.9-1.1 mm (0.0354-0.0433 in.)
F. 0.8-1.2 mm (0.0315-0.0472 in.)

EXHAUST
A. 28.4-28.6 mm (1.1181-1.1260 in.)
B. 5.960-5.975 mm (0.2346-0.2352 in.)
C. 45°
D. 2.26 mm (0.089 in.)
E. 0.9-1.1 mm (0.0354-0.0433 in.)
F. 0.8-1.2 mm (0.0315-0.0472 in.)

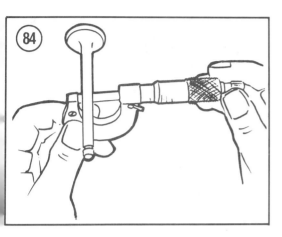

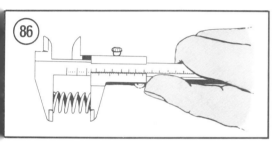

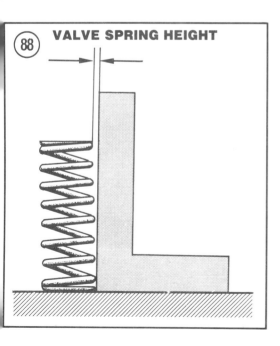

VALVE SPRING HEIGHT

6. Measure each valve guide at top, center, and bottom with a small hole gauge. Compare measurements with specifications in **Table 1** or **Table 2**.

NOTE
Step 7 assumes that all valves and valve guides have been measured and are within specifications. Replace any valves with worn stems or worn valve guides before performing Step 7.

7. Subtract the measurements in Step 4 from the measurement in Step 6. The difference between is the valve guide-to-valve stem clearance. See specifications in **Table 1** or **Table 2** for correct clearance. Replace any guide or valve that is not within tolerance.

8. Insert each valve in its guide. Hold the valve just slightly off its seat and rock it sideways. If it rocks more than slightly, the guide is probably worn and should be replaced. As a final check, take the head to a dealer and have the valve and guides measured.

9. Measure the valve spring heights with a vernier caliper (**Figure 86**). All should be of length specified in **Table 1** or **Table 2** with no bends or other distortion. Replace defective springs in pairs (inner and outer). See **Figure 87**.

10. Measure the tilt of all valve springs as shown in **Figure 88**. Compare with specifications shown in **Table 1** or **Table 2**.

11. Check the valve spring retainer and valve keepers. If they are in good condition, they may be reused.

12. Inspect valve seats (**Figure 89**). If worn or burned, they must be reconditioned. This should

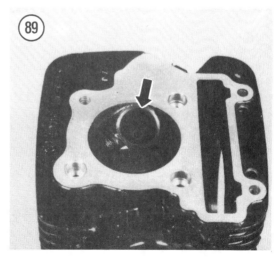

be performed by your dealer or local machine shop, although the procedure is described later in this section. Seats and valves in near-perfect condition can be reconditioned by lapping with fine carborundum paste. Lapping, however, is always inferior to precision grinding.

Installation

1. Coat the valve stems with molybdenum disulfide paste and insert into cylinder head.
2. Install bottom spring retainers and new seals (**Figure 81**).

> *NOTE*
> *Oil seals should be replaced whenever a*
> *valve is removed or replaced.*

3. Install valve springs with the narrow pitch end (end with coils closest together) facing the head (**Figure 87**) and install upper valve spring retainers.
4. Push down on upper valve spring retainers with the valve spring compressor and install valve keepers. After releasing tension from compressor, examine valve keepers and make sure they are seated correctly. See **Figure 90**.

Valve Guide Replacement

When guides are worn so that there is excessive stem-to-guide clearance or valve tipping, they must be replaced as a set. This job should be done only by a Yamaha dealer as special tools are required.

Valve Seat Reconditioning

This job is best left to your dealer or local machine shop. They have the special equipment and knowledge for this exacting job. You can still save considerable money by removing the cylinder head and taking just the head to the shop.

1. With a 30° valve seat cutter, remove just enough metal to make bottom of seat concentric (**Figure 91**).
2. With a 60° valve seat cutter, remove just enough metal from top of seat to make it concentric.
3. With a 45° valve seat cutter, cut a seat that measures 1.0-1.1 mm (0.0390-0.0433 in.). See **Figure 91**.

Valve Lapping

Valve lapping is a simple operation which can restore the valve seal without machining if the amount of wear or distortion is not too great.

1. Smear a light coating of fine grade valve lapping compound on seating surface of valve.
2. Insert the valve into the head.

3. Wet the suction cup of the lapping stick (**Figure 92**) and stick it onto the head of the valve. Lap the valve to the seat by spinning tool between hands while lifting and moving valve around seat 1/4 turn at a time.
4. Wipe off valve and seat frequently to check progress of lapping. Lap only enough to achieve a precise seating "ring" around valve head. Measure width of seat. If seat width is not within tolerance

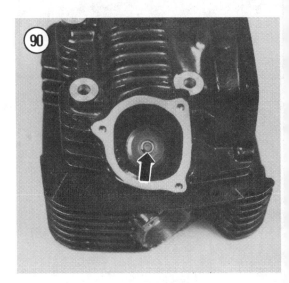

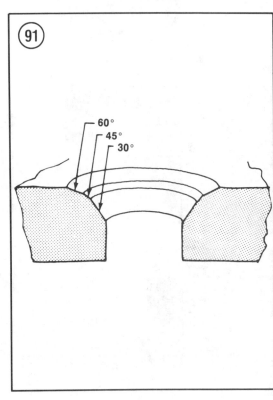

in **Figure 91**, valve seat in cylinder head must be resurfaced.

5. Closely examine valve seat in cylinder head. It should be smooth and even with a smooth, polished seating "ring."

6. Thoroughly clean the valves and cylinder head in solvent to remove all grinding compound. Any compound left on the valves or the cylinder head will end up in the engine and will cause damage.

7. After the lapping has been completed and the valve assemblies have been reinstalled into the head the valve seal should be tested. Check the seal of each valve by pouring solvent into the intake and exhaust ports. There should be no leakage past the seat. If so, combustion chamber (**Figure 93**) will appear wet. If fluid leaks past any of the seats, disassemble that valve assembly and repeat the lapping procedure until there is no leakage.

CYLINDER

Removal

1. Remove the cylinder head as described in this chapter.

2. Remove the cylinder holding bolts (**Figure 94**) from the left-hand side of the engine.

3. Loosen the cylinder by tapping around the perimeter with a rubber or plastic mallet.

4. Pull the cylinder straight up and off the crankcase studs.

5. Remove the cylinder base gasket and discard it.

6. Remove the 2 dowel pins from the left-hand side (A, **Figure 95**).

7. Remove the O-ring from the right rear stud hole (B, **Figure 95**).

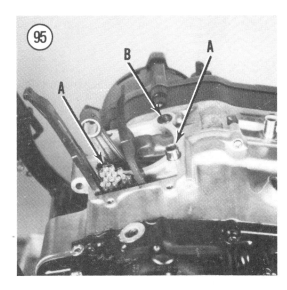

8. Install a piston holding fixture under the piston (**Figure 96**) to protect the piston skirt from damage. This fixture may be purchased or may be a homemade unit of wood. See **Figure 97**.

9. Stuff clean shop rags into the crankcase to prevent objects from falling undetected into the crankcase.

Inspection

1. Clean the cylinder thoroughly in solvent. Remove any gasket residue from the cylinder's top and bottom surfaces.

2. Measure the cylinder bores with a cylinder gauge (**Figure 98**) or inside micrometer at the points shown in **Figure 99**.

3. Measure in 2 axes—in line with the wrist pin and at 90° to the pin. If the taper or out-of-round is greater than specifications (**Table 1** or **Table 2**), the cylinder must be rebored to the next oversize and new pistons and rings installed.

> *NOTE*
> *The new piston should be obtained first before the cylinder is bored so that the piston can be measured; slight manufacturing tolerances must be taken into account to determine the actual size and the working clearance. Piston-to-cylinder clearance is specified in* **Table 1** *and* **Table 2**.

4. Check the cylinder wall (A, **Figure 100**) for scratches; if scratched the cylinder should be rebored.

5. Check the O-ring (B, **Figure 100**) at the base of the cylinder. Replace the O-ring if worn or damaged.

6. If the cylinder is going to be left off of the engine for some time, coat the cylinder lining with new engine oil and wrap it in a clean shop cloth or plastic parts bag.

Installation

1. If the base gasket is stuck to the bottom of the cylinder it should be removed and the cylinder surface cleaned thoroughly.

2. Check that the top cylinder surface is clean of all old gasket material.

3. Install 2 dowel pins on the left-hand crankcase stud holes and the O-ring on right-hand rear stud hole. See **Figure 95**.

4. Install a new cylinder base gasket. Make sure all holes align.

5. Install a piston holding fixture under the piston (**Figure 96**).

6. Carefully install the cylinder over the piston. Slowly work the piston past each piston ring.

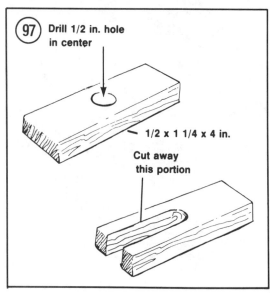

Drill 1/2 in. hole in center

1/2 x 1 1/4 x 4 in.

Cut away this portion

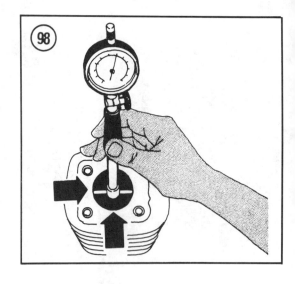

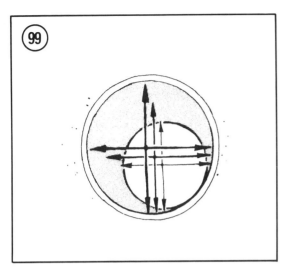

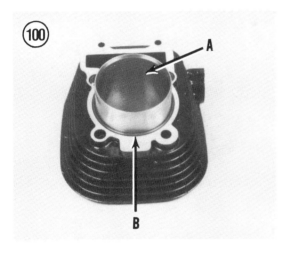

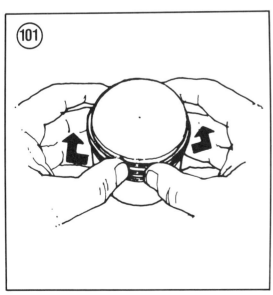

7. Continue to slide the cylinder down until it bottoms on the piston holding fixture.

8. Remove the piston holding fixture and push the cylinder down until it bottoms on the crankcase.

9. Install the cylinder holding bolts (**Figure 94**) and tighten them to specifications in **Table 3**.

10. Install the cylinder head as described in this chapter.

PISTON AND PISTON PIN

The piston is made of an aluminum alloy and should be handled carefully during all service operations. The piston pin is made of steel and is machined to a precision fit in the piston. The piston pin is held in place by a clip at each end.

Piston Removal

1. Remove the cylinder head and cylinder as described in this chapter.

2. Stuff the crankcase with a clean shop rag to prevent objects from falling into the crankcase.

> *WARNING*
> *The edges of all piston rings are very sharp. Be careful when handling them to avoid cut fingers.*

3. Remove the top ring first by spreading the ends with your thumbs just enough to slide it up over the piston (**Figure 101**). Repeat for the remaining rings.

> *NOTE*
> *If the rings are difficult to remove, they can be removed with a ring expander tool.*

4. Before removing the piston, hold the rod tightly and rock piston as shown in **Figure 102**. Any rocking motion (do not confuse with the normal

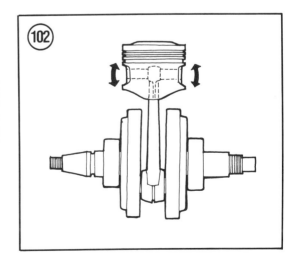

sliding motion) indicates wear on the wrist pin, rod bushing, pin bore, or more likely, a combination of all three.

5. Remove the circlips from the piston pin bore (**Figure 103**).

6. Try to remove the piston pin by pushing it out with your fingers. If the piston pin is tight, remove it using a homemade tool as shown in **Figure 104**.

> *NOTE*
> *It is necessary to remove both piston pin clips when using the homemade tool described in **Figure 104**.*

7. Lift the piston off the connecting rod.

Piston Inspection

1. Carefully clean the carbon from the piston crown with a chemical remover or with a soft scraper (**Figure 105**). Do not remove or damage the carbon ridge around the circumference of the piston above the top ring (**Figure 106**). If the piston, rings, and cylinder are found to be dimensionally correct and can be reused, removal of the carbon ring from the top of piston or the carbon ridge from the cylinder will promote excessive oil consumption.

> *WARNING*
> *The rail portions of the oil scraper can be very sharp. Be careful when handling them to avoid cut fingers.*

> *CAUTION*
> *Do not wire brush piston skirts.*

2. Examine each ring groove for burrs, dented edges, and wide wear. Pay particular attention to the top compression ring groove, as it usually wears more than the others.

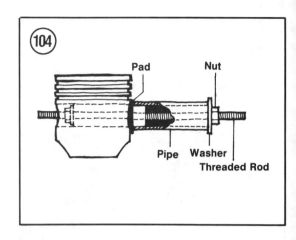

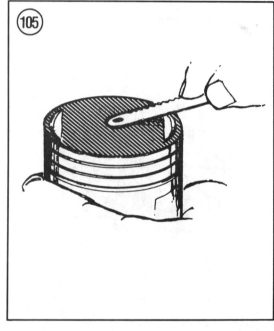

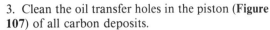

3. Clean the oil transfer holes in the piston (**Figure 107**) of all carbon deposits.

4. Measure piston-to-cylinder clearance as described under *Piston Clearance* in this chapter.

5. If damage or wear indicate piston replacement, select a new piston as described under *Piston Clearance Measurement* in this chapter.

Piston Clearance Measurement

1. Make sure the piston and cylinder walls are clean and dry.

2. Measure the inside diameter of the cylinder bore at a point 13 mm (1/2 in.) from the upper edge with a bore gauge (**Figure 98**).

3. Measure the outside diameter of the piston at a point 7.5 mm (5/16 in.) from the lower edge of the piston 90° to piston pin axis (**Figure 108**).

4. Piston clearance is the difference between the maximum piston diameter and the minimum cylinder clearance. Subtract the dimension of the piston from the cylinder dimension. If the clearance exceeds specifications (**Table 1** or **Table 2**), the cylinder should be rebored to the next oversize and a new piston installed.

5. Obtain a new piston before having the cylinder bored. Measure the new piston and add the specified clearance to determine the proper cylinder bore dimension.

Piston Installation

1. Apply molybdenum disulfide grease to the inside surface of the connecting rod.

2. Oil the piston pin with assembly oil and install it in the piston until its end extends slightly beyond the inside of the boss (**Figure 109**).

3. Place the piston over the connecting rod. Make sure the arrow on the piston crown (**Figure 110**) is facing toward the front of the engine.

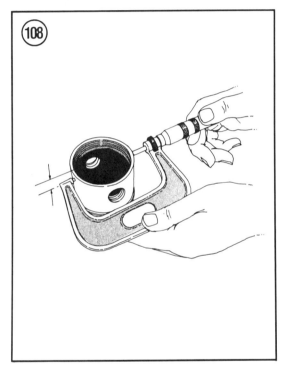

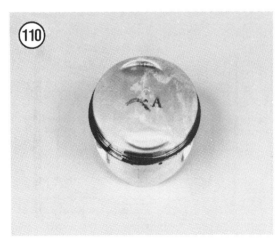

4. Line up the piston pin with the hole in the connecting rod and push the piston pin through the connecting rod and into the other side of the piston until it is even with the piston pin clip grooves.

CAUTION
*If pin is difficult to install, use the homemade tool (**Figure 104**) but eliminate the piece of pipe.*

NOTE
*In the next step, install the clips with the gap away from the cutout in the piston (**Figure 111**).*

5. Install new piston pin clips in both ends of the pin boss. Make sure they are seated in the grooves in the piston.

6. Check the installation by rocking the piston back and forth around the pin axis and from side to side along the axis. It should rotate freely back and forth but not from side to side.

7. Install the piston rings as described in this chapter.

8. Install the cylinder and cylinder head as described in this chapter.

PISTON RINGS

Replacement

WARNING
The edges of all piston rings are very sharp. Be careful when handling them to avoid cut fingers.

1. Remove the old rings with a ring expander tool or by spreading the ring ends with your thumbs and lifting the rings up evenly (**Figure 101**).

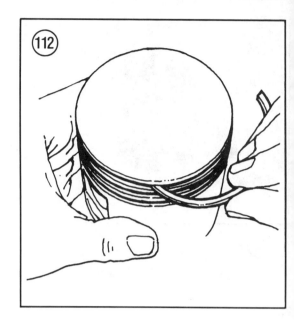

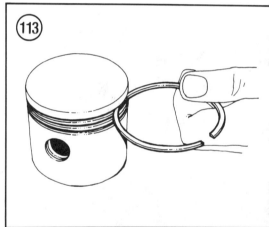

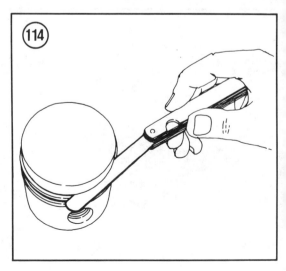

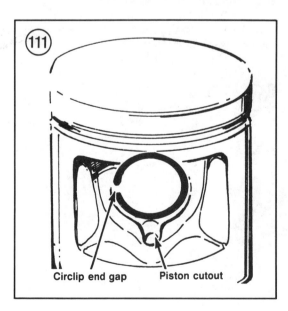

Circlip end gap   Piston cutout

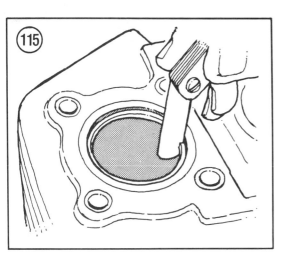

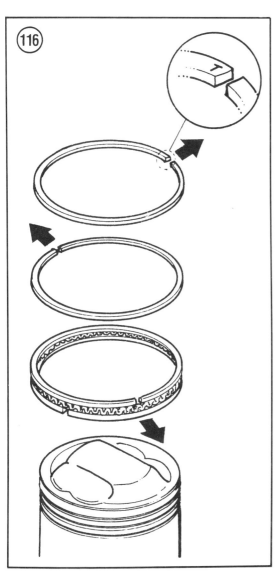

2. Using a broken piston ring, remove all carbon from the piston ring grooves (**Figure 112**). Inspect grooves carefully for burrs, nicks, or broken or cracked lands. Recondition or replace piston if necessary.

3. Roll each ring around its piston groove as shown in **Figure 113** to check for binding. Minor binding may be cleaned up with a fine cut file.

4. Measure the side clearance of each ring in its groove with a flat feeler gauge (**Figure 114**) and compare to specifications in **Table 1** or **Table 2**. If the clearance is greater than specified, the rings must be replaced. If the clearance is still excessive with the new rings, the piston must also be replaced.

5. Check end gap of each ring. To check ring, insert the ring into the bottom of the cylinder bore and square it with the cylinder wall by tapping with the piston. The ring should be in about 20 mm (3/4 in.). Insert a feeler gauge as shown in **Figure 115**. Compare gap with **Table 1** or **Table 2**. If the gap is greater than specified, the rings should be replaced. When installing new rings, measure their end gap in the same manner as for old ones. If the gap is less than specified, carefully file the ends with a fine-cut file until the gap is correct.

6. Install the piston rings in the order shown in **Figure 116**.

NOTE
*Install all rings with their markings
facing up.*

7. Install oil ring in oil ring groove with a ring expander tool or spread the ends with your thumbs.

8. Install 2 compression rings carefully with a ring expander tool or spread the ends with your thumbs.

9. Distribute ring gaps around piston as shown in **Figure 116**. The important thing is that the ring gaps are not aligned with each other when installed.

10. If new rings were installed, measure the side clearance of each ring in its groove with a flat feeler gauge (**Figure 114**). Compare to specifications given in **Table 1** or **Table 2**.

11. Follow the *Break-in Procedure* in this chapter if a new piston or piston rings have been installed or the cylinder was rebored or honed.

OIL PUMP

The oil pump is located on the right-hand side of the engine behind the clutch assembly. The oil pump can be removed with the engine in the frame.

Removal/Installation

1. Remove the clutch assembly as described in Chapter Five.

2. Turn the pump gear and align slots in gear with 3 oil pump attachment screws. Then remove 3 screws and remove oil pump assembly. See **Figure 117**.

3. Inspect all parts as described in this chapter.

4. Install by reversing the removal steps, noting the following.

5. Check that the oil pump gasket is installed on the backside of the pump or on the engine case (**Figure 118**) and that it is not torn or installed incorrectly. Install a new gasket if necessary.

Disassembly/Inspection/Assembly

1. Inspect the outer housing for cracks.

2. Remove the gasket from the backside of the housing.

3. Remove the screw (**Figure 119**) securing the oil pump housings. Then lift the rear housing off (**Figure 120**).

4. Remove the outer (**Figure 121**) and inner (**Figure 122**) rotors.

5. Remove the pin (**Figure 123**) and separate the pump gear from the front housing (**Figure 124**).

6. Clean all parts (**Figure 125**) in solvent and thoroughly dry with compressed air.

NOTE
If any part is found to be worn or damaged, the oil pump must be replaced with a new unit; replacement parts are not available from Yamaha.

7. Check the inner housing rotor surface for any signs of wear or galling.

8. Check the oil pump gear and shaft (**Figure 126**) for gear breakage, wear or shaft galling.

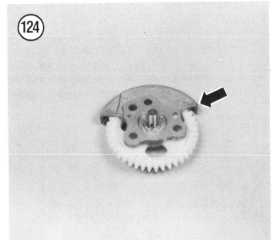

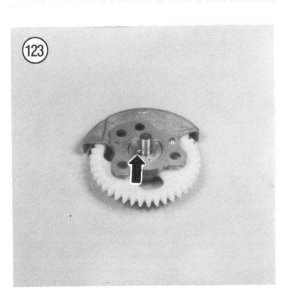

4

9. Measure the rotor widths with a vernier caliper (**Figure 127**). Replace the oil pump if the rotor widths are less than 6 mm (0.236 in.).

10. Install the inner rotor and check the clearance between the inner and outer rotor (**Figure 128**) with a flat feeler gauge. The clearance should be within the specifications listed in **Table 1** or **Table 2**. If the clearance is greater, replace the oil pump.

NOTE
Proceed with Step 11 only when the above inspection and measurement steps indicate that the parts are in good condition.

11. Assembly is the reverse of disassembly. Coat all parts with fresh engine oil prior to assembly.

PRIMARY DRIVE AND BALANCER GEARS

The primary drive and balancer gears may be removed with the engine in the frame. See **Figure 129**.

Removal/Installation

NOTE
*The gears are identified in **Figure 130**: A, primary drive gear; B, balancer driven gear; C, balancer drive gear.*

1. Remove the clutch assembly as described in Chapter Five.

2. Remove the oil pump as described in this chapter.

3. Flatten the balancer driven gear lockwasher (A, **Figure 131**). Then place a folded rag between the balancer drive gear and balancer driven gear at the point indicated in B, **Figure 131** and loosen the locknut.

4. Remove the following parts in order:
   a. Balancer driven gear nut (A, **Figure 131**).
   b. Balancer driven gear lockwasher (**Figure 132**).
   c. Balancer driven gear (**Figure 133**).
   d. Woodruff key (**Figure 134**).
   e. Primary drive gear circlip (**Figure 135**).

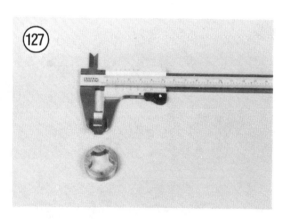

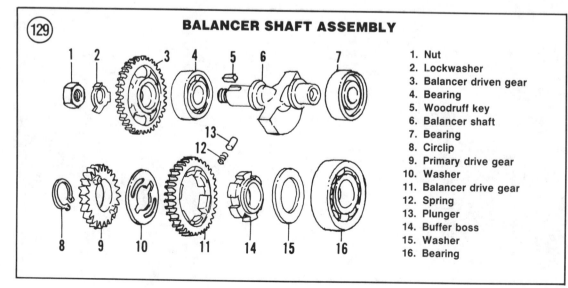

BALANCER SHAFT ASSEMBLY

1. Nut
2. Lockwasher
3. Balancer driven gear
4. Bearing
5. Woodruff key
6. Balancer shaft
7. Bearing
8. Circlip
9. Primary drive gear
10. Washer
11. Balancer drive gear
12. Spring
13. Plunger
14. Buffer boss
15. Washer
16. Bearing

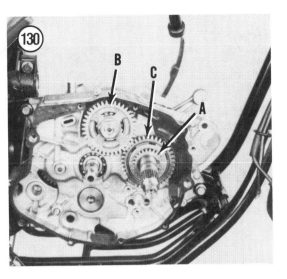

f. Primary drive gear (**Figure 136**).

g. Large washer (**Figure 137**).

> *NOTE*
> *The balancer drive gear (**Figure 138**) has 6 springs and 3 pins that may fall out when the gear is removed. Carefully remove the gear to prevent this.*

h. Balancer drive gear (**Figure 138**).

5. Removal and installation of the buffer boss (**Figure 139**) requires special Yamaha tools. It is best to refer removal to a Yamaha dealer. The engine, however, can be split with the buffer boss installed. Removal of the buffer boss is only required for its replacement, crankshaft service or replacement of the right-hand crankcase bearing.

6. Inspect the drive and balancer gears as described in this section.

7. Installation is the reverse of these steps, noting the following.

8. The balancer drive gear is equipped with 6 springs and 3 pins. To assemble the balancer gear, place a pin and spring at every other slot position. Then place the springs in the remaining slots. The arrows in **Figure 140** identify positions for springs and pins.

9. When installing the primary drive gear, align the tabs on the back of the gear with the 2 washer slots. See **Figure 141**.

10. When installing the balancer drive and driven gears, align the timing marks on both gears as shown in **Figure 142**.

11. Tighten the balancer driven gear and primary drive locknuts to the specifications in **Table 3**.

12. After tightening the locknuts, bend the lockwasher tabs over the locknuts.

Inspection

After the drive and balancer gears have been cleaned, visually inspect the components for excessive wear. Any burrs, pitting or roughness on the teeth of a gear will cause wear on the mating gear.

> *NOTE*
> *Defective gears should be replaced. It's a good idea to replace the mating gear on the other shaft, even though it may not show as much wear or damage, to prevent excessive wear to the new gear.*

CRANKCASE AND CRANKSHAFT

Disassembly of the crankcase (splitting the cases) and removal of the crankshaft require that the engine be removed from the frame.

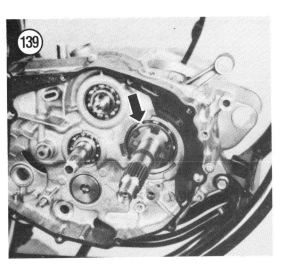

The crankcase is made in 2 halves of precision diecast aluminum alloy and is of the "thin-walled" type. To avoid damage, do not hammer or pry on any of the interior or exterior projected walls. These areas are easily damaged. The cases on all models are manufactured as a matched set. Thus if one case is damaged, both cases must be replaced. The cases are assembled with sealer; dowel pins align the halves when they are bolted together.

The crankshaft assembly is made up of 2 flywheels pressed together on a hollow crankpin. The connecting rod big-end bearing on the crankpin is a needle bearing assembly. The crankshaft assembly is supported by 2 ball bearings in the crankcase. Service to the crankshaft for the home mechanic is limited to removal and installation. However, well-equipped Yamaha dealers or machine shops can disassemble and rebuild the crankshaft when necessary.

Crankcase Disassembly

1. Remove the engine as described in this chapter.
2. Remove the exterior engine assemblies as described in this chapter and other related chapters:

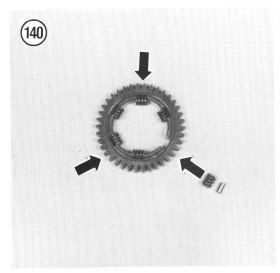

   a. Cylinder head.
   b. Cylinder.
   c. Piston.
   d. Alternator.
   e. Camshaft chain and guides.
   f. Clutch assemblies.
   g. Oil pump.
   h. Primary drive and balancer gears.
   i. External shift mechanism.
   j. Remove the middle gear or reverse gear cover on drive shaft models.

NOTE
To prevent crankcase warpage, loosen the bolts in a crisscross pattern.

3. Remove the screws from the right-hand crankcase (**Figure 143**).

4. Remove the screws from the left-hand crankcase (**Figure 144**).

NOTE
Set the engine on wood blocks or fabricate a holding fixture of 2×4 inch wood.

5. Perform the following to separate the crankcase assemblies:

 a. Place the engine assembly on wood blocks with the right-hand side facing up (**Figure 145**).

 b. Work the right-hand crankcase assembly loose by carefully tapping the cases with a plastic faced hammer. Continue this action until the crankshaft and crankcase separate (**Figure 146**). The crankshaft will stay in the left-hand crankcase (**Figure 146**).

6. If the crankcase and crankshaft will not separate using this method, check to make sure that all screws are removed. If you still have a problem, take the crankcase assembly to a dealer and have it separated.

CAUTION
Never pry between the case halves. Doing so may result in oil leaks, requiring replacement of the case halves.

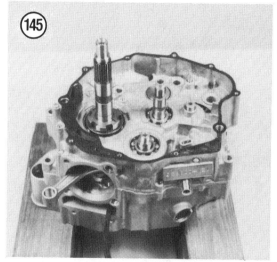

7. Don't lose the 3 locating dowels (**Figure 147**) if they came out of the case. They do not have to be removed from the case if they are secure.

8. Referring to **Figure 148**, lift up and carefully remove the following parts:
   a. Shift fork shafts (A).
   b. Shift forks (B).
   c. Shift drum (C).

9. Remove the transmission shafts (D, **Figure 148**) as described in Chapter Five.

10. Remove the balancer shaft (**Figure 149**).

> *NOTE*
> *Step 11 describes crankshaft removal. It should be noted that special Yamaha tools are required for removal and installation.*

11. Push the crankshaft assembly (**Figure 150**) from the left-hand crankcase with the Yamaha puller (YU-01135) and adaptor (YM-33278). See **Figure 151**.

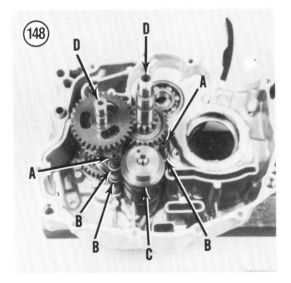

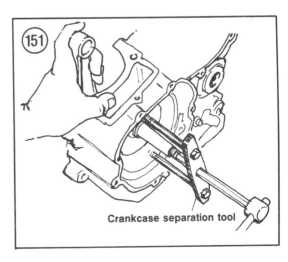

Crankcase separation tool

12. Inspect the crankcase halves, crankshaft and balancer shaft as described later in this chapter.

Crankcase Assembly

1. Apply assembly oil to the inner race of all bearings in both crankcase halve.

> *NOTE*
> *Set the left-hand crankcase assembly on wood blocks or the wood holding fixture shown in the disassembly procedure.*

2. The following Yamaha tools will be required to install the crankshaft:
   a. Crankshaft installer (YU-90050). See A, **Figure 152**.
   b. Adapter No. 11 (YM-33279). See B, **Figure 152**.
   c. Pot extension (YM-33280). See C, **Figure 152**.
3. Pull the crankshaft into right-hand crankcase using the Yamaha tool as shown in **Figure 153**.
4. Place the left-hand crankcase on wood blocks as shown in **Figure 154**.
5. Install the balancer shaft (**Figure 149**).
6. Install the transmission assemblies, shift shafts and shift drum into the crankcase. Lightly oil all shaft ends. Refer to Chapter Five for the correct procedure.

> *NOTE*
> *Make sure the mating surfaces are clean and free of all old sealant.*

7. Install the 3 locating dowels (**Figure 147**) if they were removed.

8. Apply a light coat of non-hardening liquid gasket (**Figure 155**) such as Yamabond No. 4, 4-Three Bond or equivalent to the mating surfaces of both crankcase halves.
9. Set the upper crankcase half over the one on the blocks. Push it down squarely into place until it reaches the crankshaft bearing, usually with about 1/2 inch left to go.
10. Lightly tap the case halves together with a plastic or rubber mallet until they seat. After the cases are assembled tap on the end of each shaft to make sure it is free and rotates smoothly.

> *CAUTION*
> *Crankcase halves should fit together without force. If the crankcase halves do not fit together completely, do not attempt to pull them together with the crankcase screws. Separate the crankcase halves and investigage the interference. If the transmission shafts were disassembled, recheck to make sure that a gear is not installed backwards. Crankcase halves are very expensive. Do not risk damage by trying to force the cases together.*

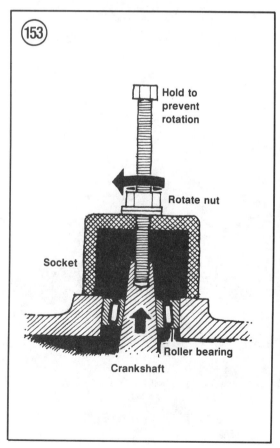

(153)

Hold to prevent rotation

Rotate nut

Socket

Roller bearing

Crankshaft

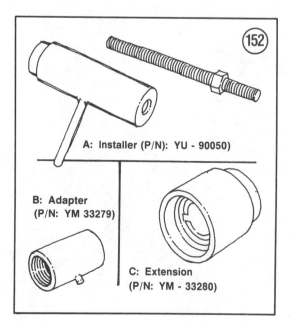

(152)

A: Installer (P/N): YU - 90050)

B: Adapter (P/N: YM 33279)

C: Extension (P/N: YM - 33280)

11. Install all the crankcase screws and tighten only finger-tight at first.

12. Securely tighten the screws in 2 stages in a crisscross pattern until they are firmly hand-tight.

13. After the crankcase halves are completely assembled, rotate the crankshaft and transmission shafts to make sure there is no binding. If any is present, disassemble the crankcase and correct the problem.

14. Install all exterior engine assembles as described in this chapter and other related chapters:

    a. Middle gear or reverse gear housings (shaft drive models).

    b. External shift mechanism.

    c. Primary drive and balancer gears.

    d. Oil pump.

    e. Clutch assemblies.

    f. Cam chain and guides.

    g. Alternator.

    h. Piston.

    i. Cylinder.

    j. Cylinder head.

Crankcase and Crankshaft Inspection

1. Clean both crankcase halves inside and out with cleaning solvent. Thoroughly dry with compressed air and wipe off with a clean shop cloth. Be sure to remove all traces of old gasket material from all mating surfaces.

2. Check the transmission and balancer shaft bearings (**Figure 156** and **Figure 157**) and the shift

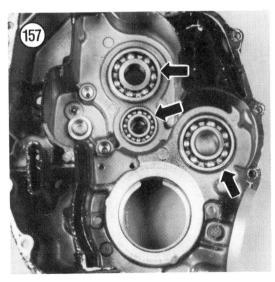

drum bearing (**Figure 158**) for roughness, galling and play by rotating them slowly by hand. If any roughness or play can be felt in the bearing it must be replaced.

3. Carefully inspect the cases for cracks and fractures, especially in the lower areas; they are vulnerable to rock damage. Also check the areas around the stiffening ribs, bearing bosses and threaded holes. If any are found, replace the crankcases.

4. Check that bolt threads in cases are clean and free of any thread damage. See **Figure 159** and **Figure 160**. Clean thread holes by blowing out with compressed air. If threads are damaged, use a tap of the correct size to repair them.

5. Check the crankshaft main bearings (**Figure 161** and **Figure 162**) for roughness, pitting, galling and play by rotating them slowly by hand. If any roughness or play can be felt in the bearing it must be replaced. Replace the crankcase bearing (**Figure 162**) as described in this chapter. The bearing on the crankshaft (**Figure 161**) should be removed by a dealer as special tools are required.

6. Inspect the cam chain sprocket (**Figure 163**) for wear or missing teeth. If damaged, the crankshaft will have to be split and the left crank wheel replaced. Refer this service to a dealer as special tools are required.

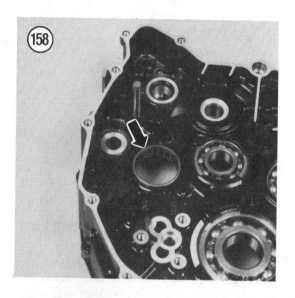

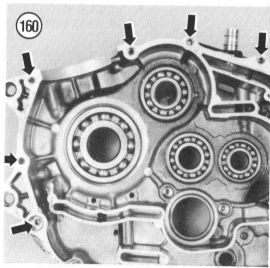

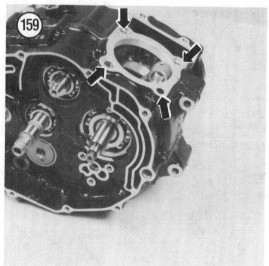

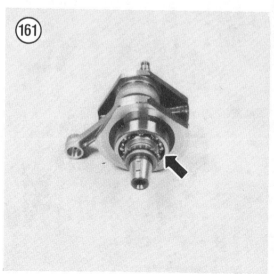

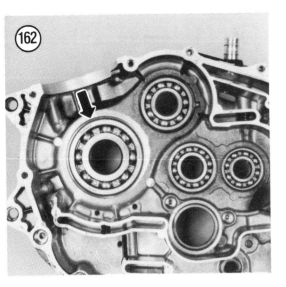

NOTE
*If the cam chain sprocket requires replacement, the camshaft sprocket and cam chain (**Figure 164**) should also be replaced to prevent premature wear to the new part.*

7. Check the connecting rod small end (**Figure 165**) for any signs of galling or discoloration. If damaged, replace the connecting rod and piston pin.

8. Check the connecting rod big end bearing by grasping the rod in one hand and lifting up on it. With the heel of your other hand, rap sharply on the top of the rod. A sharp metallic sound, such as a click, is an indication that the bearing or crankpin or both are worn; the crankshaft assembly should be disassembled and new parts installed.

9. Check the connecting rod-to-crankshaft side clearance with a flat feeler gauge (**Figure 166**). Compare to dimensions given in **Table 1** or **Table**

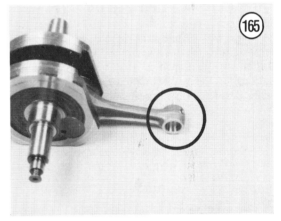

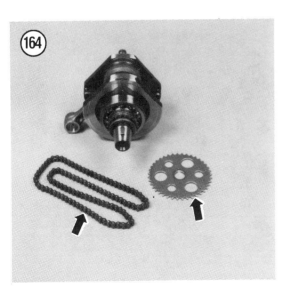

2. If the clearance is greater than specified the crankshaft assembly should be disassembled and new parts installed.

10. Check the balancer shaft bearing surfaces (**Figure 167**) for any signs of wear or discoloration and the keyway for any signs of damage. If damage is found, replace the balancer shaft.

11. Check the crankshaft runout with a set of V-blocks or in a lathe as shown in **Figure 168**. Compare specifications to those listed in **Figure 168**. Note that specifications for left and right sides are different. Have a Yamaha dealer or machine shop true the crankshaft if necessary.

12. Replace the oil seals as described in this chapter. They should always be replaced when the crankcase is disassembled.

Bearing and Oil Seal Replacement

Whenever replacing oil seals and bearings, always place the crankcase halves on wood blocks to protect the sealing surfaces from damage.

1. Pry out the oil seals (**Figure 169**) with a small screwdriver, taking care not to damage the crankcase bore. If the seals are old and difficult to remove, heat the cases as described in Step 2 and use an awl to punch a small hole in the steel backing of the seal. Install a small sheet metal screw partway into the seal and pull the seal out with a pair of pliers.

> *CAUTION*
> *Do not install the screw too deep or it may contact and damage the bearing behind it.*

2. The bearings are installed with a slight interference fit. The crankcase must be heated in an oven to a temperature of about 212° F (100° C). An easy way to check the proper temperature is to drop tiny drops of water on the case; if they sizzle and evaporate immediately, the temperature is correct. Heat only one case at a time.

> *CAUTION*
> *Do not heat the cases with a torch (propane or acetylene); never bring a flame into contact with the bearing or case. The direct heat will destroy the case hardening of the bearing and will likely cause warpage of the case.*

3. Remove the case from the oven and hold onto the 2 crankcase studs with a kitchen pot holder, heavy gloves or heavy shop cloths—*it is hot*.

4. Hold the crankcase with the bearing side down and tap it squarely on a piece of soft wood.

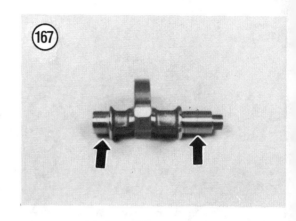

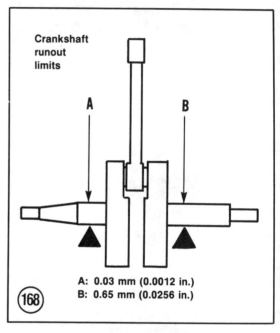

Crankshaft runout limits

A B

A: 0.03 mm (0.0012 in.)
B: 0.65 mm (0.0256 in.)

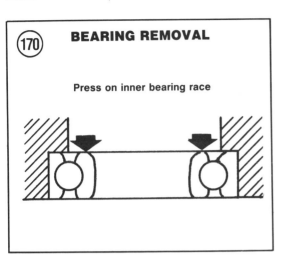

BEARING REMOVAL

Press on inner bearing race

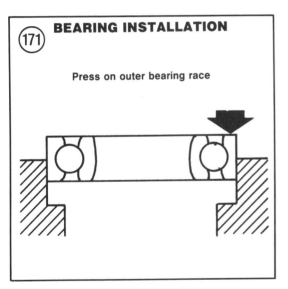

BEARING INSTALLATION

Press on outer bearing race

Continue to tap until the bearing(s) fall out. Repeat for the other half.

CAUTION
Be sure to tap the crankcase squarely on the piece of wood. Avoid damaging the sealing surface of the crankcase.

5. If the bearings are difficult to remove, they can be gently tapped out with a socket or piece of pipe the same size as the bearing race (**Figure 170**).

NOTE
If the bearings or seals are difficult to remove or install, don't take a chance on expensive damage. Have the work performed by a dealer or competent machine shop.

6. While heating up the crankcase halves, place the new bearings in a freezer if possible. Chilling them will slightly reduce their overall diameter while the hot crankcase is slightly larger due to heat expansion. This will make bearing installation much easier.
7. While the crankcase is still hot, press each new bearing(s) into place in the crankcase (**Figure 171**) until it seats completely. If the bearing is tapped in, hit on the outer race (**Figure 171**) only. Do not force it in. If the bearing will not seat, remove it and cool it again. Reheat the crankcase and install the bearing again.
8. Oil seals can be installed with a proper size socket or piece of pipe. Make sure that the bearings and oil seals are not cocked in the crankcase hole and that they are seated properly.
9. After installing bearings and seals, apply a light amount of lightweight lithium base grease to the seal lips. Coat the bearings with engine oil to prevent rust.

ALTERNATOR ROTOR, STARTER CLUTCH ASSEMBLY AND GEARS

The alternator, starter clutch assembly and gears can be removed with the engine in the frame. The starter motor can be left in place, if desired.

Removal/Installation

1. Remove the recoil starter as described in this chapter.
2. Drain the engine oil as described in Chapter Three.
3. Disconnect the battery negative terminal.
4. Disconnect the alternator electrical connector (**Figure 172**).

5. Remove the bolts securing the alternator cover and remove the cover (**Figure 173**), gasket and the electrical harness from the frame. Note the path of the wire harness as it must be routed the same during installation.

6. Remove the following in order:

    a. Spacer (**Figure 174**).

    b. Starter idler gear shaft (A, **Figure 175**).

    c. Starter idler gear (B, **Figure 175**).

7. Remove the alternator rotor (**Figure 176**) with a 3-way universal puller (**Figure 177**).

8. Refer to **Figure 178**. Remove the washer (A) and Woodruff key (B).

9. Remove the starter idler gear (**Figure 179**).

10. Remove the washer (**Figure 180**).

Inspection

1. Check the starter clutch roller assembly as follows:

    a. Remove the roller (**Figure 181**), plunger and coil spring (**Figure 182**) from each recess.

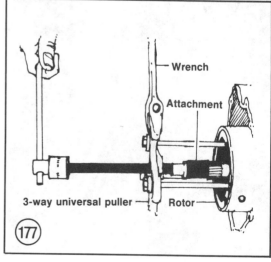

Wrench

Attachment

3-way universal puller — Rotor

b. Check the springs (A, **Figure 183**) for stretching or apparent damage.

c. Check the plungers (B, **Figure 183**) for tip wear.

d. Check the rollers (C, **Figure 183**) for uneven or excessive wear.

e. Replace the roller assembly if any one component is bad.

f. Install the spring, plunger and roller into each receptacle in the starter clutch.

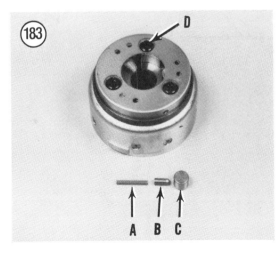

2. Check the starter clutch Allen bolts (D, **Figure 183**) for looseness. If a bolt is loose, replace it with a new one and tighten to 30 N•m (22 ft.-lb.). Apply Loctite 242 to the bolt before installation.

3. Check the idler gear teeth (**Figure 184**) for cracks, deep scoring, or excessive wear. Replace the gear if necessary.

4. Check the starter idler gear (A, **Figure 185**) where it rides against the rollers (B, **Figure 185**). Replace the gear if worn or scored in this area. If the gear is bad, replace the roller assembly also.

5. Inspect the alternator cover oil seal (**Figure 186**) for wear or damage. If necessary, replace the oil seal as described under *Bearing and Oil Seal Replacement* in this chapter.

Installation

1. Install the following parts in order:
   a. Washer (**Figure 180**).
   b. Starter idler gear (**Figure 179**).
   c. Washer (A, **Figure 178**).
   d. Woodruff key (B, **Figure 178**).

2. Carefully inspect the inside of the rotor (**Figure 187**) for small bolts, washers or other metal "trash" that may have been picked up by the magnets. These small bits can cause severe damage to the alternator stator assembly.

3. Align the keyway in the alternator with the Woodruff key (B, **Figure 178**) and install the alternator.

4. Refer to **Figure 175**. Install the following in order:
   a. Idler gear (B, **Figure 175**).
   b. Idler gear shaft (A, **Figure 175**).
   c. Spacer (**Figure 174**).

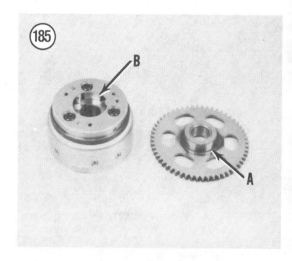

5. Install the 2 alternator cover dowel pins (**Figure 188**) and install a new alternator cover gasket.

6. Install the alternator cover (**Figure 173**) and tighten the screws securely.

7. Route the alternator stator wire harness through the frame. Clean the wire connectors of all dirt and grit and connect the electrical connectors (**Figure 172**).

8. Install the recoil starter assembly as described in this chapter.

9. Refill the engine oil as described in Chapter Three.

RECOIL STARTER

Removal/Installation

Refer to **Figure 189** (chain drive) or **Figure 190** (shaft drive) for this procedure.

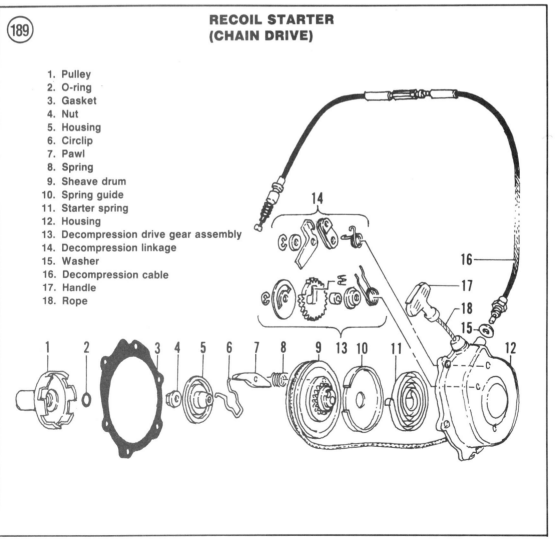

RECOIL STARTER (CHAIN DRIVE)

1. Pulley
2. O-ring
3. Gasket
4. Nut
5. Housing
6. Circlip
7. Pawl
8. Spring
9. Sheave drum
10. Spring guide
11. Starter spring
12. Housing
13. Decompression drive gear assembly
14. Decompression linkage
15. Washer
16. Decompression cable
17. Handle
18. Rope

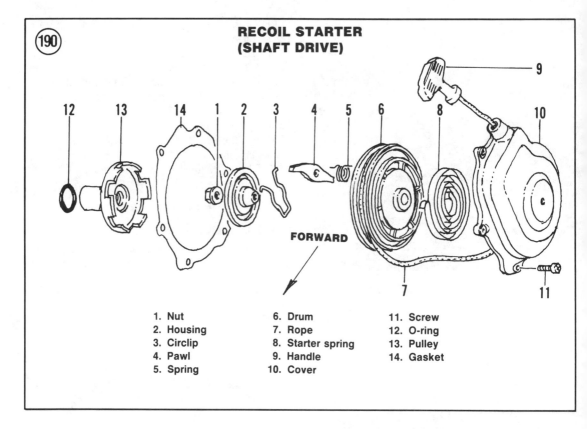

RECOIL STARTER (SHAFT DRIVE)

FORWARD

1. Nut
2. Housing
3. Circlip
4. Pawl
5. Spring
6. Drum
7. Rope
8. Starter spring
9. Handle
10. Cover
11. Screw
12. O-ring
13. Pulley
14. Gasket

1. Park the vehicle on level ground and set the parking brake.

2. *Models with reverse:* Remove the reverse lever bracket bolts at the recoil starter housing and remove the bracket (**Figure 191**). Then remove the reverse lever bolt at the middle/reverse gear housing (**Figure 192**) and remove the reverse lever assembly.

3. Shift the transmission into NEUTRAL and remove the gearshift lever.

4. Remove the bolts securing the recoil starter pull-housing (**Figure 193**) and remove it.

5. Secure the starter pulley with a universal type holding tool (**Figure 194**) and remove the pulley bolt.

6. Pull the starter pulley (**Figure 195**) off of the crankshaft.

7. Installation is the reverse of these steps, noting the following.

8. Refer to **Figure 196**. Check the starter pulley tabs (A) and O-ring (B) for wear or damage. Replace the O-ring by carefully prying it out of the pulley with a pointed tool. Replace the starter pulley if the pulley tabs are worn or damaged.

9. Secure the starter pulley with the same tool used during removal when tightening the pulley nut. Tighten the nut to the specifications in **Table 3**.

Disassembly and Starter Rope Removal (Chain Drive Models)

Refer to **Figure 189** for this procedure.

WARNING
The return spring is under pressure and may jump out during the disassembly procedure. It is not a very strong spring, but it may cut fingers or cause eye injury. Wear safety glasses and gloves when disassembling and assembling.

1. Refer to **Figure 197**. Remove the starter handle as follows:

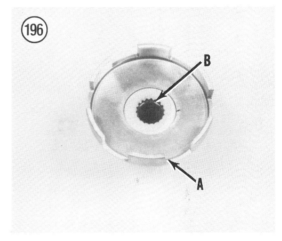

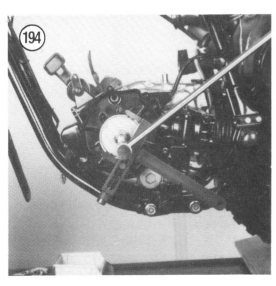

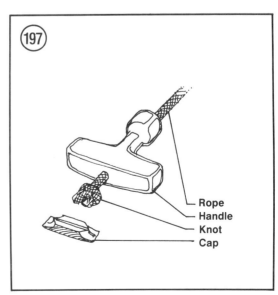

Rope

Handle

Knot

Cap

a. Place the recoil starter housing on the bench with the gears facing down.

b. Secure the starter rope with Vise Grips pliers.

c. Pry the cap from the end of the handle.

d. Slide the handle away from the rope knot and untie the knot.

e. Remove the starter handle.

f. Remove the Vise Grips and slowly allow the rope to wind into the starter housing.

2. Place the recoil starter housing on the bench with the gears facing up.

3. Remove the drive housing nut. Then remove the following parts in order:

a. Drive housing.

b. Drive pawl.

c. Drive pawl spring.

4. Slowly lift the sheave drum (**Figure 198**) up and remove the starter housing.

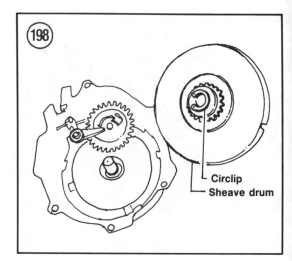

> *NOTE*
> *If you are disassembling the starter assembly to replace the starter rope, this is as far as you need to go. Install a new starter rope by beginning with Step 4 under* **Installation***.*

5. Remove the decompression linkage assembly as follows:

a. Remove the circlip.

b. Remove the washer.

c. Lift the decompression linkage out of the starter housing.

d. Disconnect the decompression cable.

e. Remove the cable attachment and spring.

6. Remove the decompression drive gear as follows:

a. Remove the circlip.

b. Remove the washer.

c. Remove the decompression gear assembly.

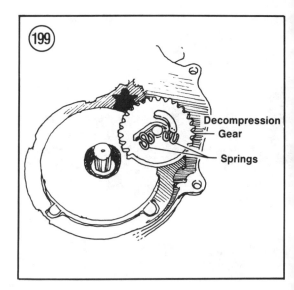

> *NOTE*
> *The drive gear assembly uses two different types of springs (**Figure 199**). Make sure to mark each spring as to position, as it must be reinstalled in the same position.*

d. Remove the spring retainer and stopper springs.

> *NOTE*
> *Generally, it is not necessary to remove the starter spring unless replacement is necessary.*

> *WARNING*
> *The recoil spring may jump out at this time. Protect yourself accordingly.*

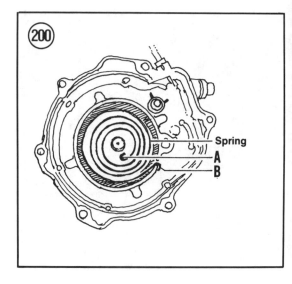

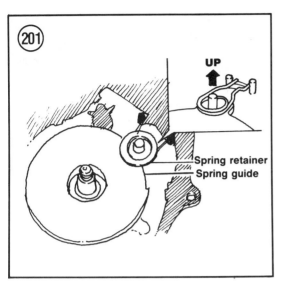

Spring retainer
Spring guide

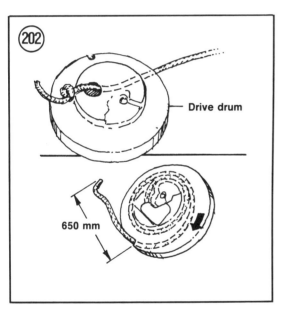

Drive drum

650 mm

7. Slowly remove the starter spring guide and starter spring from the case.

8. Clean all parts in solvent (except starter rope) and thoroughly dry.

9. Inspect all parts for wear or damage and replace as necessary.

**Assembly and
Starter Rope Installation
(Chain Drive Models)**

1. Referring to **Figure 200**, install the recoil spring in the housing as follows:

  a. Place the housing on the workbench before you as shown in **Figure 200**.

  b. Insert the end of the recoil spring into the slot in the center post (A, **Figure 200**).

  c. Bend a coat hanger or welding rod into a small hook and hook it onto the end of the spring.

  d. Carefully wind the recoil spring counterclockwise until it fits inside the retaining posts. Then hook the *end of the spring* onto the retaining post shown in B, **Figure 200**.

  e. After attaching the recoil spring at both ends, make sure the entire spring is within all retaining posts in the housing and that the spring faces in the direction shown in **Figure 200**.

  f. Lubricate the entire spring with waterproof grease.

  g. Install the starter spring guide (**Figure 201**).

2. Install the decompression gear assembly as follows:

  a. Install the decompression gear spring into the starter housing as shown in **Figure 201**. Make sure the spring arms engage the inside of the posts.

  b. Install the spring retainer (**Figure 201**).

  c. Install the decompression gear and 2 springs. Install the 2 springs in their original positions as marked during disassembly. See **Figure 199**.

  d. Install the washer and circlip.

3. Install the decompression linkage assembly as follows:

  a. Attach the decompression cable to the linkage joint.

  b. Install the spring and linkage joint.

  c. Install the linkage arm and secure it with the washer and circlip.

4. Install a new starter rope in the drive drum (**Figure 202**) and tie a special knot at the end (**Figure 203**). Pull the knot away from the drive

drum and apply heat from a match to the knot to *slightly* melt the nylon rope. This will hold the knot securely.

5. Coil the rope into the drive drum clockwise (**Figure 202**). Then hook the rope into the drum, leaving approximately 650 mm (25 in.) of the rope hanging out of the drum as shown in **Figure 202**. The drive drum is now ready to install in the housing.

6. Align the cutout on the bottom of the drive drum with the start of the spring and install the drive drum into the housing.

7. Rotate the drive drum until it drops slightly. Then rotate the drive drum until you can feel the spring tension.

8. Insert the rope through the hole in the housing.

9. Hold the rope with Vise Grips and insert the handle over the rope (**Figure 197**). Tie the end of the rope using the same special knot as shown in **Figure 203**. Apply heat to the knot (a match is sufficient) and *slightly* melt the nylon rope. This will hold the knot securely.

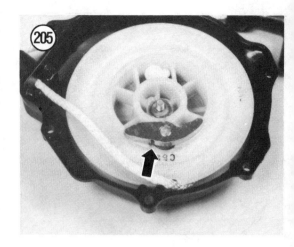

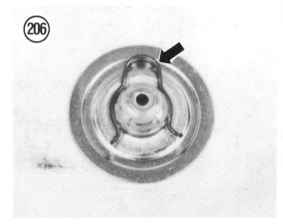

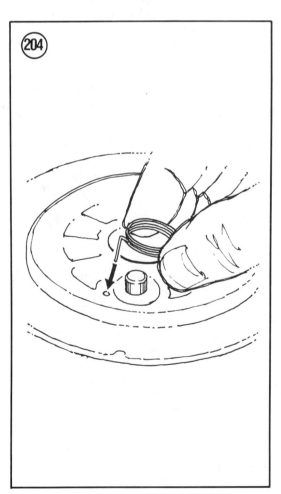

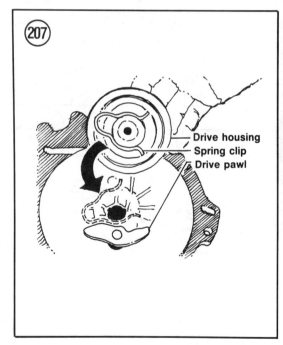

Drive housing
Spring clip
Drive pawl

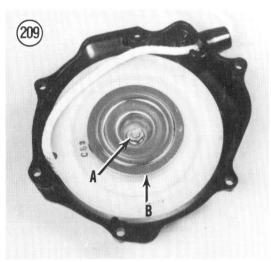

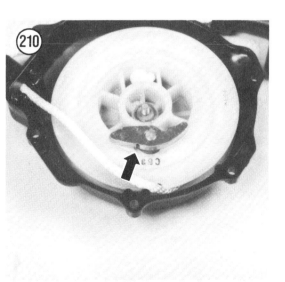

10. Install the drive pawl spring and drive pawl as follows:
   a. Insert the long end of the pawl spring (**Figure 204**) into the drive drum spring hole.
   b. Install the drive pawl onto the spring so that the short pawl spring end fits into the drive pawl notch. See **Figure 205**.
   c. Preload the drive pawl spring by turning the drive pawl one turn counterclockwise. Then push the drive pawl into the drive drum cutout.

11. Install the spring clip onto the drive housing as shown in **Figure 206**. Then align the spring clip with the drive housing as shown in **Figure 207**.

12. Install the drive housing nut and tighten to 10 N•m (7.2 ft.-lb.).

13. Remove the Vise Grips from the rope. Then rotate the drive drum 4 turns clockwise to preload the spring.

14. After assembly is complete, check the operation of the recoil starter by pulling on the handle. Make sure the drive pulley rotates freely and returns completely. Also make sure the ratchet moves out and in correctly. If either does not operate correctly, disassemble and correct the problem.

Disassembly and Starter Rope Removal (Shaft Drive Models)

Refer to **Figure 190** for this procedure.

WARNING
The return spring is under pressure and may jump out during the disassembly procedure. It is not a very strong spring, but it may cut fingers or cause eye injury. Wear safety glasses and gloves when disassembling and assembling.

1. Remove the starter handle as follows:
   a. Pull the handle out partway. Then carefully pry the starter rope out from around the drum and engage it with the slot in the drive drum as shown in **Figure 208**.
   b. Pry the cap from the end of the handle.
   c. Slide the handle away from the rope knot and untie the knot.
   d. Remove the starter handle.
   e. Slowly allow the rope to unwind into the starter housing.

2. Remove the drive housing nut (A, **Figure 209**). Then remove the following parts in order:
   a. Drive housing (B, **Figure 209**).
   b. Drive pawl (**Figure 210**).

c. Drive pawl spring (**Figure 211**).

3. Slowly lift the drive drum (**Figure 212**) up and remove it.

> *WARNING*
> *The recoil spring may jump out at this time—protect yourself accordingly.*

4. Refer to **Figure 213**. If necessary, disengage the recoil spring from the outer sping post and slowly allow the spring to unwind. Then disengage the spring from the center post and remove it.

5. Clean all parts in solvent and thoroughly dry.

6. Inspect the pawl and spring (**Figure 214**) for wear or damage. Replace if necessary.

Assembly and
Starter Rope Installation
(Shaft Drive Models)

1. Referring to **Figure 213**, install the recoil spring in the housing as follows:

  a. Place the housing on the workbench before you as shown in **Figure 213**.

  b. Insert the start of the recoil spring into the slot in the center post.

  c. Bend a coat hanger or welding rod into a small hook and hook it onto the end of the spring.

  d. Carefully wind the recoil spring counterclockwise until it fits inside the retaining posts. Then hook the *end of the spring* onto the retaining post shown in **Figure 213**.

  e. After attaching the recoil spring at both ends, make sure the entire spring is within all retaining posts in the housing and that the spring faces in the direction shown in **Figure 213**.

  f. Lubricate the entire spring with waterproof grease.

2. Install a new starter rope in the drive drum (**Figure 215**) and tie a special knot at the end (**Figure 203**). Pull the knot away from the drive drum and apply heat from a match to the knot to *slightly* melt the nylon rope. This will hold the knot securely.

3. Coil the rope into the drive drum clockwise. Then hook the rope into the drum, leaving approximately 400 mm (15 in.) of the rope hanging out of the drum as shown in **Figure 216**. Engage the rope with the notch in the drum as shown in **Figure 216**. The drive drum is now ready to install in the housing.

4. Align the cutout on the bottom of the drive drum with the start of the spring and install the drive drum into the housing. See **Figure 217**.

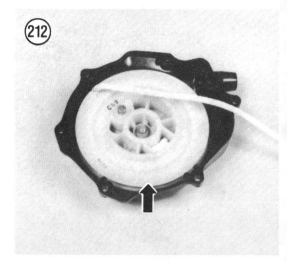

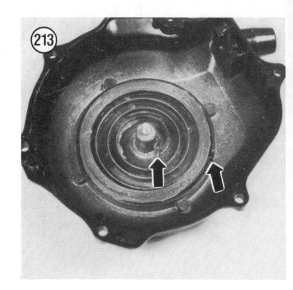

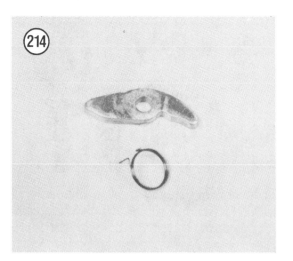

5. Rotate the drive drum until it drops slightly. Then rotate the drive drum until you can feel the spring tension.

6. Insert the rope through the hole in the housing (**Figure 218**).

NOTE
Make sure the rope still engages the notch in the drive drum as shown in ***Figure 218***. *If the rope will not stay in the notch, secure it with Vise Grips pliers.*

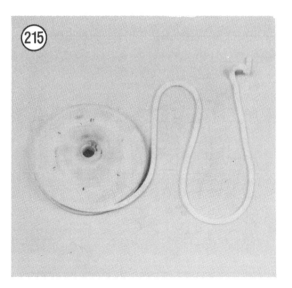

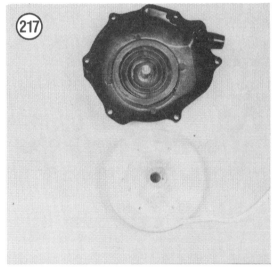

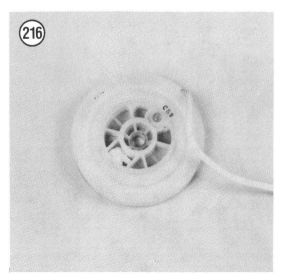

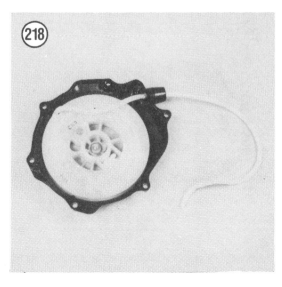

7. Insert the handle over the rope (**Figure 219**). Tie the end of the rope (**Figure 220**) using the same special knot as shown in **Figure 203**. Apply heat to the knot (a match is sufficient) and *slightly* melt the nylon rope. This will hold the knot securely.

8. Install the drive paw spring and drive paw as follows:

   a. Insert the long end of the pawl spring (**Figure 211**) into the drive drum spring hole.

   b. Install the drive pawl onto the spring so that the short pawl spring end fits into the drive pawl notch. See **Figure 210**.

   c. Preload the drive pawl spring by turning the drive pawl one turn counterclockwise. Then push the drive pawl into the drive drum cutout.

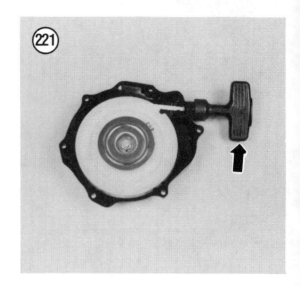

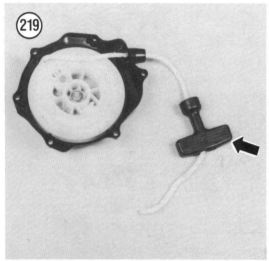

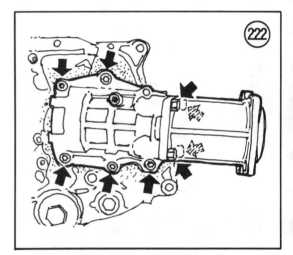

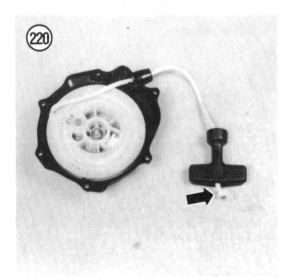

9. Install the spring clip onto the drive housing as shown in **Figure 206**. Then install the spring clip with the drive housing as shown in **Figure 207**.

10. Install the drive housing nut and tighten to 10 N•m (7.2 ft.-lb.).

11. Remove the rope from the notch in the drive drum. Then rotate the drive drum 4 turns clockwise to preload the spring.

12. After assembly is complete, check the operation of the recoil starter by pulling on the handle (**Figure 221**). Make sure the drive pulley rotates freely and returns completely. Also make sure the ratchet moves out and in correctly. If either does not operate correctly, disassemble and correct the problem.

MIDDLE GEAR CASE

These procedure pertains to shaft drive models with forward gears only.

Removal/Installation

1. Remove the engine from the frame as described in this chapter.

2. Remove the bolts securing the gear case to the left-hand crankcase half (**Figure 222**).

3. If necessary, remove the drive pinion gear (**Figure 223**) as described in Chapter Five under *Transmission Disassembly*.

4. Install by reversing these removal steps.

Disassembly/Inspection/Assembly

Middle gear case disassembly and reassembly requires a number of special Yamaha tools. The price of these tools could be more than the cost of most repairs done by a dealer. Refer all service to a Yamaha dealer.

MIDDLE/REVERSE GEAR CASE

This procedure pertains to shaft drive models with reverse.

Removal/Inspection/Installation

1. Remove the engine from the frame as described in this chapter.

2A. *YTM200ERN:* Referring to **Figure 224**, perform the following:

   a. Remove the middle/reverse gear case bolts and remove the gear case from the engine.

   b. If necessary, remove the drive shaft housing bolts and pull the housing away from the middle/reverse gear case.

2B. *All other models:* Perform the following:

   a. Remove the front (**Figure 225**) and rear (A, **Figure 226**) case bolts and lift the gear case (**Figure 227**) off of the engine crankcase.

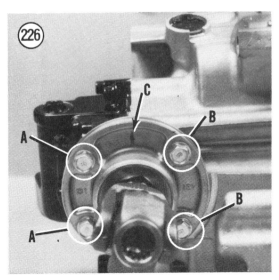

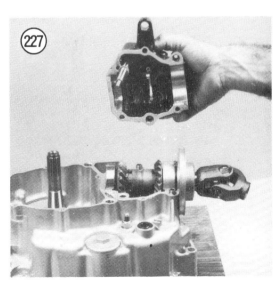

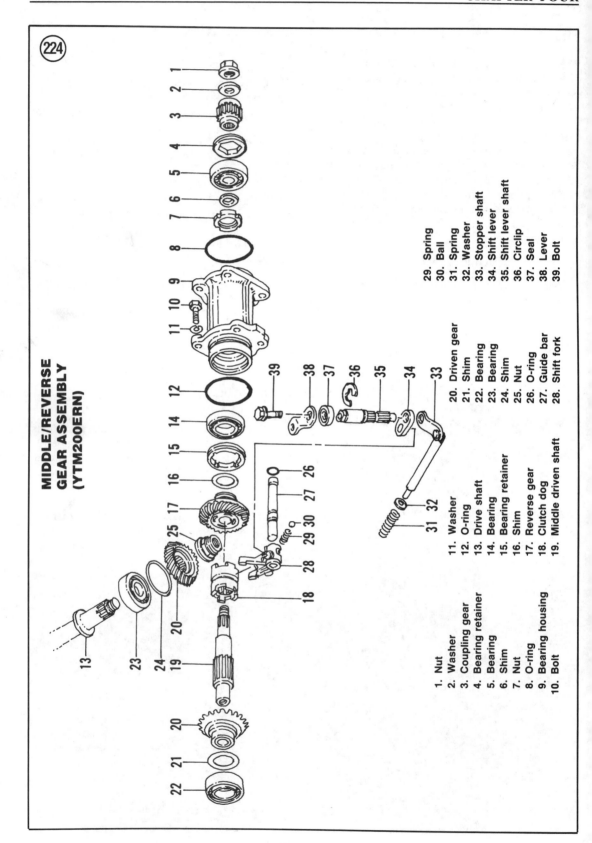

MIDDLE/REVERSE GEAR ASSEMBLY (YTM200ERN)

1. Nut
2. Washer
3. Coupling gear
4. Bearing retainer
5. Bearing
6. Shim
7. Nut
8. O-ring
9. Bearing housing
10. Bolt
11. Washer
12. O-ring
13. Drive shaft
14. Bearing
15. Bearing retainer
16. Shim
17. Reverse gear
18. Clutch dog
19. Middle driven shaft
20. Driven gear
21. Shim
22. Bearing
23. Bearing
24. Shim
25. Nut
26. O-ring
27. Guide bar
28. Shift fork
29. Spring
30. Ball
31. Spring
32. Washer
33. Stopper shaft
34. Shift lever
35. Shift lever shaft
36. Circlip
37. Seal
38. Lever
39. Bolt

b. Remove the 2 bolts (B, **Figure 226**) and lift the middle driven gear shaft (**Figure 228**) out of the crankcase.

3. If necessary, remove the shift fork assembly as follows:

    a. Remove the spring (**Figure 229**) and washer (**Figure 230**).

    b. Pull the guide bar partway out (A, **Figure 231**). Then slide the shift fork out (B, **Figure 231**) off of the bar and remove it. Remove the shift fork ball and spring (**Figure 232**).

4. If necessary, remove the stopper rod assembly as follows:

    a. Remove the circlip from the shaft groove (**Figure 224**).

    b. Push the lever toward the stopper rod.

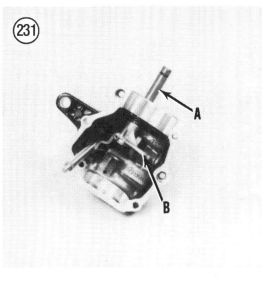

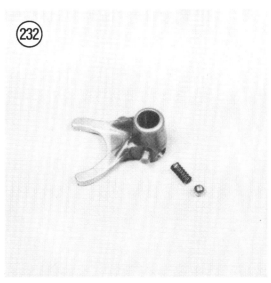

c. Remove the stopper rod (**Figure 233**) assembly.

5. Clean all components thoroughly in solvent.

6. Check the shift fork and shaft (**Figure 234**) for irregular wear patterns or damage. Replace worn or damaged parts.

7A. *YTM200ERN:* Do not attempt to disassemble the drive shaft assembly. Refer all service to a Yamaha dealer.

7B. *All other models:* Check the middle driven shaft assembly for wear (**Figure 235**). If wear is apparent, refer service to a Yamaha dealer. Do not attempt to disassemble the assembly. Check the universal joint pivot points for play (**Figure 236**). Rotate the joint in both directions. If there is noticeable side play the universal joint must be replaced. Replace the O-ring (**Figure 237**) if worn or damaged.

8. Installation is the reverse of these steps, noting the following.

9. Make sure the gear case dowel pins are installed in the crankcase (**Figure 238**).

BREAK-IN

Following cylinder servicing (boring, honing, new rings, etc.) and major lower end work, the engine should be broken in just as if it were new. The performance and service life of the engine depends greatly on a careful and sensible break-in.

For the first 2 hours, no more than one-third throttle should be used and speed should be varied as much as possible within the one-third throttle limit. Prolonged, steady running at one speed, no matter how moderate, is to be avoided, as is hard acceleration.

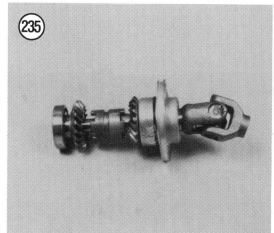

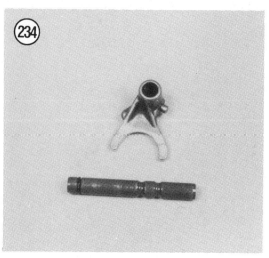

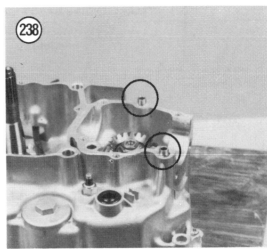

4

Table 1 ENGINE SPECIFICATIONS—YTM200 AND YFM200

Item	Specifications mm (in.)	Wear limit mm (in.)
General		
Type	4-stroke, air-cooled, SOHC	
Number of cylinders	1	
Bore and stroke		
YTM200, YFM200	67×55.7	
	(2.6×2.2)	
Displacement		
YTM200, YFM200	196 cc	
Compression ratio	8.5:1	
Lubrication	Wet sump	
Cylinder		
Bore		
YTM200, YFM200	67.97-67.02	—
	(2.637-2.639)	—
Taper	—	0.005 (0.0002)
Cylinder head		
Warp limit	—	0.03 (0.0012)
Piston		
Size	66.935-66.985	—
	(2.352-2.6372)	—
Clearance	0.025-0.045	—
	(0.0010-0.0018)	—
Measuring point	See text	—
Piston Rings		
Number of rings		
Compression	2	—
Oil control	1	—
End gap		
Top/second	0.15-0.30	0.4
	(0.0059-0.0138)	(0.016)
Oil	0.3-0.9	—
	(0.012-0.036)	—
	(continued)	

Table 1 ENGINE SPECIFICATIONS—YTM200 AND YFM200

Item	Specifications mm (in.)	Wear limit mm (in.)
Piston Rings (continued)		
Side clearance		
Top	0.03-0.07 (0.0012-0.0028)	0.12 (0.0047)
Second	0.02-0.06 (0.0008-0.0024)	0.12 (0.0047)
Camshaft		
Clearance	0.020-0.061 (0.0008-0.0024)	— —
Runout	—	0.03 (0.0012)
Lobe height		
Intake	36.537-36.637 (1.438-1.442)	—
Exhaust	36.577-36.677 (1.440-1.444)	—
Diameter		
Intake		
YFM200DXS	30.131-30.231 (1.186-1.190)	— —
All other models	31.131-31.221 (1.228-1.232)	—
Exhaust	30.214-30.314 (1.188-1.192)	—
Rocker Arm/Shaft		
Clearance	0.0009-0.037 (0.0004-0.0016)	— —
Inside diameter	12.000-12.018 (0.4700-0.4707)	12.03 (0.474)
Shaft diameter	11.985-11.991 (0.4694-0.4696)	11.94 (0.470)
Valve		
Stem runout	—	0.02 (0.0008)
Valve seat width	0.9-1.1 (0.0351-0.0429)	—
Valve spring free length		
Inner	35.5 (1.40)	—
Outer	37.2 (1.46)	—
Crankshaft		
Big end side clearance	0.35-0.65 (0.014-0.026)	— —
Small end side clearance	0.8-1.0 (0.03-0.04)	2.0 (0.08)
Runout	See text	—
Oil pump		
Side clearance	0.04-0.09 (0.0016-0.0035)	— —
Tip clearance	0.15 (0.0059)	—

Table 2 ENGINE SPECIFICATIONS—YFM225

Item	Specifications mm (in.)	Wear limit mm (in.)
General		
Type	4-stroke, air-cooled, SOHC	
Number of cylinders	1	
Bore and stroke	70×58	
	(2.76×2.28)	
Displacement	223.2 cc	
Compression ratio	8.8:1	
Lubrication	Wet sump	
Cylinder		
Bore	69.97-70.02	—
	(2.7547-2.7567)	—
Taper	—	0.005 (0.0002)
Cylinder head		
Warp limit	—	0.03 (0.0012)
Piston		
Size	69.935-69.985	—
	(2.7533-2.7553)	—
Clearance	0.035-0.055	—
	(0.0014-0.0022)	—
Measuring point	See text	—
Piston Rings		
Number of rings		
Compression	2	—
Oil control	1	—
End gap		
Top/second	0.15-0.30	—
	(0.0059-0.0138)	—
Oil	0.3-0.9	—
	(0.0118-0.0354)	—
Side clearance		
Top	0.03-0.07	—
	(0.0012-0.0028)	—
Second	0.02-0.06	—
	(0.0008-0.0024)	—
Camshaft		
Clearance	0.020-0.061	—
	(0.0008-0.0024)	—
Runout	—	0.03 (0.0012)
Lobe height		
Intake	36.537-36.637	—
	(1.438-1.442)	—
Exhaust	36.577-36.677	—
	(1.440-1.444)	—
Diameter		
Intake	30.131-30.231	—
	(1.1863-1.1902)	—
Exhaust	30.214-30.314	—
	(1.1895-1.1935)	—
Rocker Arm/Shaft		
Clearance	0.0009-0.037	—
	(0.0004-0.0015)	—
Inside diameter	12.000-12.018	12.03
	(0.4724-0.4731)	(0.474)

(continued)

4

Table 2 ENGINE SPECIFICATIONS—YFM225 (continued)

Item	Specifications mm (in.)	Wear limit mm (in.)
Rocker Arm/Shaft (continued)		
Shaft diameter	11.985-11.991	11.94
	(0.4718-0.4721)	(0.470)
Valve		
Stem runout	—	0.03 (0.001)
Valve seat width	0.9-1.1	—
	(0.0354-0.0433)	—
Valve spring free length		
Inner	35.5	—
	(1.40)	—
Outer	37.2	—
	(1.46)	—
Crankshaft		
Big end side clearance	0.35-0.65	—
	(0.014-0.026)	—
Small end side clearanc		
	—	2.0 (0.08)
Runout	See text	—
Oil pump		
Side clearance	0.04-0.09	—
	(0.0016-0.0035)	—
Tip clearance	0.15 (0.0059)	—

Table 3 TIGHTENING TORQUES

Item	N·m	ft.-lb.
Cylinder head		
Bolt (M6)	7	5.1
Flange bolt (M8)	22	16
Bolt (M8)	20	14
Oil galley bolt	7	5.1
Cam sprocket cover	7	5.1
Valve tappet cover	10	7.2
Rocker arm shaft stopper bolt	8	5.8
Cylinder bolt	10	7.2
Balancer shaft nut	50	36
Recoil starter pulley bolt	50	36
Valve adjuster lock nut	14	10
Sprocket cam bolt	60	43
Oil pump screw	7	5.1
Engine drain plug	43	31
Oil filter cover	10	7.2
Oil filter cover drain bolt	10	7.2
Exhaust pipe flange	10	7.2
Crankcase screws	7	5.1
Crankcase spacer		
Left-hand	7	5.1
Right-hand	7	5.1
Bearing retainer		
Left-hand	7	5.1
Right-hand	10	7.2
Shift cam segment screw	12	8.7

Table 4 ENGINE MOUNT TIGHTENING TORQUES

	N·m	ft.-lb.
Front bracket and engine bolt	33	24
Front bracket and engine nut	33	24
Upper engine bracket		
At frame	33	24
At engine	33	24
Rear engine upper and lower nut		
At frame	44	32

4

Table 5 DRIVE SHAFT TIGHTENING TORQUES

	N·m	ft.-lb.
Middle gear case cover bolt	10	7.2
Bearing retainer		
Drive axle	25	18
Housing		
YFM225DXS	25	18
All other models	60	43
Bearing housing nut and bolt	23	17
Coupling gear nut	60	43

CHAPTER FIVE

CLUTCH AND TRANSMISSION

This chapter describes removal, inspection and installation of the clutch, transmission, and shift mechanism (external and internal) assemblies. **Table 1** (clutch wear limits) and **Table 2** (clutch tightening torques) are found at the end of the chapter.

CLUTCH

All models in this manual use both a centrifugal and manual clutch mechanism to transmit power from the engine to the transmission. All clutch types are immersed in the oil supply they share with the engine and transmission.

During disassembly pay particular attention to the location and positioning of spacers and washers to make assembly easier.

Both clutch units can be removed with the engine in the frame.

Removal

Refer to **Figure 1** for this procedure.
1. Park the vehicle on level ground and set the parking brake.
2. Drain the engine oil as described in Chapter Three.
3. Remove the seat and fenders.

4. Remove the oil filter (**Figure 2**) from the clutch cover as described in Chapter Three.

> *CAUTION*
> *An impact driver with a Phillips bit (described in Chapter One) will be necessary to loosen the clutch cover screws in Step 5. Attempting to loosen the screws with a Phillips screwdriver may ruin the screw heads.*

5. Remove the screws securing the clutch cover (**Figure 3**) and remove the cover.
6. Remove the gasket and 2 locating dowels. See **Figure 4**.
7. Remove the shift guide pawl assembly as follows:
   a. Remove the spring (**Figure 5**).
   b. Remove the No. 1 shift guide (**Figure 6**).
   c. Remove the pawl holder (**Figure 7**).
   d. Remove the No. 2 shift guide (**Figure 8**).

> *NOTE*
> *Steps 8-11 describe removal of the primary (centrifugal) clutch assembly.*

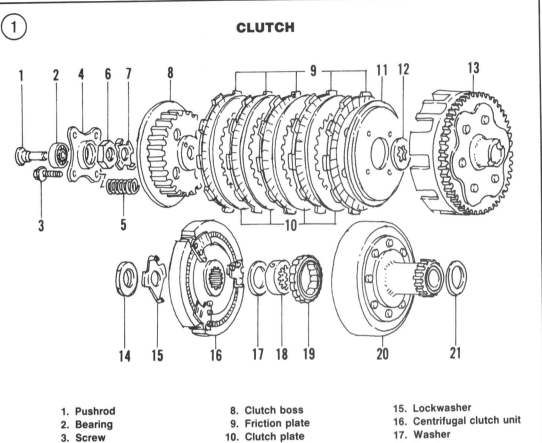

CLUTCH

1. Pushrod
2. Bearing
3. Screw
4. Guide
5. Spring
6. Nut
7. Lockwasher
8. Clutch boss
9. Friction plate
10. Clutch plate
11. Pressure plate
12. Thrust washer
13. Clutch housing
14. Nut
15. Lockwasher
16. Centrifugal clutch unit
17. Washer
18. Bearing
19. Bearing
20. Clutch housing
21. Washer

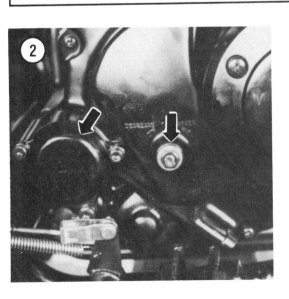

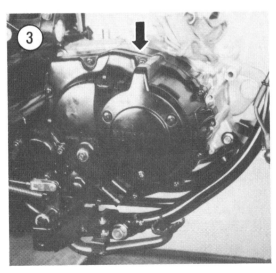

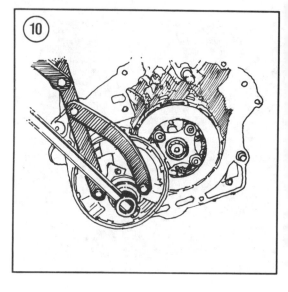

8. Using a large-bladed screwdriver or chisel, carefully pry the lockwasher tab away from the clutch nut (**Figure 9**).

9. Secure the primary clutch assembly with a universal holding tool (**Figure 10**) and remove the clutch nut and washer.

> *NOTE*
> *The secondary clutch housing has 2 notches machined into it to allow removal of the primary gear when removing the primary clutch. **Figure 11** shows one of the notches with the primary clutch removed for clarity.*

10. Align one of the secondary clutch housing notches (**Figure 11**) with the primary gear and slide the primary clutch assembly off of the crankshaft. See **Figure 12**.

11. Remove the washer (**Figure 13**).

> *NOTE*
> *Steps 12-19 describe removal of the secondary (manual) clutch assembly.*

12. Remove the pushrod (**Figure 14**) and bearing (**Figure 15**) from the spring plate.

13. Refer to **Figure 16**. Remove the 4 spring plate bolts (A) and remove the spring plate (B).
14. Remove the 4 clutch springs (**Figure 17**).
15. Using a large bladed screwdriver or chisel, carefully pry the lockwasher tab away from the clutch nut (A, **Figure 18**).
16. Secure the secondary clutch assembly with a universal holding tool and remove the clutch nut and washer.
17. Remove the pressure plate and clutch plates (B, **Figure 18**).
18. Remove the washer (**Figure 19**).
19. Remove the clutch housing (**Figure 20**).

Primary Clutch Inspection

1. Clean all parts in a petroleum-based solvent such as kerosene, and thoroughly dry with compressed air.

2. Rotate the one-way clutch inner race (**Figure 21**). It should only rotate *clockwise*. If if will rotate counterclockwise, even the slightest amount, it is defective and must be replaced by removing the one-way clutch assembly as a set. See **Figure 22**.
3. Inspect the inside contact surfaces of the outer drum (**Figure 23**) for scratches, scoring or heat damage (bluish tint). If there are deep grooves (deep enough to catch a fingernail) the outer drum should be replaced. If there are indications of heat damage, the outer drum may be distorted and must be replaced.
4. Inspect the teeth on the outer drum primary drive gear (**Figure 24**). Remove any small nicks on the gear teeth with an oilstone. If damage is severe, the outer drum must be replaced. Also check the drive teeth on the secondary clutch outer housing; it may need servicing or replacement.
5. Inspect the primary clutch shoe linings (**Figure 25**) for uneven wear, cracks, discoloration or

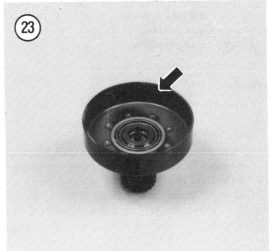

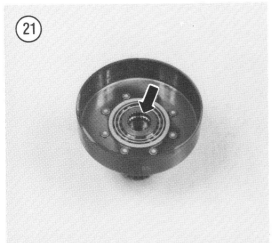

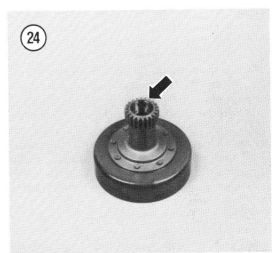

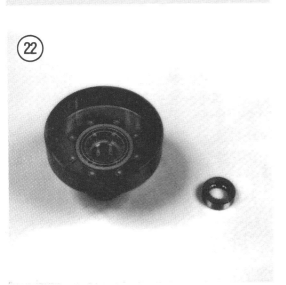

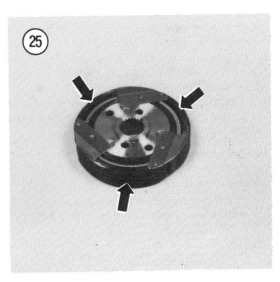

5

damaged friction material. Also measure the shoe lining depth (**Figure 26**) with a vernier caliper and compare to specifications in **Table 1**. Replace the shoe assembly if necessary.

Secondary Clutch Inspection

1. Clean all clutch parts in a petroleum-based solvent such as kerosene, and thoroughly dry with compressed air.

2. Measure the free length of each clutch spring with a caliper (**Figure 27**). Replace any springs that are too short (**Table 1**).

3. Check the clutch metal plates (**Figure 28**) for warpage using a flat surface and a feeler gauge as shown in **Figure 29**. If any plate is warped more than specified (**Table 1**), replace the entire set of plates. Do not replace only one or 2 plates.

4. Measure the thickness of each friction disc (**Figure 30**) at several places around the disc as shown in **Figure 31**. See **Table 1** for specifications. Replace all friction discs if any one is found too thin. Do not replace only one or 2 discs.

5. Check the tangs on the outside of the friction discs (**Figure 30**). If any plate is worn or damaged, the discs must be replaced as a set.

6. Inspect the clutch housing (**Figure 32**) and the clutch boss assembly (**Figure 33**) for cracks or galling in the grooves where the clutch plates slide. They must be smooth for consistent clutch operation. If damage is only minor, remove any small burrs with a fine cut file; if damage is severe, replace the component.

7. Check the teeth on the clutch housing gear (**Figure 34**). If the teeth are damaged, replace the clutch housing assembly. Also check the teeth on the outer drum primary drive gear; it may also need replacing.

8. Check the pressure plate screw studs (**Figure 35**) for cracks or damage. Check the threads for stripping or other damage. Thread damage may be cleaned with a M6×1.25 tap. Replace the pressure plate if necessary.

9. Check the clutch spring plate push rod and bearing for wear or damage. Replace worn or damaged parts as necessary.

Assembly/Installation

> *NOTE*
> *If either or both friction discs and clutch plates have been replaced with new ones, apply new engine oil to all surfaces to avoid having the clutch plates wear prematurely when used for the first time.*

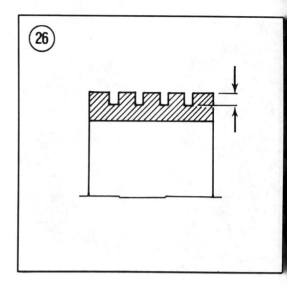

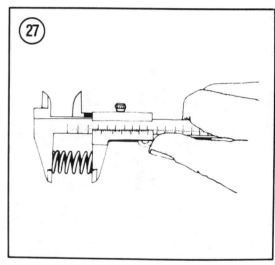

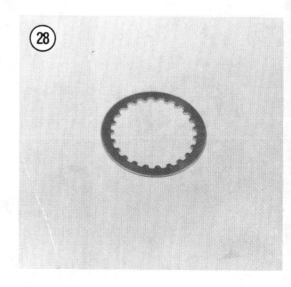

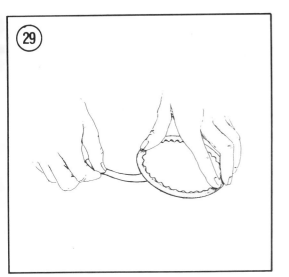

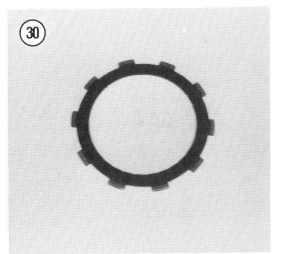

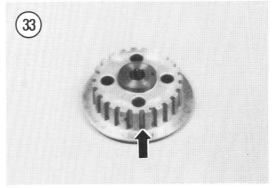

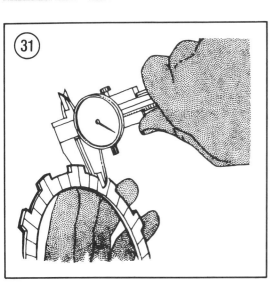

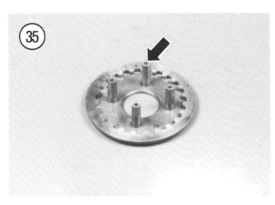

5

1. Lubricate all bearing surfaces with clutch/transmission oil.

> *NOTE*
> *Steps 2-12 describe installation of the secondary (manual) clutch assembly.*

2. Slide the clutch housing (**Figure 20**) onto the mainshaft.

3. Install the thrust washer (**Figure 19**).

> *NOTE*
> *The clutch housing must be partially assembled before installation.*

4. Place the clutch boss on the workbench so that back side faces up (**Figure 33**).

> *CAUTION*
> *If either or both friction and/or clutch plates have been replaced with new ones or if they were cleaned, apply new clutch/transmission oil to all plate surfaces. This will prevent the plates from burning up when used for the first time.*

5. Install a friction plate (**Figure 36**) and a steel clutch plate (**Figure 37**). Alternate until all plates are installed (**Figure 38**). The last plate installed should be a friction plate.

6. Align the arrow on the clutch boss (**Figure 39**) with the arrow or round mark on the pressure plate (**Figure 40**) and install the pressure plate. See **Figure 41**.

7. Install a spring, washer and bolt into the pressure plate to lock the sub-assembly together. See **Figure 42**.

8. Align the subassembly with the clutch housing and install it onto the transmission main shaft. See **Figure 43**.

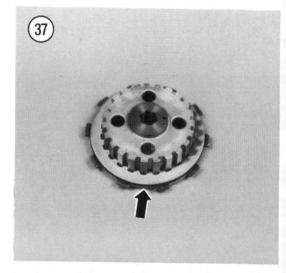

9. Remove the bolt, washer and clutch spring installed in Step 6. Then install the secondary clutch lockwasher and clutch nut. Hold the clutch assembly with the same tool used during disassembly and tighten the clutch nut to specifications in **Table 2**. Bend the lockwasher tab over the nut to lock it.

> *NOTE*
> *If all of the clutch nut lockwasher tabs have been used, install a new lockwasher.*

10. Install the clutch springs (**Figure 17**) and the spring plate (**Figure 16**). Install the 4 clutch spring bolts. Tighten the bolts in a crisscross pattern in 2-3 stages to the specifications in **Table 2**.

11. Install the bearing (**Figure 15**).

12. Install the pushrod (**Figure 14**).

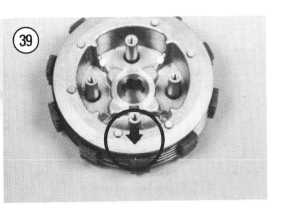

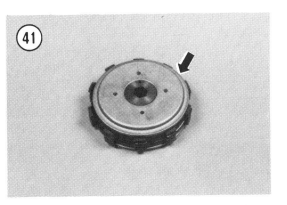

Steps 13-16 describe installation of the primary (centrifugal) clutch assembly.

13. Align the notch in the secondary clutch housing with the crankshaft (**Figure 11**).

14. Install the primary clutch washer (**Figure 13**).

15A. If the primary clutch assembly was not disassembled, slide it (**Figure 12**) onto the crankshaft.

15B. If the primary clutch was disassembled, assemble it as follows:
   a. Install the primary clutch housing (**Figure 44**).

5

b. Install the washer (**Figure 45**).

c. Install the primary clutch friction plate assembly (**Figure 46**).

16. Install the primary clutch lockwasher and clutch nut. Hold the clutch assembly with the same tool used during disassembly and tighten the clutch nut to specifications in **Table 2**. Bend the lockwasher tab over the nut to lock it.

17. Install the shift guide pawl assembly as follows:

a. Align the notch in the No. 2 shift guide with the shift shaft arm and install the guide (**Figure 47**).

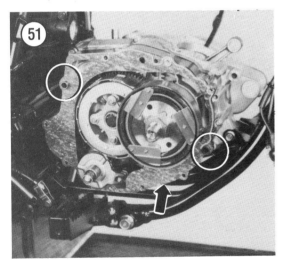

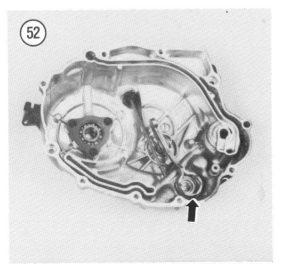

b. Slide the pawl holder onto the shift shaft (**Figure 48**).

c. Align the notch in the No. 1 shift guide with the shift shaft arm and install the guide (**Figure 49**).

d. Install the spring (**Figure 50**).

18. Install the 2 clutch cover dowel pins and a new clutch cover gasket. See **Figure 51**.

19. Align the shift guide spring (**Figure 50**) with the clutch lever (**Figure 52**) and install the clutch cover.

CAUTION
Do not install any of the clutch cover screws until the cover is snug against the crankcase surface. Do not try to force the cover into place with the screws. This is a sure way to break the cover. If the cover will not fit up against the crankcase, remove it and repeat Step 19.

20. Install the clutch cover screws. Install and tighten all screws in a crisscross pattern.

NOTE
Use an impact driver with a Phillips bit to tighten the clutch cover screws and to prevent damaging the Phillips screw heads.

21. Install the oil filter and refill the engine oil as described in Chapter Three.

22. Adjust the clutch as described in Chapter Three.

23. Install the seat and fender assembly.

CLUTCH LEVER AND EXTERNAL SHIFT MECHANISM

The clutch lever mechanism is located both within the clutch cover and on the external shift mechanism. When the gearshift lever is moved to shift gears it also activates the clutch lever, releasing the clutch. The clutch lever can be removed with the engine in the frame.

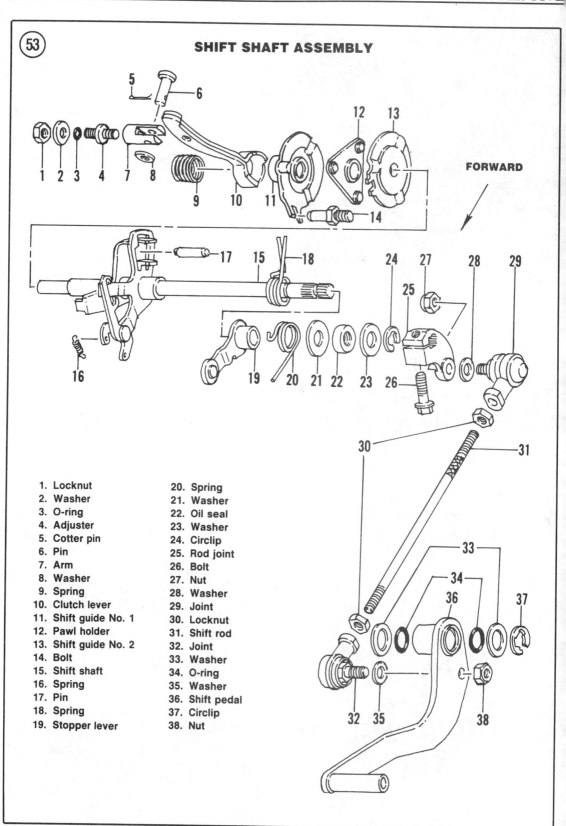

SHIFT SHAFT ASSEMBLY

FORWARD

1. Locknut
2. Washer
3. O-ring
4. Adjuster
5. Cotter pin
6. Pin
7. Arm
8. Washer
9. Spring
10. Clutch lever
11. Shift guide No. 1
12. Pawl holder
13. Shift guide No. 2
14. Bolt
15. Shift shaft
16. Spring
17. Pin
18. Spring
19. Stopper lever
20. Spring
21. Washer
22. Oil seal
23. Washer
24. Circlip
25. Rod joint
26. Bolt
27. Nut
28. Washer
29. Joint
30. Locknut
31. Shift rod
32. Joint
33. Washer
34. O-ring
35. Washer
36. Shift pedal
37. Circlip
38. Nut

Refer to **Figure 53** for this procedure.

1. Remove the clutch cover as described in this chapter.

2. Remove the shift guide pawl assembly as follows:

    a. Remove the spring (**Figure 50**).

    b. Remove the No. 1 shift guide (**Figure 49**).

    c. Remove the pawl holder (**Figure 48**).

    d. Remove the No. 2 shift guide (**Figure 47**).

3. Remove the clutch as described in this chapter.

NOTE
The gearshift lever is subject to a lot of abuse. If the bike has been in a hard spill, the gearshift lever may have been hit and the shift shaft bent. It is very hard to straighten the shaft without subjecting the crankcase to abnormal stress where the shaft enters the case. If the shaft is bent enough to prevent it from being withdrawn from the crankcase, it is necessary to cut the shaft off with a hacksaw very close to the crankcase. Then file the end of the shaft to remove all burrs before withdrawing the shaft. It is much cheaper in the long run to replace the shaft than risk damaging a very expensive crankcase.

4. Remove the gearshift lever (**Figure 54**) from the left-hand side.

5. Remove the circlip (**Figure 55**) and washer (**Figure 56**) from the left-hand side.

6. Refer to **Figure 57**. Lift the shift arm away from the shift drum segment (A) and withdraw the shift lever assembly (B).

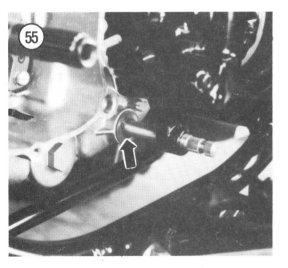

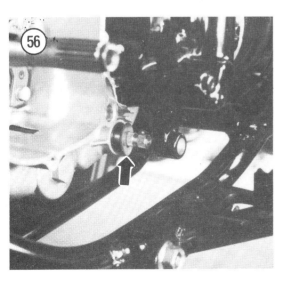

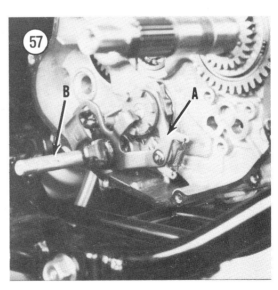

7. Using a T-30 Torx bit, remove the screw (A, **Figure 58**) and the shift cam segment (B, **Figure 58**).

Inspection

1. Clean all parts in solvent and thoroughly dry with compressed air.

2. Inspect the balls in the pawl holder. They must rotate freely in the holder but not be so loose that they would fall out. Check the balls for evidence of wear, pitting or excessive heat (bluish tint). Replace if necessary.

3. Inspect the grooves and inside surfaces of both shift guides where the balls ride. Both surfaces must be smooth and free of burrs or scoring. Replace as necessary.

4. Check the movement of the clutch lever within the clutch cover (**Figure 52**). It must pivot freely or be replaced.

5. To remove the clutch lever, remove the cotter pin (**Figure 53**) and washer and push the pin out of the pivot joint. Lift off the clutch lever (**Figure 52**).

6. Slide the stopper lever, spring and washers off of the shift shaft. See **Figure 59**.

7. Check the external shift shaft (A, **Figure 60**). Make sure the shaft is not bent.

8. Examine the splines on the end of the shift shaft (B, **Figure 60**). If the splines are damaged, the shift shaft should be replaced. Eventually the splines will deteriorate to a point where the shift lever will slip during shifting.

9. Refer to **Figure 61**. Check the large (A) and small (B) tension springs. Replace the springs if fatigued or if they show signs of cracks or other

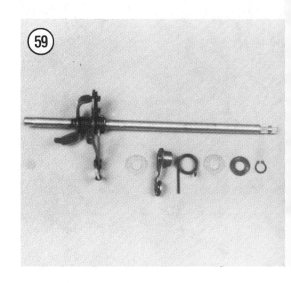

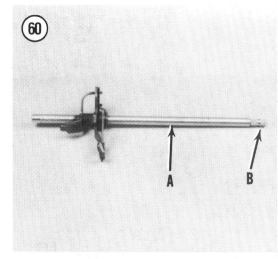

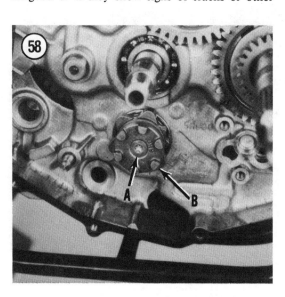

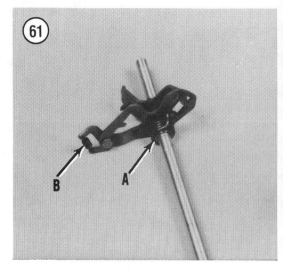

damage. If the springs are replaced, make sure they are installed as shown in **Figure 61**.

10. Refer to **Figure 62**. Inspect the stopper lever (A) and spring (B). Look for signs of wear at all contact points. Check the spring for fatigue or cracks. Replace any worn or damaged parts.

11. Examine all shift cam segment contact points (**Figure 63**) for wear or damage. Also check the 4 small and 1 large (**Figure 64**) segment pins. The pins can be replaced individually if worn or damaged. When installing the pins, make sure the pins are placed in the segment as shown in **Figure 64**. There will be one hole with no pin.

12. Install the clutch lever by reversing the procedure in Step 5.

13. Assemble the shift shaft assembly in the order shown in **Figure 59**.

Installation

1. Align the long pin on the shift cam segment (**Figure 64**) with the hole in the shift cam (**Figure 65**) and install the segment.

2. Coat the shift cam segment screw with Loctite 242 and install it (A, **Figure 58**). Tighten the secrew with a T-30 Torx socket. Tighten the screw securely.

3. Install the shift shaft partway. Then from the left-hand side, install the washer (**Figure 56**) and circlip.

4. Install the shift shaft assembly (**Figure 57**) fully. Make sure the shift arm engages the shift cam segment pins.

5. After the shift shaft is installed, install the circlip into the shift shaft groove. See **Figure 55**.

5

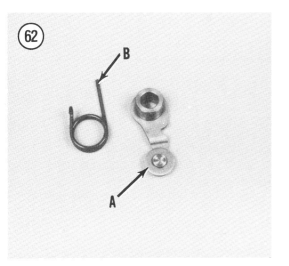

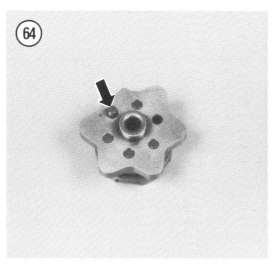

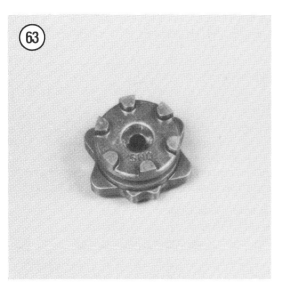

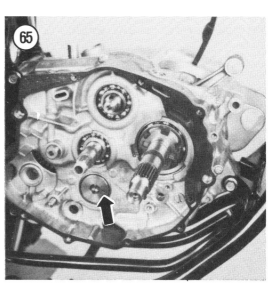

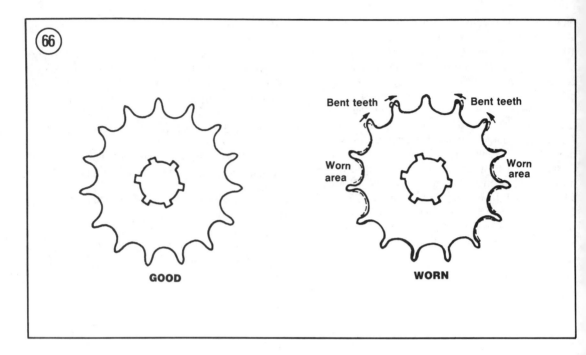

GOOD   WORN

6. Install the shift lever (**Figure 52**).

7. Install the clutch as described in this chapter.

8. Install the shift guide pawl assembly as follows:
   a. Align the notch in the No. 2 shift guide with the shift shaft arm and install the guide (**Figure 47**).
   b. Slide the pawl holder onto the shift shaft (**Figure 48**).
   c. Align the notch in the No. 1 shift guide with the shift shaft arm and install the guide (**Figure 49**).
   d. Install the spring (**Figure 50**).

9. Install the clutch cover as described in this chapter.

10. Refill the engine oil as described in Chapter Three.

DRIVE SPROCKET
(YTM200K, L, N)

Removal/Installation

1. Park the vehicle on level ground. Set the parking brake.

2. Remove the bolt securing the gearshift lever and remove the lever.

3. Remove the screws securing the drive sprocket cover and remove the cover.

4. Have an assistant hold the rear brake on while you loosen the bolts securing the drive sprocket and drive sprocket holding plate.

5. Remove the bolts securing the drive sprocket and drive sprocket holding plate.

6. Loosen the rear chain adjusters to obtain as much chain slack as possible.

7. Rotate the holding plate in either direction to disengage it from the splines on the shaft; slide off the holding plate and drive sprocket.

8. Install by reversing these removal steps, noting the following.

9. Adjust the drive chain as described in Chapter Three.

Inspection

Inspect the condition of the teeth on the drive sprocket. If the teeth are visibly worn (**Figure 66**), replace the sprocket with a new one.

If the sprocket requires replacement, replace the rear sprocket and drive chain also. Running worn and new parts at the same time will rapidly wear out the new parts.

TRANSMISSION

The crankcase must be disassembled to gain access to the transmission components. The transmission is shown in **Figure 67** (chain drive) or **Figure 68** (shaft drive).

Removal/Installation
(Chain Drive)

Refer to **Figure 67** for this procedure.

1. Remove the engine and split the crankcase as described in Chapter Four.

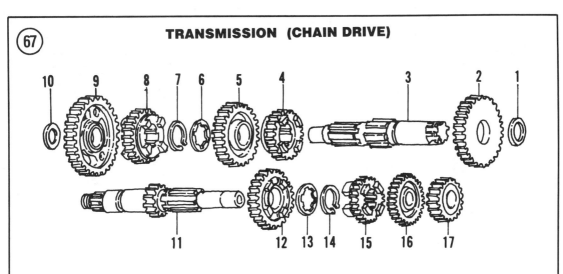

TRANSMISSION (CHAIN DRIVE)

1. Washer
2. Countershaft 2nd gear
3. Countershaft
4. Countershaft 5th gear
5. Countershaft 3rd gear
6. Washer
7. Circlip
8. Countershaft 4th gear
9. Countershaft 1st gear
10. Washer
11. Mainshaft
12. Mainshaft 4th gear
13. Washer
14. Circlip
15. Countershaft 3rd gear
16. Countershaft 5th gear
17. Countershaft 2nd gear

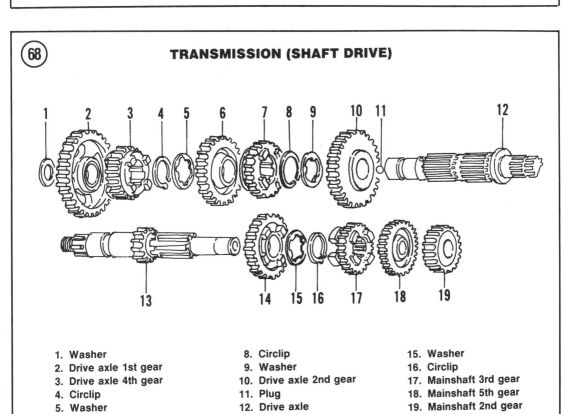

TRANSMISSION (SHAFT DRIVE)

1. Washer
2. Drive axle 1st gear
3. Drive axle 4th gear
4. Circlip
5. Washer
6. Drive axle 3rd gear
7. Drive axle 5th gear
8. Circlip
9. Washer
10. Drive axle 2nd gear
11. Plug
12. Drive axle
13. Mainshaft
14. Mainshaft 4th gear
15. Washer
16. Circlip
17. Mainshaft 3rd gear
18. Mainshaft 5th gear
19. Mainshaft 2nd gear

2. Lift up and remove the transmission components in the following order:

    a. Shift fork shafts (A, **Figure 69**).

    b. Shift drum (B, **Figure 69**).

    c. Shift forks (**Figure 70**).

    d. Transmission shafts (**Figure 71**).

3. Disassemble and inspect the shift forks and transmission assemblies as described later in this chapter.

4. Installation is the reverse of these steps, noting the following:

    a. If the transmission assemblies were disassembled, make sure all circlips are seated completely in their respective grooves.

    b. Before installation, coat all bearing and sliding surfaces of the shift forks, shafts, shift drum and transmission shafts with assembly oil.

    c. Make sure all cam pin followers are in mesh with the shift drum grooves.

    d. Spin the transmission shafts and shift through the gears using the shift drum. Make sure you can shift into all gears. This is the time to find that something may be installed incorrectly—not after the crankcase is completely assembled.

> *NOTE*
> *This procedure is best done with the aid of a helper as the assemblies are loose and do not want to spin very easily. Have the helper spin the transmission shafts while you turn the shift drum through all the gears.*

5. Assemble the crankcase as described in Chapter Four.

Mainshaft Disassembly/Assembly (Chain Drive)

Refer to **Figure 67** for this procedure.

> *NOTE*
> *A helpful "tool" that should be used for transmission disassembly is a large egg carton. As you remove a part from the shaft, identify it and then set it in one of the depressions in the exact same position from which it was removed. This is an easy way to remember the correct relationship of all parts.*

1. Place the assembled shaft into a large can or plastic bucket and thoroughly clean with solvent and a stiff brush. Dry with compressed air or let it sit on rags to drip dry.

NOTE
*A hydraulic press is required to remove second gear from the mainshaft. Before disassembly, measure the assembled gear length with a vernier caliper (*Figure* 72) and record the measurement for reassembly.*

2. Press off second gear and fifth gear (**Figure 73**).
3. Slide off third gear.
4. Remove the circlip and splined washer.
5. Slide off fourth gear.
6. Inspect the mainshaft assembly as described in this chapter.
7. Make sure that all splined gears slide smoothly on the mainshaft splines.
8. Slide on fourth gear and install the splined washer and circlip.
9. Slide on third and fifth gears.
10. Press on fifth and second gears. Be sure to install gears to specifications made before disassembly.

11. Make sure all circlips are seated correctly in the main shaft grooves.

Countershaft Disassembly/Assembly (Chain Drive)

Refer to **Figure 67** for this procedure.

NOTE
A helpful "tool" that should be used for transmission disassembly is a large egg carton. As you remove a part from the shaft, identify it and then set it in one of the depressions in the exact same position from which it was removed. This is an easy way to remember the correct relationship of all parts.

1. Place the assembled shaft into a large can or plastic bucket and thoroughly clean with solvent and a stiff brush. Dry with compressed air or let it sit on rags to drip dry.
2. Remove the washer (**Figure 74**) and slide off second gear (**Figure 75**).

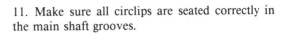

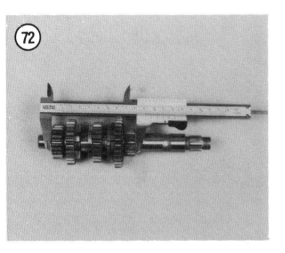

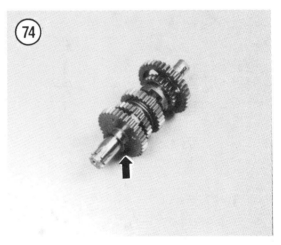

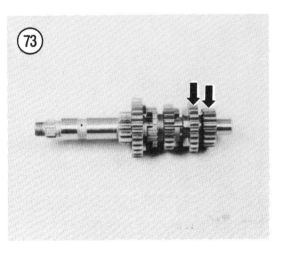

5

3. Slide off fifth gear (**Figure 76**).

4. Remove the circlip and washer (**Figure 77**).

5. Slide off third gear (**Figure 78**).

6. Slide off fourth gear (**Figure 79**).

7. Slide off first gear (**Figure 80**).

8. Inspect the countershaft assembly as described in this chapter.

9. Make sure that all gears slide smoothly on the countershaft splines.

11. Slide on second gear (**Figure 80**).

12. Slide on fourth gear (**Figure 79**).

13. Slide on third gear (**Figure 78**) and install the washer and circlip (**Figure 77**).

14. Slide on fifth gear (**Figure 76**), second gear (**Figure 75**) and install the washer (**Figure 74**).

15. After assembly is complete refer to **Figure 81** for the correct placement of all gears. Make sure all circlips are seated correctly in the countershaft grooves.

Removal/Installation
(Shaft Drive)

Refer to **Figure 68** for this procedure.

1. Remove the engine and split the crankcase as described in Chapter Four.

2. Remove the No. 1 shift fork shaft (**Figure 82**) and fork (**Figure 83**).

3. Remove the No. 2 and No. 3 shift fork shaft (**Figure 84**). Then remove the No. 2 (**Figure 85**) and No. 3 (**Figure 86**) shift forks.

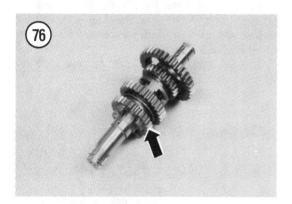

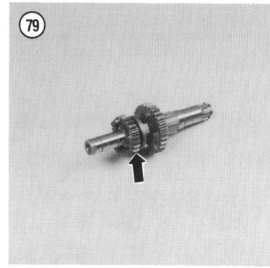

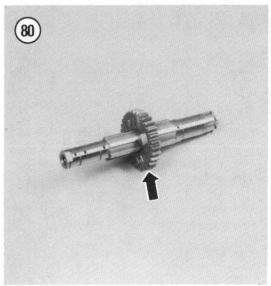

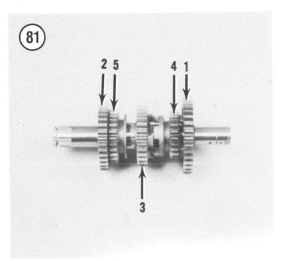

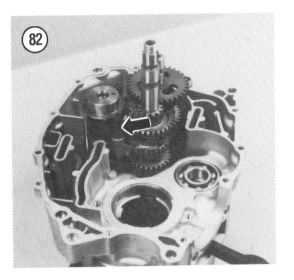

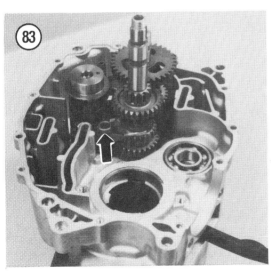

5

4. Remove the shift drum (**Figure 87**).

5. Remove the drive axle washer (**Figure 88**).

6. Remove drive axle first gear (**Figure 89**).

7. Remove drive axle fifth gear (**Figure 90**).

8. Remove the mainshaft assembly (**Figure 91**).

9. Remove the circlip (**Figure 92**) and washer (**Figure 93**).

10. Remove the drive axle third gear (**Figure 94**).

11. Remove the drive axle fourth gear (**Figure 95**).

12. Remove the circlip (**Figure 96**) and washer (**Figure 97**).

13. Remove the drive axle second gear (**Figure 98**).

14. To remove the drive axle, perform the following:

   a. Secure the drive axle (**Figure 99**) in a vise (with soft jaws) or with a suitable holding tool.

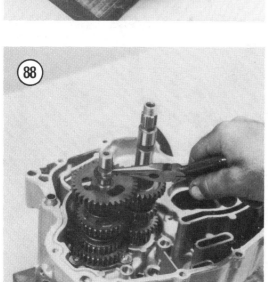

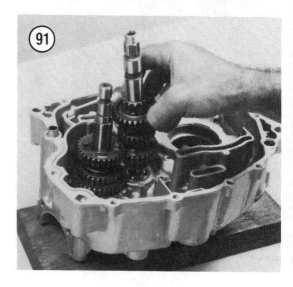

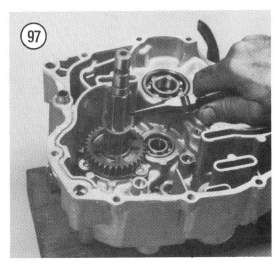

5

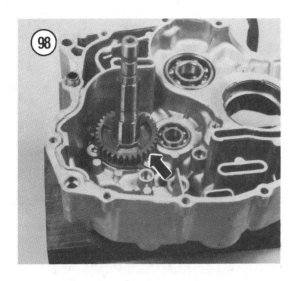

Make sure to use provisions to prevent damage to the drive axle.

b. Pry back the middle drive gear nut tab (A, **Figure 100**).

c. Loosen the middle drive gear nut (A, **Figure 100**) and remove it.

d. Remove the middle drive gear (B, **Figure 100**).

e. Remove the drive axle from the vise and remove it (**Figure 99**) from the crankcase.

15. Assembly is the reverse of these steps, noting the following.

16. Install a new middle drive gear nut (A, **Figure 100**) during installation. Tighten the nut to 60 N•m (43 ft.-lb.).

17. If the transmission assemblies were disassembled, make sure all circlips are seated completely in their respective grooves.

18. Before installation, coat all bearing and sliding surfaces of the shift forks, shafts, shift drum and transmission shafts with assembly oil.

19. Make sure all cam pin followers are in mesh with the shift drum grooves.

20. Spin the transmission shafts and shift through the gears using the shift drum. Make sure you can shift into all gears. This is the time to find that something may be installed incorrectly—not after the crankcase is completely assembled.

NOTE
This procedure is best done with the aid of a helper as the assemblies are loose and do not want to spin very easily. Have the helper spin the transmission shafts while you turn the shift drum through all the gears.

21. Assemble the crankcase as described in Chapter Four.

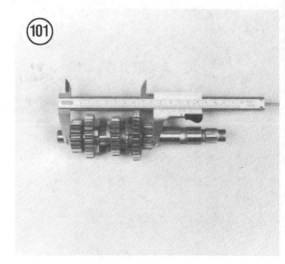

**Main Shaft Disassembly/Assembly
(Shaft Drive)**

Refer to **Figure 68** for this procedure.

*NOTE
A helpful "tool" that should be used for
transmission disassembly is a large egg
carton. As you remove a part from the
shaft, identify it and then set it in one of
the depressions in the exact same
position from which it was removed.
This is an easy way to remember the
correct relationship of all parts.*

1. Place the assembled shaft into a large can or
plastic bucket and thoroughly clean with solvent
and a stiff brush. Dry with compressed air or let it
sit on rags to drip dry.

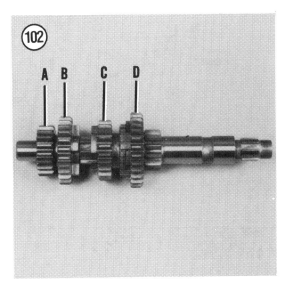

*NOTE
A hydraulic press is required to remove
second gear from the mainshaft. Before
disassembly, measure the assembled
gear length with a vernier caliper
(**Figure 101**) and record the
measurement for reassembly.*

2. Press off second gear (A, **Figure 102**) and fifth
gear (B, **Figure 102**).
3. Slide off third gear (C, **Figure 102**).
4. Remove the circlip and splined washer.
5. Slide off fourth gear (D, **Figure 102**).
6. Inspect the mainshaft assembly as described in
this chapter.
7. Make sure that all splined gears slide smoothly
on the main shaft splines.
8. Slide on fourth gear (D, **Figure 102**) and install
the splined washer and circlip.
9. Slide on third gear (C, **Figure 102**).
10. See **Figure 102**. Press on fifth (B) and second
gear (A). Be sure to install gears according to
measurements made before disassembly.
11. Make sure all circlips are seated correctly in
the main shaft grooves.

**Drive Axle
(Drive Shaft)**

The drive shaft was disassembled during
transmission removal.

Inspection

1. Clean all parts in cleaning solvent and
thoroughly dry.
2. Inspect the gears visually for cracks, chips,
broken teeth and burnt teeth. Check lugs on ends
of gears (**Figure 103**) to make sure they are not
rounded off. If lugs are rounded off, check the shift
forks as described later in this chapter. More than
likely, one or more of the shift forks is bent.
3. Check the slots in gears (**Figure 104**) for
distortion or flaking that may indicate a bent shift
fork.

NOTE
Defective gears should be replaced, and it is a good idea to replace the mating gear even though it may not show as much wear or damage. Remember that accelerated wear to new parts is normally caused by contact from worn parts.

4. Inspect all free wheeling gear bearing surfaces for wear, discoloration and galling. Inspect the mating shaft bearing surface also. If there is any metal flaking or visible damage, replace both parts.
5. Inspect the main shaft and countershaft or drive shaft splines for wear or discoloration (**Figure 105**).

Check the mating gear internal splines also. If no visible damage is apparent, install each sliding gear on its respective shaft and work the gear back and forth to make sure the gear operates smoothly.
6. Check all circlips and washers. Replace any circlips that may have been damaged during operation or removal as well as any washers that show wear.
7. If some of the transmission components were damaged, make sure to inspect the shift drum and shift forks as described later in this chapter.

Internal Shift Mechanism Inspection

Refer to **Figure 106** for this procedure.

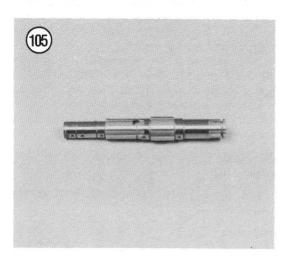

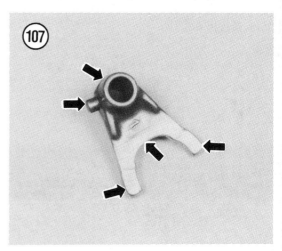

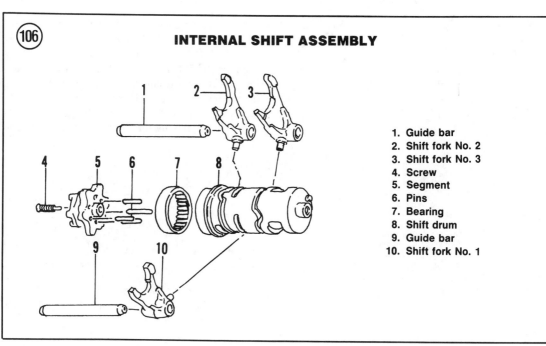

INTERNAL SHIFT ASSEMBLY

1. Guide bar
2. Shift fork No. 2
3. Shift fork No. 3
4. Screw
5. Segment
6. Pins
7. Bearing
8. Shift drum
9. Guide bar
10. Shift fork No. 1

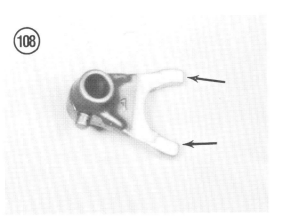

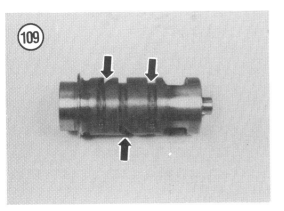

NOTE
Before removal or disassembly of any of the components, lay the assembly down on a piece of paper or cardboard and carefully trace around it. Write down the identifying numbers and letter next to the item. This will take a little extra time now but it may save some time and frustration later.

1. Inspect each shift fork (**Figure 107**) for signs of wear or cracking. Examine the shift forks at the points where they contact the slider gear. This surface should be smooth with no signs of wear or damage. Make sure the forks slide smoothly on the shaft. Make sure the shaft is not bent. This can be checked by removing the shift forks from the shaft and rolling the shaft on a piece of glass. Any clicking noise detected indicates that the shaft is bent.

2. Check for any arc-shaped wear or burned marks on the shift forks (**Figure 108**). This indicates that the shift fork has come in contact with the gear. The fork fingers have become excessively worn and the fork must be replaced.

3. Check grooves in the shift drum (**Figure 109**) for wear or roughness.

4. Check the shift drum bearing surfaces for any signs of wear or damage. Replace the shift drum if necessary.

Table 1 CLUTCH WEAR LIMITS

	mm	in.
Primary clutch		
Shoe thickness		
YTM200K, L, N	2.5	0.098
All other models	1.5	0.0591
Secondary clutch		
Friction plate	2.8	0.11
Clutch plate warp limit	0.2	0.008
Clutch spring fee length	32.9	1.30

Table 2 CLUTCH TIGHTENING TORQUES

	N·m	ft.-lb.
Clutch cover screws	7	5.1
Primary clutch nut	78	56
Clutch spring screw	6	4.3
Clutch boss nut	50	36
Shift cam segment screw	12	8.7
Clutch adjuster nut	15	11

CHAPTER SIX

FUEL AND EXHAUST SYSTEMS

The fuel system consists of the fuel tank, shutoff valve, a single carburetor and air cleaner. The exhaust system consists of an exhaust pipe assembly and spark arrester.

This chapter includes service procedures for all parts of the fuel and exhaust systems. **Table 1** and **Table 2** are at the end of the chapter.

AIR CLEANER

The air cleaner must be cleaned frequently. Refer to Chapter Three for specific procedures and service intervals.

CARBURETOR OPERATION

For proper operation, a gasoline engine must be supplied with fuel and air mixed in proper proportions by weight. A mixture in which there is an excess of fuel is said to be rich. A lean mixture is one which contains insufficient fuel. A properly adjusted carburetor supplies the proper mixture to the engine under all operating conditions.

Mikuni carburetors consist of several major systems. A float and float valve mechanism maintain a constant fuel level in the float bowl. The pilot system supplies fuel at low speeds. The main fuel system supplies fuel at medium and high speeds. Finally, a starter (choke) system supplies the very rich mixture needed to start a cold engine.

CARBURETOR SERVICE

Major carburetor service (removal and cleaning) should be performed whenever the engine is decarbonized or when poor engine performance, hesitation, and little or no response to mixture adjustment is observed. The service interval will become natural to you after owning and running the vehicle for a period of time.

Carburetor Identification

Refer to **Table 1** at the end of this chapter for carburetor specifications.

Removal/Installation

1. Park the vehicle on level ground. Set the parking brake.
2. Turn the fuel shutoff valve (**Figure 1**) to the OFF position.
3. Remove the tank side panels (**Figure 2**).
4. Disconnect the fuel line at the carburetor (**Figure 3**).
5. Pull the rubber cover off of the carburetor cap (A, **Figure 4**). Loosen the cap slightly but do not remove it.
6A. *Chain drive*: Loosen the 2 carburetor clamps.
6B. *Shaft drive*: Remove the 2 front carburetor-to-intake manifold bolts (B, **Figure 4**) and loosen the rear boot clamp (C, **Figure 4**).

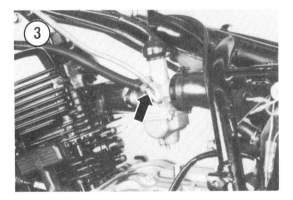

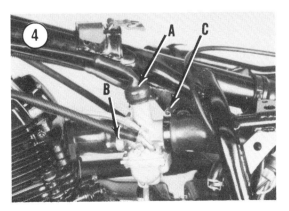

7. Work the carburetor away from the rubber boot(s) and remove it.

8. Loosen the cap and pull the throttle valve out of the carburetor (**Figure 5**).

9. Loosen the choke valve and remove it (**Figure 6**).

NOTE
If the top cap and throttle valve assembly are not going to be removed from the throttle cable for cleaning, wrap them in a clean shop cloth or place them in a plastic bag to help keep them clean.

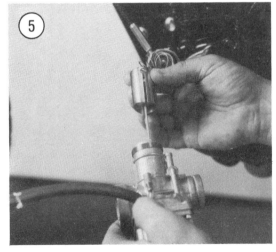

10. If necessary, remove the throttle valve assembly as follows:

   a. Hold the carburetor cap (A, **Figure 7**) and push the throttle valve (B, **Figure 7**) up. Then move the throttle cable end over to the larger hole in the throttle valve and withdraw the cable out through the top and remove it.

   b. Remove the throttle valve and spring (**Figure 8**).

   c. Remove the cable guide (**Figure 9**) from the throttle valve.

   d. Remove the jet needle (**Figure 10**).

11. Take the carburetor to a workbench for disassembly and cleaning.

12. Install by reversing these removal steps, noting the following.

13. Install the cable clip onto the jet needle (**Figure 11**) before installing the needle into the throttle valve.

14. When installing the throttle valve, make sure to align the slot in the throttle valve with the pin in the carburetor bore. See **Figure 5**. Adjust the throttle cable as described in Chapter Three.

Disassembly/Cleaning/Inspection/Assembly

   Refer to **Figure 12** (chain drive) or **Figure 13** (shaft drive) for this procedure.

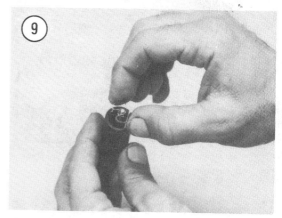

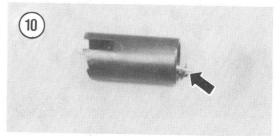

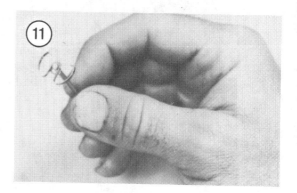

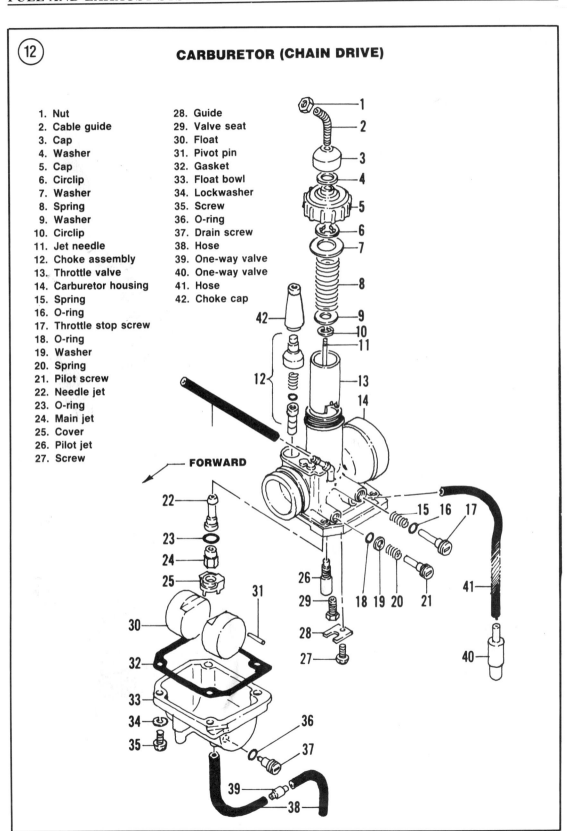

CARBURETOR (CHAIN DRIVE)

1. Nut
2. Cable guide
3. Cap
4. Washer
5. Cap
6. Circlip
7. Washer
8. Spring
9. Washer
10. Circlip
11. Jet needle
12. Choke assembly
13. Throttle valve
14. Carburetor housing
15. Spring
16. O-ring
17. Throttle stop screw
18. O-ring
19. Washer
20. Spring
21. Pilot screw
22. Needle jet
23. O-ring
24. Main jet
25. Cover
26. Pilot jet
27. Screw
28. Guide
29. Valve seat
30. Float
31. Pivot pin
32. Gasket
33. Float bowl
34. Lockwasher
35. Screw
36. O-ring
37. Drain screw
38. Hose
39. One-way valve
40. One-way valve
41. Hose
42. Choke cap

FORWARD

6

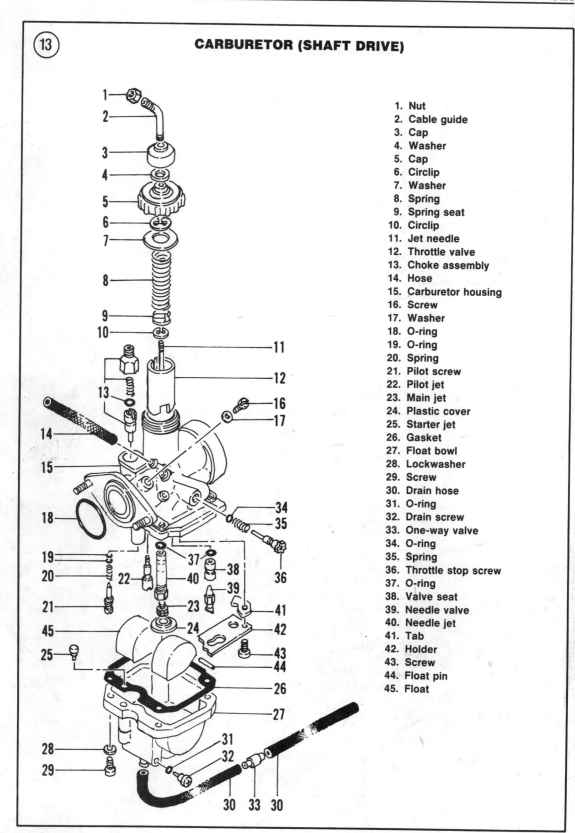

CARBURETOR (SHAFT DRIVE)

1. Nut
2. Cable guide
3. Cap
4. Washer
5. Cap
6. Circlip
7. Washer
8. Spring
9. Spring seat
10. Circlip
11. Jet needle
12. Throttle valve
13. Choke assembly
14. Hose
15. Carburetor housing
16. Screw
17. Washer
18. O-ring
19. O-ring
20. Spring
21. Pilot screw
22. Pilot jet
23. Main jet
24. Plastic cover
25. Starter jet
26. Gasket
27. Float bowl
28. Lockwasher
29. Screw
30. Drain hose
31. O-ring
32. Drain screw
33. One-way valve
34. O-ring
35. Spring
36. Throttle stop screw
37. O-ring
38. Valve seat
39. Needle valve
40. Needle jet
41. Tab
42. Holder
43. Screw
44. Float pin
45. Float

Both carburetors are basically the same, even though minor variations exist between different models. Where differences occur they are identified. The carburetor for shaft drive models (**Figure 13**) is photographed in the following procedure.

1. Remove all drain and overflow hoses.
2. *Shaft drive*: Remove the spigot O-ring (**Figure 14**).

> *CAUTION*
> *If the float bowl is on tight in the next step, tap it with a plastic tipped hammer to loosen it. Do not pry it off or you may damage the casting.*

3. Remove the screws securing the float bowl (**Figure 15**) and remove it and its gasket.
4. Remove the main jet plastic cover (**Figure 16**).
5. Remove the float pin (**Figure 17**).
6. Remove the float (**Figure 18**).

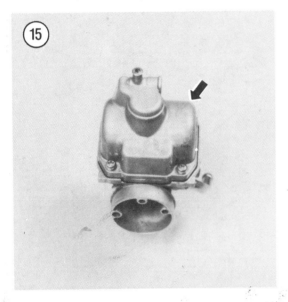

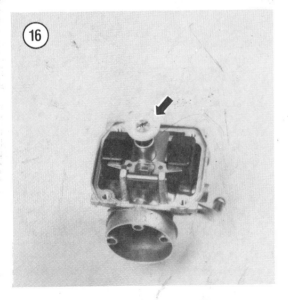

NOTE
*The float valve needle is attached to the float arm. See **Figure 19**.*

7A. *Chain drive:* Remove the screw and washer and remove the float valve seat.

7B. *Shaft drive:* Remove the float valve seat as follows:

   a. Remove the screw securing the plate and remove it and the plate (**Figure 20**).
   b. Remove the washer (**Figure 21**) under the plate.
   c. Remove the float valve seat (**Figure 22**).

8. Remove the main jet (**Figure 23**).

9. Remove the needle jet (**Figure 24**).

10. Remove the pilot jet (**Figure 25**).

11. Remove all O-rings from all jets and needles (**Figure 26**).

12. Remove the rubber gaskets and covers from the carburetor cap (**Figure 27**).

NOTE
Before removing the carburetor adjustment screws in Step 13 and Step 14, count the number of turns required to close each screw and record this measurement.

9. Adjust the float by carefully bending the tang on the float arm (**Figure 34**). Bend the float tang upward very slightly to lower the fuel level; bend the float tang downward to raise the fuel level. If the float level is set too high, the result will be a rich air/fuel mixture. If it is set too low, the mixture will be too lean.

10. Install the carburetor and repeat this procedure until the fuel level is correct.

Needle Jet Adjustment

The position of the needle jet (**Figure 35**) can be adjusted to affect the fuel/air mixture for medium throttle openings.

The top of the carburetor must be removed for this adjustment.

1. Unscrew the carburetor top cap and pull the throttle valve assembly up and out of the carburetor.

> *NOTE*
> *Before removing the top cap, thoroughly clean the area around it so no dirt will fall into the carburetor.*

2. At the end of the throttle cable, push up on the throttle valve (slide) spring. Then remove the cable guide.

3. Move the throttle cable end over to the larger hole in the throttle valve and withdraw the cable out through the top and remove it.

4. Remove the needle jet (**Figure 36**) from the throttle valve assembly.

5. Slide the needle jet out of the connector and note the position of the clip. Raising the needle (lowering the clip) will enrich the mixture during mid-throttle opening, while lowering it (raising the clip) will lean the mixture. Refer to **Figure 35**.

6. Refer to **Table 1** at the end of the chapter for standard clip position for all models.

7. Reassemble and install the top cap.

Pilot Screw and
Idle Speed Adjustment

Before starting this procedure the air cleaner must be clean, otherwise this procedure cannot be done properly.

1A. *Chain drive:* Turn the pilot air screw (**Figure 37**) in until it lightly seats. Back the screw out the correct number of turns for your model (**Table 1**).

1B. *Shaft drive:* The pilot screw on these models is only accessible by removing the carburetor from the vehicle and removing the float bowl. Perform the following:

   a. Remove the carburetor from the vehicle as described in this chapter. It is not necessary to

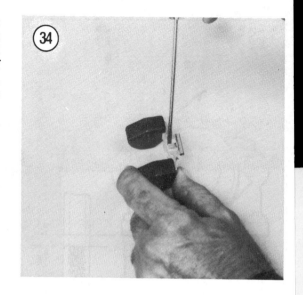

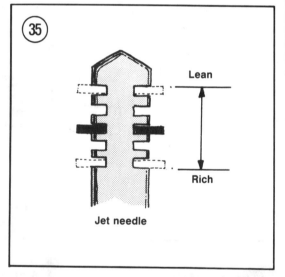

Lean

Rich

Jet needle

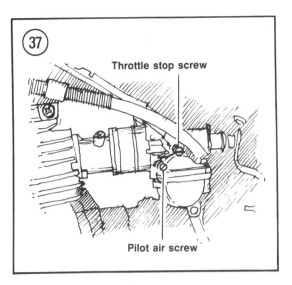

Throttle stop screw

Pilot air screw

disconnect the throttle valve or choke assemblies.

WARNING
Fuel will flow out of the carburetor when performing the next step. Take precautions to prevent the fuel from contacting the engine and exhaust pipes (if hot) and work away from all open flames.

b. Remove the float bowl (**Figure 15**).
c. Turn the pilot air screw (**Figure 29**) in until it lightly seats. Then back it out the specified number of turns (**Table 1**).
d. Reinstall the float bowl and install the carburetor as described in this chapter.

2. Start the engine and let it reach normal operating temperature.
3. Turn the throttle stop screw in or out to achieve the desired idle speed. See **Figure 38** and **Figure 39**. **Table 1** lists the correct idle speed for all models.

WARNING
With the engine idling, move the handlebar from side to side. If idle speed increases during this movement, the throttle cable needs adjusting or it may be incorrectly routed through the frame. Correct this problem immediately. Do not ride the vehicle in this unsafe condition.

High Altitude Adjustment (Main Jet Replacement)

If the vehicle is going to be operated for any sustained period of time in high elevations (above 5,000; 1,500 m), the main jet should be changed to a one-stop smaller jet; never change the jet by more than one size at a time without test riding the bike and running a spark plug test. Refer to *Reading Spark Plugs* in Chapter Three.

The carburetor is set with the standard jet for normal sea level conditions. But if the vehicle is run at higher altitudes or under heavy load—deep sand or mud—the main jet should be replaced or it will run too rich and carbon up quickly.

CAUTION
If the vehicle has been rejetted for high altitude operation (smaller jet), it must be changed back to the standard main jet if ridden at altitudes below 5,000 ft. (1,500 m); engine overheating and piston seizure may occur.

Refer to **Table 1** (end of chapter) for standard main jet sizes.

1. Turn the fuel shutoff valve to the OFF position and disconnect the fuel line.

2. Remove the carburetor from the vehicle as described in this chapter. It is not necessary to disconnect the throttle valve or choke assemblies.

3. Loosen the drain screw and drain out all fuel in the bowl.

WARNING
*Place a metal container under the cover to catch the fuel that will flow out. Do not let it drain out onto the engine or the vehicle's frame as it presents a real fire danger. **Do not perform this procedure with a hot engine**. Dispose of the fuel properly; wipe up any that may have spilled on the bike and the floor (if inside a garage).*

4. On all models, remove the float bowl (**Figure 15**).

5. The main jet is directly under the cover. Remove the plastic cover (**Figure 16**) and remove the main jet (**Figure 17**). Replace it with a different one. Remember, only one jet size at a time.

6. Install the float bowl. Tighten it securely.

7. Install the carburetor. Tighten the clamping band screws and reinstall the carburetor fuel line.

THROTTLE CABLE

Removal

1. Park the vehicle on level ground and set the parking brake.

2. Remove the side covers and seat.

3. Remove the fuel tank as described in this chapter.

4. Clean the area around the carburetor cap thoroughly so that no dirt will fall into the carburetor. Then unscrew the cap and pull the throttle valve assembly up and out of the carburetor (**Figure 40**). Depress the throttle valve spring (**Figure 41**), then remove the throttle valve and spring and remove the throttle cable from the throttle valve.

NOTE
Place a clean shop rag over the top of the carburetor to keep any foreign matter from falling into the carburetor bore.

5. Remove the screws securing the throttle cover (A, **Figure 42**) and remove it.

6. Slide the rubber protector (B, **Figure 42**) away from the throttle housing.

7. Disconnect the throttle cable (**Figure 43**) at the throttle lever.

NOTE
The piece of string attached in the next step will be used to pull the new throttle cable(s) back through the frame so it will be routed in the exact same position as the old one.

8. Tie a piece of heavy string or cord (approximately 6-8 ft./1.8-2.4 m long) to the carburetor end of the throttle cable. Wrap this end with masking or duct tape. Do not use an excessive amount of tape as it will be pulled through the frame loop during removal. Tie the other end of the string to the frame.

9. At the twist grip end of the cable, carefully pull the cable (and attached string) out through the frame loop and from behind the headlight housing

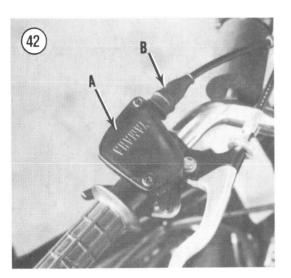

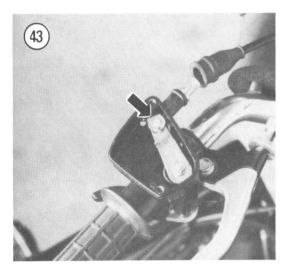

(**Figure 44**). Make sure the attached string follows the same path of the cable through the frame and behind the headlight.

10. Remove the tape and untie the string from the old cable.

Installation

1. Lubricate the new cable as described in Chapter Three.

2. Tie the string (used during *Removal*) to the new throttle cable and wrap them with tape.

3. Carefully pull the string back through the frame routing the new cable through the same path as the old one.

4. Remove the tape and untie the string from the cable and the frame.

5. Reverse Steps 1-7 of *Removal*, noting the following.

6. Operate the throttle lever and make sure the carburetor is operating correctly and with no binding. If operation is incorrect or there is binding carefully check that the cable is attached correctly and there are no tight bends in the cable.

7. Adjust the throttle lever as described in Chapter Three.

8. Test ride the bike to make sure the throttle is operating correctly.

FUEL TANK

Removal/Installation

1. Park the vehicle on level ground. Set the parking brake.

2. Turn the fuel shutoff valve to the OFF position and remove the fuel line to the carburetor (**Figure 45**).

3. Remove the seat.

4. Remove the fuel tank covers. See **Figure 46** (YTM200 and YTM225) or **Figure 47** (YFM200).

5. Remove the bolts securing the the fuel tank and remove it.

6. Inspect the rubber cushions on the frame where the fuel tank is held in place. See **Figure 48** (front) and **Figure 49**. Replace as necessary if damaged or starting to deteriorate.

7. Install by reversing these removal steps.

FUEL SHUTOFF VALVE

Removal/Cleaning/Installation

The integral fuel filter in the fuel shutoff valve removes particles in the fuel which might otherwise enter into the carburetor. This could cause the float needle to stay in the open position or clog one of the jets.

1. Place the fuel hose into a clean, sealable metal container. This fuel can be reused if kept clean.

2. Turn the fuel shutoff valve to the RES position and open the fuel filler cap. This will speed up the flow of fuel. Drain the tank completely.

3. Remove the fuel tank.

4. Remove the screws securing the fuel shutoff valve to the tank and remove the valve. See **Figure 50**.

5. After removing the valve, insert a corner of a clean shop rag into the opening in the tank to stop the dribbling of fuel onto the engine and frame.

6. Clean the screen in solvent with a soft toothbrush, then dry. Check the O-ring gasket. Replace it if it is starting to deteriorate or get hard. Make sure the lever spring is not broken or getting soft. Replace if necessary.

7. Reassemble the valve and install it on the tank. Don't forget the O-ring gasket. Check for fuel leakage after installation is completed.

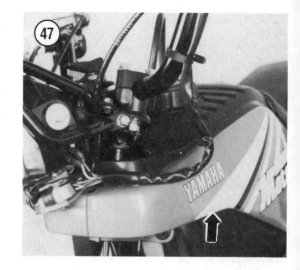

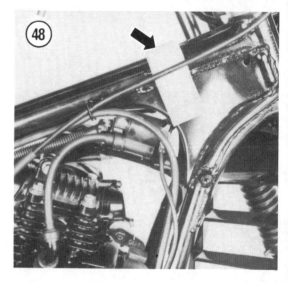

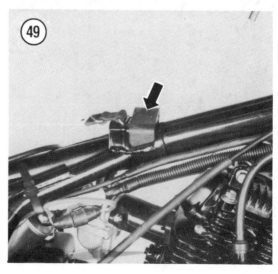

EXHAUST SYSTEM

The exhaust system is a vital performance component and frequently, because of its design, it is a vulnerable piece of equipment. Check the exhaust system for deep dents and fractures and repair them or replace parts immediately. Check the muffler frame mounting flanges for fractures and loose bolts. Check the cylinder head mounting flange for tightness. A loose exhaust pipe connection will not only rob the engine of power, it could also damage the piston and cylinder.

The exhaust system consists of an exhaust pipe, muffler and spark arrestor.

Removal/Installation

1. Park the vehicle on level ground. Set the parking brake.
2. Remove the fuel tank covers. See **Figure 46** or **Figure 47**.
3. Remove the bolts securing the header pipe to the cylinder (**Figure 51**) and slide the pipe bracket away from the engine.
4. On models with separate muffler and header pipe assemblies, loosen the pipe clamp bolt (**Figure 52**).
5. On models with one-piece exhaust systems, move the exhaust system to the rear and remove it. On two-piece exhaust systems, remove the muffler (**Figure 53**) and header pipe separately.
6. Inspect the condition of the gaskets at all joints; replace as necessary.
7. Installation is the reverse of these steps, noting the following.

6

8. To minimize exhaust leaks, install all exhaust system components before tightening the fasteners.

9. Tighten all fasteners securely.

10. Make sure the head pipe is correctly seated in the exhaust port.

11. After installation is complete, start the engine and make sure there are no exhaust leaks.

Carbon Removal

The spark arrester should be removed and cleaned every 6 months.

1. Remove the screw and pull the spark arrester out of the muffler.

2. Using a wire brush and solvent, clean the spark arrester of all carbon build-up.

3. After the carbon build-up, clean the spark arrester with solvent and allow to dry.

4. Reverse to install.

Table 1 CARBURETOR SPECIFICATIONS

Item	YTM200K, L, N	YTM200EK, EL
Type	Mikuni VM22	Mikuni VM22
I.D.	21V00	23W00
Main jet	102.5	112.5
Main air jet	1.5	1.7
Jet needle/Position	4L25/3	4H23/3
Needle jet	N-8	N-6
Slide cutaway	3.5	4.0
Pilot jet	35	25
Pilot air jet	1.3	1.3
Pilot screw (turns)	2 1/4	1 1/2
Valve seat	2.0	1.8
Starter jet	65	65

Item	YTM200ERN	YTM225DXK, DXL, DXN
Type	Mikuni VM22SH	Mikuni VM22
I.D.	24W01	29U00
Main jet	112.5	112.5
Main air jet	1.7	1.6
Jet needle/Position	4H23/3	5L10/3
Needle jet	N-6	N-8
Slide cutaway	4.0	3.5
Pilot jet	25	20
Pilot air jet	130	60
Pilot screw (turns)	2 1/2	1 1/2
Valve seat	1.8	1.8
Starter jet	85	65

Item	YTM225DRN	YTM225DRS
Type	Mikuni VM22	Mikuni VM24
I.D.	29U01	1NV00
Main jet	112.5	112.5
Main air jet	1.6	1.6
Jet needle/Position	5L10/3	5L10/4
Needle jet	N-8	0-0
Slide cutaway	3.5	3.5
Pilot jet	20	20
Pilot air jet	60	120
Pilot screw (turns)	1 1/2	1 3/4
Valve seat	1.8	1.8
Starter jet	80	60

Item	YFM200N	YFM200DXS
Type	Mikuni VM22SH	Mikuni VM22SH
I.D.	52H-00	1NU00
Main jet	115	117.5
Main air jet	1.7	1.7
Jet needle/Position	4DH1/3	4D11/3
Needle jet	N-6	N-6
Slide cutaway	4.0	4.0
Pilot jet	27.5	20
Pilot air jet	130	—
Pilot outlet	—	0.7
Pilot screw (turns)	1 1/2	2.0
Valve seat	1.8	1.8
Starter jet	85	—

6

Table 2 CARBURETOR FUEL AND FLOAT LEVELS

Fuel level	
YFM200DXS	2.5-3.5 mm (0.10-0.14 in.)
All other models	2.0-3.0 mm (0.08-0.12 in.)
Float height	21.5 ±0.5 mm (0.85 ±0.02 in.)

CHAPTER SEVEN

ELECTRICAL SYSTEM

This chapter contains operating principles and service procedures for all electrical and ignition components.

The electrical systems include:
a. Charging system.
b. Ignition system.
c. Starting system.
d. Lighting system.

Refer to Chapter Three for routine ignition system maintenance. Electrical system specifications are found in **Tables 1-4**. **Tables 1-6** are at the end of the chapter.

CHARGING SYSTEM (SHAFT DRIVE MODELS)

The charging system consists of the battery, alternator and a solid state rectifier/voltage regulator. See **Figure 1**.

The alternator generates an alternating current (AC) which the rectifier converts to direct current (DC). The regulator maintains the voltage to the battery and load (lights, ignition, etc.) at a constant level regardless of variations in engine speed and load. Refer to Chapter Three for battery service.

Charging System Output Test

Whenever the charging system is suspected of trouble, make sure the battery is fully charged

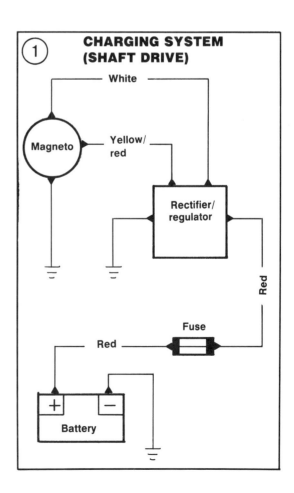

CHARGING SYSTEM (SHAFT DRIVE)

before going any further. Clean and test the battery
as described in Chapter Three. If the battery is in
good condition, test the charging system as follows.
1. Remove the rear fender assembly.
2. Connect a 0-20 volt DC voltmeter onto the
battery terminals as shown in **Figure 2**. The battery
is shown in **Figure 3**.
3. Start the engine and idle it at 5,000 rpm. Check
the output and compare to the specifications in
Tables 2-4.
4. If charging voltage is lower than specified, check
the alternator and voltage regulator/rectifier. It is
less likely that the charging voltage is too high;
however, in that case the regulator is probably
faulty. Test the separate charging system
components as described in this chapter.

CHARGING SYSTEM
(CHAIN DRIVE MODELS)

The AC generator charging system performance
test is described in the lighting system section of
this chapter. Refer to *Lighting Voltage Test* for
testing information.

ALTERNATOR

The alternator is a form of electrical generator in
which a magnetized field called a rotor revolves
within a set of stationary coils called a stator. As

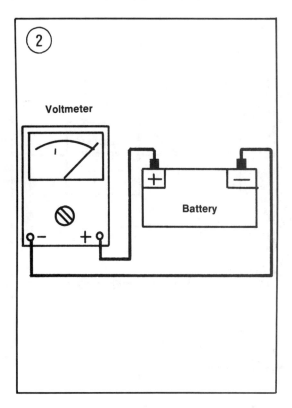

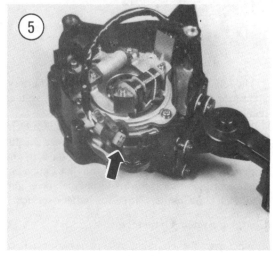

the rotor revolves, alternating current is induced in the stator. The current is then rectified to direct current and used to operate the electrical accessories on the motorcycle and to charge the battery (if so equipped). The rotor is a permanent magnet.

Charge Coil Testing

It is not necessary to remove the stator assembly to perform the following tests. It is shown removed in the following procedures for clarity.

In order to get accurate resistance measurements the stator assembly and coil must be approximately 68° F (20° C).

1. Remove the seat and fender assembly.
2. Disconnect the alternator connector (**Figure 4**).
3. Connect an ohmmeter between the white and black (shaft drive) or the brown to black (chain drive) wires as shown in **Figure 5**. The specified resistance is listed in **Tables 1-4**.
4. If the value is not within the specified range, check the electrical wires to and within the connector. If they are okay, remove and inspect the stator and rotor as described in this chapter.

Rotor Removal

1. Remove the recoil starter as described in Chapter Four.
2. Drain the engine oil as described in Chapter Three.
3. Disconnect the battery negative terminal (if so equipped).
4. Disconnect the alternator electrical connector (**Figure 5**).

> *CAUTION*
> *An impact driver with a Phillips bit (described in Chapter One) will be necessary to loosen the alternator cover screws in Step 5. Attempting to loosen the screws with a Phillips screwdriver may ruin the screw heads.*

5. Remove the bolts securing the alternator cover and remove the cover (**Figure 6**), gasket and the electrical harness from the frame. Note the path of the wire harness as it must be routed the same during installation.
6. Remove the following parts in order:
   a. Spacer (**Figure 7**).
   b. Starter idler gear shaft (A, **Figure 8**).
   c. Starter idler gear (B, **Figure 8**).

7. Remove the alternator rotor (**Figure 9**) with a 3-way universal puller (**Figure 10**).

Rotor Inspection

1. Inspect the alternator cover oil seal (**Figure 11**) for wear or damage. If necessary, replace the oil seal as described under *Bearing and Oil Seal Replacement* in Chapter Four.

2. Check the alternator cover bearing (**Figure 12**). Make sure the bearing spins freely without excessive noise or roughness. If necessary, replace the bearing by first removing the stator coils as described in this chapter. Then refer to *Bearing and Oil Seal Replacement* in Chapter Four.

Rotor Installation

1. Carefully inspect the inside of the rotor (**Figure 13**) for small bolts, washers or other metal "trash"

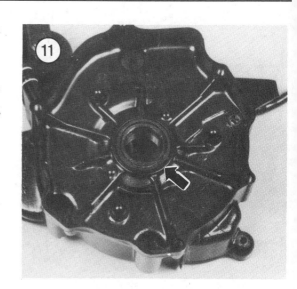

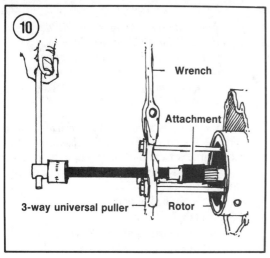

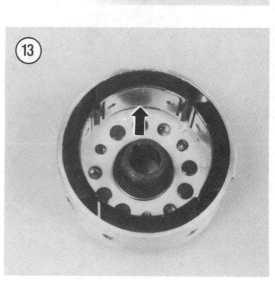

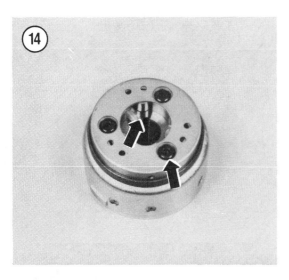

that may have been picked up by the magnets. These small bits can cause severe damage to the alternator stator assembly.

2. *Electric start models:* If the rollers and springs in the starter clutch ring (**Figure 14**) have become loose or fallen out, refer to ***Alternator Rotor, Starter Clutch Assembly and Gears*** in Chapter Four.

3. Align the keyway in the rotor with the Woodruff key (**Figure 15**) and install the rotor (**Figure 13**).

4. Install the following parts in order:
    a. Idler gear (B, **Figure 8**).
    b. Idler gear shaft (A, **Figure 8**).
    c. Spacer (**Figure 7**).

5. Install the 2 alternator cover dowel pins (**Figure 16**) and install a new alternator cover gasket.

6. Install the alternator cover (**Figure 6**) and tighten the screws securely.

NOTE
Use an impact driver with a Phillips bit to tighten the alternator cover screws and to prevent damaging the Phillips screw heads.

7. Route the alternator stator wire harness through the frame. Clean the wire connectors of all dirt and grit and connect the electrical connectors (**Figure 4**).

8. Install the recoil starter assembly as described in Chapter Four.

9. Refill the engine oil as described in Chapter Three.

Stator Assembly
Removal/Installation

1. Perform Steps 1-5 under *Rotor Removal* in this chapter.

2. Install by reversing these removal steps. Route the electrical wires in their original position. Make sure to keep them away from the exhaust system.

Coil Replacement

When replacing an individual coil, it will be necessary to heat the wire connection at the bad coil with a soldering iron before disconnecting the wire. When the solder has melted, pull the wire away from the connection. This step will give you enough wire to work with when resoldering. If the wire is cut at the connection, it could cause the wire to fall short at the connection. During reassembly, rosin core solder must be used—never use acid core solder on electrical connections—to reconnect the wire.

1. Remove the alternator cover as described in this chapter under *Rotor Removal*.

2. Remove the screws securing the coils to the stator plate. See **Figure 17**.

3. Carefully unsolder the wire from the bad coil.

4. Resolder the new coil to the wire.

5. Install by reversing these removal steps.

6. Make sure all electrical connections are tight and free from corrosion. This is absolutely necessary with electronic ignition systems.

Voltage Regulator/Rectifier
Removal/Installation

1. Remove the seat and fender assembly.

2. Disconnect the battery negative lead.

3. Disconnect the electrical connector from the regulator/rectifier and remove the unit (**Figure 18**).

4. Install by reversing these removal steps. Make sure all electrical connections are clean and tight.

Voltage Regulator/Rectifier
Testing

1. Disconnect the electrical connector from the rectifier. See **Figure 18**. The rectifier connector contains 4 wires (red, black, white and yellow/red).

2. Connect an ohmmeter positive lead to the red wire and the negative lead to the white wire. The ohmmeter should show continuity.

3. Reverse the ohmmeter leads and repeat Step 2. This time the ohmmeter should show no continuity.

4. If the rectifier fails to pass the tests in Step 2 and Step 3, the unit is defective and must be replaced.

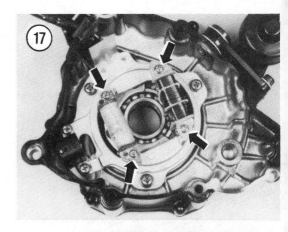

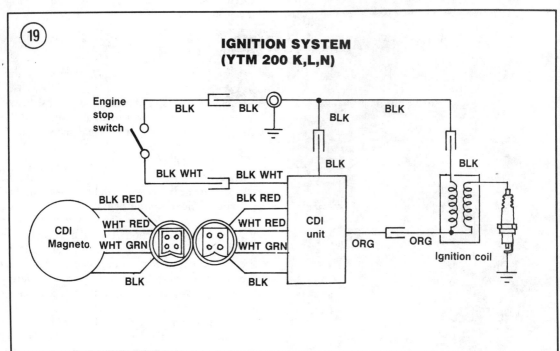

IGNITION SYSTEM
(YTM 200 K,L,N)

IGNITION SYSTEM
(FULLY TRANSISTORIZED)

All models are equipped with a capacitor discharge ignition (CDI) system which is a solid-state system that uses no breaker points. Refer to **Figure 19** or **Figure 20** for the ignition circuit for your model.

Alternating current from the alternator is rectified to direct current and is used to charge the capacitor. As the piston approaches the firing position, a pulse from the pick-up coil is used to trigger the silicone controlled rectifier. The rectifier in turn allows the capacitor to discharge quickly into the primary circuit of the ignition coil, where the voltage is stepped up in the secondary circuit to a value sufficient to fire the spark plug.

NOTE
The electric starter can only be used to start the engine when the transmission is in NEUTRAL. This is due to the installation of a starting circuit. When the transmission is in gear, current cannot reach the starter motor.

Precautions

Certain measures must be taken to protect the capacitor discharge system.

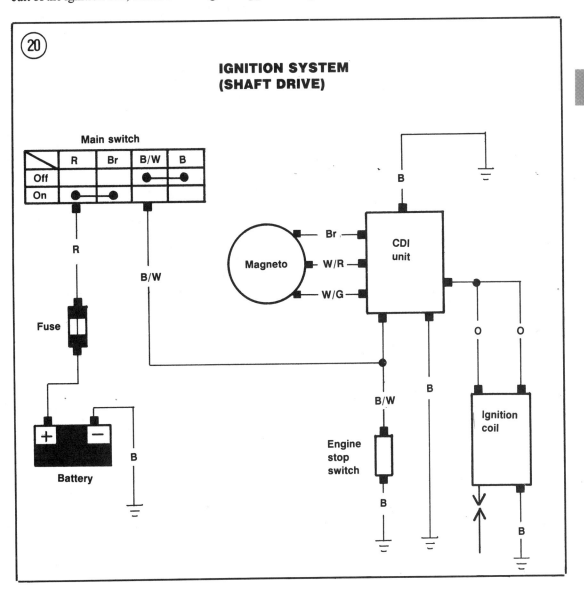

IGNITION SYSTEM (SHAFT DRIVE)

1. Never connect the battery backwards. If the battery polarity is wrong, damage will occur to the voltage regulator, alternator and ignition unit.

2. Do not disconnect the battery while the engine is running. A voltage surge will occur which will damage the voltage regulator and possibly burn out the lights.

3. Keep all connections between the various units clean and tight. Be sure that the wiring connectors are pushed together firmly.

4. Each solid state unit is mounted on a rubber vibration isolator. Always be sure that the isolators are in place when replacing any units.

Troubleshooting

Problems with the capacitor discharge ignition system are usually limited to the production of a weak spark or no spark at all. Test procedures for troubleshooting the ignition system are found in Chapter Two.

IGNITION UNIT

Removal/Installation

1. Remove the seat and fender assembly.

2. Disconnect the battery negative lead.

3. Disconnect the electrical connectors from the ignition unit and remove it. See **Figure 21**.

4. Install by reversing these removal steps. Before connecting the electrical wire connectors at the CDI unit, make sure the connectors are clean of any dirt or moisture.

Testing

The ignition unit should be tested by a Yamaha mechanic familar with capacitor discharge ignition testing. Improper testing of a good unit can damage it.

IGNITION COIL

Removal/Installation

1. Disconnect the battery negative lead from the battery.

2. Remove the fuel tank as described in Chapter Six.

3. Disconnect the spark plug lead (**Figure 22**) and the coil primary electrical wires at the electrical connector (**Figure 23**).

4. Remove the 2 nuts and lockwashers securing the coil to the frame and remove the coil (**Figure 24**).

5. Install by reversing these removal steps. Make sure to correctly connect the primary electrical wires to the coils and the spark plug leads to the

correct spark plug. In addition, make sure the ground wire is attached correctly.

Testing

The ignition coil is a form of transformer which develops the high voltage required to jump the spark plug gap. The only maintenance required is that of keeping the electrical connections clean and tight and occasionally checking to see that the coil is mounted securely.

If the coil condition is doubtful, there are several checks which may be made.

First, as a quick check of coil condition, disconnect the high voltage lead from the spark plug (**Figure 22**). Remove the spark plug from the cylinder head. Connect a new or known good spark plug to the high voltage lead and place the spark plug base on a good ground like the engine cylinder head (**Figure 25**). Position the spark plug so you can see the electrode.

> *WARNING*
> *Do not hold the high voltage lead by hand. The high voltage generated by the CDI could produce serious or fatal shocks.*

Turn the engine over with the recoil starter. If a fat blue spark occurs, the coil is in good condition; if not, proceed as follows. Make sure that you are using a known good spark plug for this test. If the spark plug used is defective, the test results will be incorrect.

Reinstall the spark plug in the cylinder head.

Refer to **Figure 26** for this procedure. Disconnect all ignition coil wires before testing.

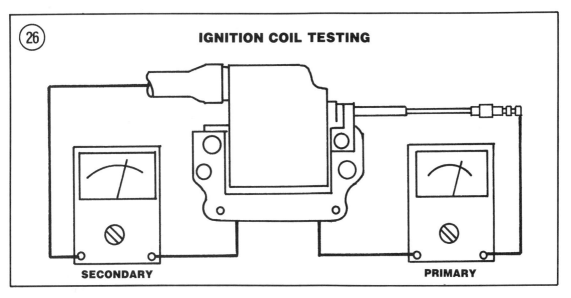

IGNITION COIL TESTING

SECONDARY

PRIMARY

NOTE
To get accurate resistance measure-
ments the coil must be at approximately
60° F (20° C).

1. Measure the coil primary resistance using an ohmmeter set at R × 1. Measure between the primary terminal (orange wire) and ground. Resistance is specified in **Tables 1-4**.
2. Measure the secondary resistance using an ohmmeter set at R × 100. Measure between the secondary lead (spark plug lead) and the orange wire. Resistance is specified in **Tables 1-4.**
3. Replace the coil if the spark plug lead shows visible damage or if it does not test within the specifications in Step 1 or Step 2.

PICKUP COIL

Removal/Installation

Remove the alternator coil assembly as described under *Rotor Removal* in this chapter. If necessary, replace the pickup coil as described under *Coil Replacement* in this chapter.

Magneto Coil Testing

It is not necessary to remove the stator plate to perform the following tests. It is shown removed in the following procedures for clarity.

To get accurate resistance measurements the stator assembly and coil must be approximately 68° F (20° C).

Source coil resistance

Use an ohmmeter set at R × 10 and check resistance between the brown and black wires. See **Figure 4** and **Figure 27**. If there is continuity (specified resistance listed in **Tables 1-4**) the coil is good. If there is no continuity or the resistance is much less or more than specified, the coil is bad and must be replaced.

Pickup coil resistance

Use an ohmmeter set at R × 10 and check resistance between the white/red and white/green wires. See **Figure 28**. If there is continuity (specified resistance listed in **Tables 1-4**), the coil is good. If there is no continuity or the resistance is much less or more than specified, the coil is bad and must be replaced.

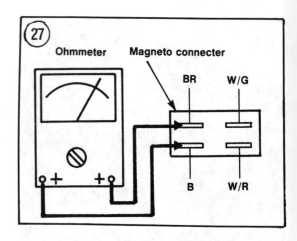

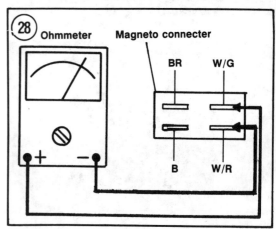

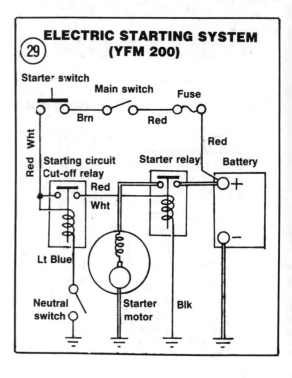

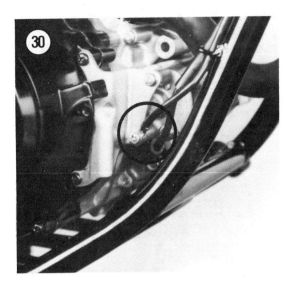

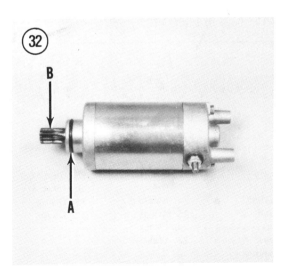

SPARK PLUGS

The spark plugs recommended by the factory are usually the most suitable for your machine. If riding conditions are mild, it may be advisable to go to spark plugs one step hotter than normal. Unusually severe riding conditions may require slightly colder plugs. See Chapter Two and Chapter Three for details.

STARTING SYSTEM

The starting system consists of the starter motor, starter solenoid, starter circuit cutoff relay and the starter button.

The starting system is shown in **Figure 29**. When the starter button is pressed, it engages the solenoid switch that closes the circuit. The electricity flows from the battery to the starter motor.

> *CAUTION*
> *Do not operate the starter for more than five seconds at a time. Let it rest approximately ten seconds, then use it again.*

When the engine stop switch and the main switch are turned to ON, the engine can only be started if the transmission is in NEUTRAL.

If the above conditions are not met, the starting circuit cut-off relay will prevent the starter from operating.

The starter gears are covered in Chapter Four.

Table 5 lists starter specifications.

Troubleshooting

Starter troubleshooting tips and procedures are described in Chapter Two.

Removal/Installation

1. Park the vehicle on level ground.
2. Make sure the ignition switch is in the OFF position.
3. Remove the seat and fender assembly.
4. Disconnect the negative lead from the battery.
5. See **Figure 30**. Pull back on the rubber boot and disconnect the electrical cable. Remove the screw and disconnect the ground cable.
6. Remove the starter mounting bracket (A, **Figure 31**).
7. Pull the starter (B, **Figure 31**) to the right and remove it from the engine.
8. Installation is the reverse of these steps, noting the following.
9. Grease the starter O-ring (A, **Figure 32**) and insert the starter into the crankcase. Do not damage the O-ring during installation.

10. During installation, the starter gear (B, **Figure 32**) should engage with the starter idler gear (**Figure 33**).

11. Tighten the starter bracket bolts securely.

Starter Disassembly/Assembly

The overhaul of a starter motor is best left to an expert. This section shows how to determine if the unit is defective. Refer to **Figure 34** for this procedure.

1. Remove the starter motor case bolts (**Figure 35**) and separate the case.

2. Clean all grease, dirt, and carbon dust from the armature, case and end covers.

> *CAUTION*
> *Do not immerse brushes or the wire windings in solvent or the insulation might be damaged. Wipe the windings with a cloth slightly moistened with solvent and dry thoroughly.*

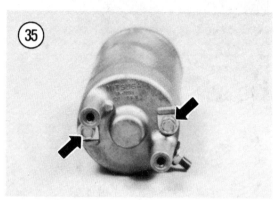

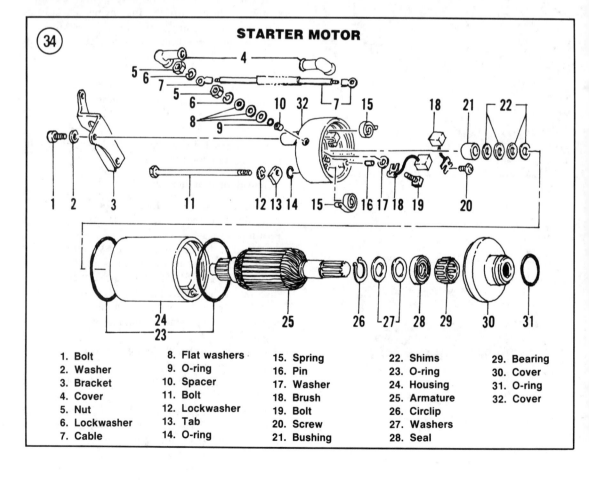

STARTER MOTOR

1. Bolt	8. Flat washers	15. Spring	22. Shims	29. Bearing
2. Washer	9. O-ring	16. Pin	23. O-ring	30. Cover
3. Bracket	10. Spacer	17. Washer	24. Housing	31. O-ring
4. Cover	11. Bolt	18. Brush	25. Armature	32. Cover
5. Nut	12. Lockwasher	19. Bolt	26. Circlip	
6. Lockwasher	13. Tab	20. Screw	27. Washers	
7. Cable	14. O-ring	21. Bushing	28. Seal	

3. Pull back the spring from behind the brushes and remove the brushes from their guides. Measure the length of each brush with a vernier caliper (**Figure 36**). If they are worn to less than the minimum (**Table 5**), replace them.

4. Check the spring tension by comparing to a new set of springs. Replace if necessary.

5. Inspect the condition of the commutator. The mica in a good commutator is below the surface of the copper bars (**Figure 37**). A worn commutator is indicated by the copper and mica being level with each other. A worn commutator can be undercut, but it requires a specialist. Take the job to a dealer or electrical repair shop.

6. Inspect the commutator bars for discoloration. If a pair of bars are discolored, that indicates grounded armature coils.

7. Use an ohmmeter and check the electrical continuity between pairs of commutator bars (**Figure 38**) and between the commutator bars and the shaft mounting (**Figure 39**). If there is a short, the armature should be replaced.

8. Inspect the field coil by checking continuity from the cable terminal to the motor case with an ohmmeter; there should be no continuity. Also check from the cable terminal to each brush wire; there should be continuity. If the unit fails either of these tests, the case/field coil assembly must be replaced.

9. Check the end bushing and bearings in the end cover. If either is worn or damaged, the starter motor must be replaced. Replacement bushings and bearings are not available through Yamaha dealers.

10. When the armature is inserted through the case, make sure each of the 2 brushes contact the commutator evenly. Then attach the cable terminal to the end cover and install the end cover.

Starter Solenoid
Removal/Installation

1. Park the vehicle on level ground.
2. Remove the seat and rear fender assembly.

7

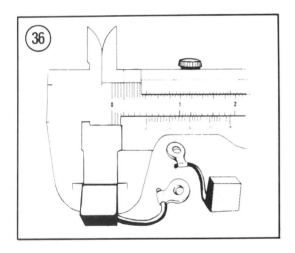

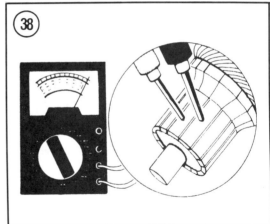

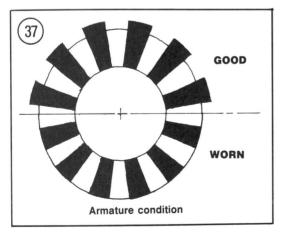

Armature condition

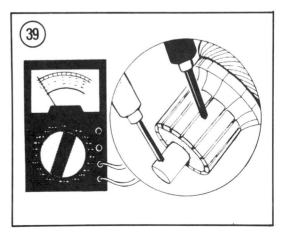

3. Pull the solenoid (A, **Figure 40**) partway out of its holder.

4. Disconnect both starter cables and the electrical connector at the solenoid and remove it.

5. Installation is the reverse of these steps.

Troubleshooting

1. Remove the seat and fender assembly.

2. Disconnect both starter cables at the solenoid.

> *NOTE*
> *Do not disconnect the solenoid electrical connector.*

3. Connect an ohmmeter at the starter solenoid as shown in **Figure 41**. Set the ohmmeter scale to read ohms×1. Turn the ignition switch ON and shift the transmission into NEUTRAL. Press the starter button and measure the resistance between the terminals shown in **Figure 41**. If the solenoid is operating correctly, the solenoid should click once and the ohmmeter should read zero ohms. If not, replace the solenoid.

> *NOTE*
> *If the solenoid did not click in Step 3, check the lead from the starter switch (black) to the starting circuit cut-off relay (red/white) for damage.*

4. Turn the ignition switch OFF.

5. Connect an ohmmeter between the solenoid black and red/white leads as shown in **Figure 42**. Set the ohmmeter scale to read ohms×1. The ohmmeter should read 3.4 ohms. If the reading is incorrect, replace the solenoid.

Starting Circuit Cut-Off Relay
Testing

All models with electric start are equipped with a cut-off switch in the ignition circuit. On these models, the bike cannot be started (with the electric starter) unless the transmission is in NEUTRAL.

If the engine will not start and you've made all the other checks listed previously, perform the following tests.

Resistance check

Use an ohmmeter set at R×10 and check resistance at the cut-off relay connector as shown in **Figure 43** or **Figure 44**. If there is continuity (specified resistance listed in **Table 5**), the relay is good. If there is no continuity or the resistance is much less or more than specified, the relay is bad and must be replaced.

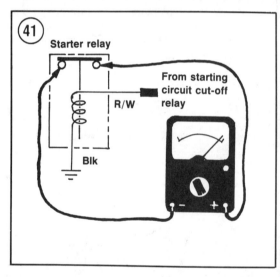

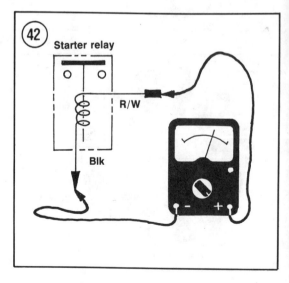

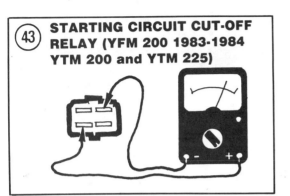

STARTING CIRCUIT CUT-OFF
RELAY (YFM 200 1983-1984
YTM 200 and YTM 225)

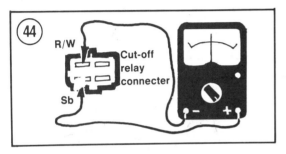

R/W

Cut-off
relay
connecter

Sb

STARTING CIRCUIT CUT-OFF
RELAY (YFM 200 1983-1984
YTM 200 and YTM 225)

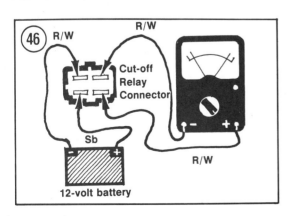

Cut-off
relay
connecter

12-volt battery

R/W

R/W

Cut-off
Relay
Connector

Sb

R/W

12-volt battery

Voltage check

Connect a 12V DC voltmeter and battery to the cut-off relay connector as shown in **Figure 45** or **Figure 46**. When the negative battery terminal is disconnected, the voltage reading should be 0 volts; with the negative terminal connected, the reading should be 12 volts. If the cut-off relay tested incorrectly, replace it.

LIGHTING SYSTEM

The lighting system consists of a headlight, taillight and indicator bulbs.

Always use the correct wattage bulb. A larger wattage bulb will give a dim light and a smaller wattage bulb will burn out prematurely. **Table 6** lists bulb sizes.

Headlight Bulb Replacement

1. If so equipped, remove the headlight cover (**Figure 47**).
2. Remove the screws at the bottom of the headlight housing (A, **Figure 48**) and pull the lens assembly out of the housing.

7

3. Turn the bulb holder counterclockwise and remove it. Remove the bulb from the socket. Replace with a new bulb.

> *NOTE*
> *Do not touch the bulb with your fingers*
> *or bulb life will be shortened.*

4. To remove the lens, carefully remove the spring clips from the backside of the headlight trim bezel and remove the headlight lens unit.

5. Install by reversing these removal steps.

Headlight Beam Adjustment

The headlight beam on all models can be set for vertical adjustment.
1. Park the vehicle on level ground.
2. *Headlight without cover:* To adjust, loosen the bolts securing the headlight housing and turn the housing up or down as necessary to adjust the beam direction. See B, **Figure 48**.
3. *Headlight with cover:* To adjust, turn the adjusting screw counterclockwise (lower beam) or clockwise (raise beam). See **Figure 49**.

Taillight Replacement

Remove the screws securing the lens and remove the lens (**Figure 50**). Wash the lens with a mild detergent and wipe dry.

Inspect the lens gasket and replace it if damaged or deteriorated.

Turn the bulb counterclockwise and remove it (**Figure 51**). Reverse to install. When installing the lens, do not overtighten the screws as the lens may crack.

Indicator Bulbs

Electric start models are equipped with a neutral indicator light and models with reverse are equipped with a reverse indicator light. The neutral indicator (green) lights when the transmission is in NEUTRAL. The reverse indicator (red) lights when the transmission is in REVERSE. Both indicator lights are mounted on the instrument panel beside the main switch. To replace a bulb, remove its connector from underneath the instrument panel and replace the bulb. Reverse to install.

Lighting Voltage Test

> *NOTE*
> *While this test is performed on all*
> *models, it also is used to determine the*
> *condition of the charging system for*
> *YTM200K, L and N models (chain*
> *drive).*

1. Disconnect the headlight connector from behind the headlight assembly (**Figure 52**).

2. Use a multimeter set to AC20 volts. Connect the positive test lead to the yellow headlight wire connector and the negative test lead to ground. See **Figure 53**.

3. Start the engine and, with the lights operating, check the output voltage at the specified rpm in **Tables 1-4**. Compare voltage to specifications in **Tables 1-4**.

4. If the output voltage is incorrect, check for bad or dirty wire connections, damaged wires or bulbs of incorrect wattage. If the problem cannot be corrected by checking and repairing these components, perform the *Lighting Coil Resistance Check* in this chapter.

Lighting Coil Resistance Check

Use an ohmmeter set at R×1 and check resistance between the yellow/red wire (from the ignition unit) and ground (black wire). See **Figure 54**. If there is continuity (specified resistance listed in **Tables 1-4**), the coil is good. If there is no continuity or the resistance is much less or more than specified, the coil is bad and must be replaced as described in this chapter under *Coil Replacement*.

SWITCHES

Switches can be tested with an ohmmeter (Chapter One) or with a homemade test light (**Figure 55**). To test a switch, disconnect its electrical connector. Identify its terminals by referring to the continuity diagram in each test procedure. **Figure 56** shows a typical continuity

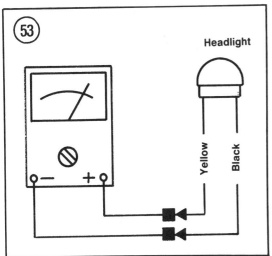

Headlight

Yellow   Black

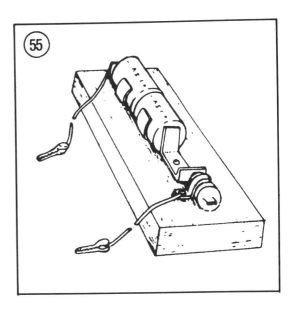

diagram. It tells which terminals should show continuity when the switch is in a given position.

When the switch is in the OFF position, there should be continuity between wire connectors R and E. This is indicated by the line on the continuity diagram. An ohmmeter connected between these wire connectors should indicate little or no resistance.

When the switch is in the ON position, there should be continuity between wire connectors B, R and E. An ohmmeter connected between these connectors should indicate little or no resistance.

If the switch doesn't perform correctly, replace it. Refer to the appropriate figure for switch continuity diagrams for your model:

    a. **Figure 57**: (YTM200K, L, N).
    b. **Figure 58**: (YTM200EK, EL, ERN; all 1983-1984 YTM225).

    c. **Figure 59**: (1985-1986 YTM225 and all YFM200).

Handlebar Switch Replacement

The stop, lighting and electric starter (if so equipped) switches are all mounted in the left-hand handlebar switch housing (**Figure 60**). If one switch is bad, the complete switch housing must be replaced as a unit. Replace the housing by disconnecting the switch connectors and removing the switch screws (**Figure 60**). Reverse to install.

Main Switch Replacement (Electric Start Only)

Electric start models are equipped with a main switch mounted on the instrument panel (**Figure 61**). Replace the switch by disconnecting the

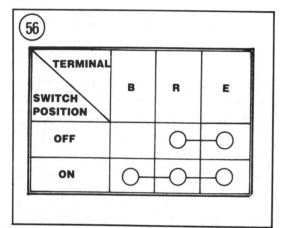

(56)

TERMINAL / SWITCH POSITION	B	R	E
OFF		○—○	
ON	○—○—○		

---

(57) SWITCHES (YTM 200 K, L, N)

ENGINE STOP SWITCH

SWITCH POSITION	Wire code	
	B	B/W
STOP	●—●	
RUN		
STOP	●—●	

LIGHT SWITCH

SWITCH POSITION	Wire code			
	Y/R	L	G	Y
HI	●—●	●		●
LO	●—●	●—●		
OFF				

---

(58) SWITCHES (YTM 200 EK, EL, ERN; 1983-1984 YTM 225)

MAIN SWITCH

Switch Position	Wire code					
	B/W	B	R	Br	L	L/B
ON			●—●		●—●	
OFF	●—●					
LIGHT	●—●		●			●

STARTER SWITCH

Switch position	Wire code	
	R/W	Br
ON	●—●	
OFF		

STOP SWITCH

Switch position	Wire code	
	B	B/W
OFF	●—●	
RUN		

LIGHT SWITCH

Switch position	Wire code				
	Y/R	L	L/B	G	Y
HI	●—●		●		●
LO	●—●		●—●		
OFF					

SWITCHES: (YFM 200; YTM 1984-1985)

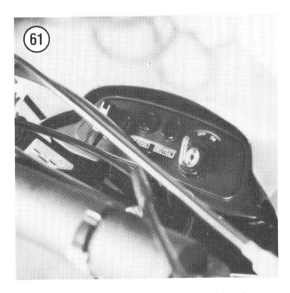

59

MAIN SWITCH

Switch position	Wire code			
	B/W	B	R	Br
ON			●━━━━●	
OFF	●━━━●			

STARTER SWITCH

Switch position	Wire code	
	R/W	Br
ON	●━━━━━━━●	
OFF		

ENGINE STOP SWITCH

Switch Postion	Wire code	
	B	B/W
OFF	●━━━━●	
RUN		

LIGHT SWITCH

Switch Position	Wire code			
	Y/R	L	G	Y
HI	●━━━●		●
LO	●━━❤━━●		
OFF				

connectors and removing the top switch nut. Pull the switch out of the panel. Reverse to install.

Neutral Switch
Replacement

The neutral switch is located on the left-hand crankcase near the shift lever. Replace the switch as follows:

1. Remove the shift lever assembly as required to to gain access to the neutral switch (**Figure 62**).
2. Drain the engine oil as described in Chapter Three.
3. Remove the screw and disconnect the wire at the neutral switch.
4. Unscrew the neutral switch.
5. Remove the neutral switch and gasket.

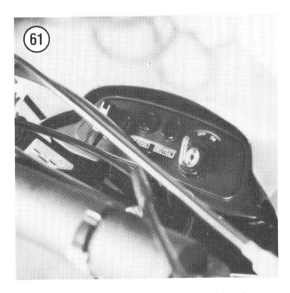

61

7

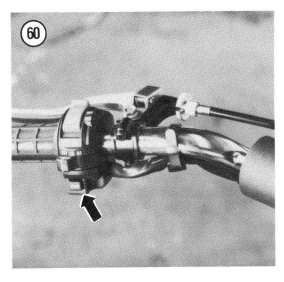

60

62

6. Reverse to install. Note the following.

7. Refill the engine oil as described in Chapter Three.

Reverse Switch Replacment

The reverse switch is located on the reverse gear housing (**Figure 63**). Replace the switch as follows:

1. Drain the engine oil as described in Chapter Three.

2. Remove the screw and disconnect the wire at the reverse switch (**Figure 63**).

3. Unscrew the reverse switch.

4. Remove the reverse switch and gasket.

5. Reverse to install. Note the following.

6. Refill the engine oil as described in Chapter Three.

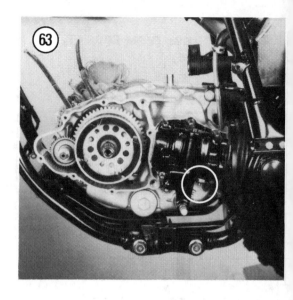

FUSE
(ELECTRIC START MODELS)

There is only one fuse. It is the 10-amp main fuse (**Figure 64**). Fuse location varies among the different models. The fuse in **Figure 64** is shown mounted to the upper right-hand frame tube. On other models, the fuse is located underneath the seat.

NOTE
Always carry a spare fuse.

Whenever a fuse blows, find out the reason for the failure before replacing the fuse. Usually the trouble is a short circuit in the wiring. This may be caused by worn-through insulation or a disconnected wire shorting to ground.

CAUTION
Never substitute metal foil or wire for a fuse. Never use a higher amperage fuse than specified. An overload could result in fire and complete loss of the vehicle.

Table 1 ELECTRICAL SPECIFICATIONS—YTM200K, L, N

Charging/lighting system	
Lighting voltage	12 volts or more @ 3,000 rpm
	18 volts or less @ 8,000 rpm
Lighting coil	
Resistance	0.78 ohms ±10%*
Wire connector colors	Yellow/red to black
Charging coil	
Resistance	0.4 ohms ±10%*
Wire connector colors	White to ground
Ignition system	
Pickup coil	
Resistance	196 ohms ±10%*
Wire connector colors	White/red to white/green
Ignition coil	
Primary	0.85 ohms ±20%*
Secondary	5.9K ohms ±20%*
* Test @ 68° F (20° C).	

7

Table 2 ELECTRICAL SPECIFICATIONS—YTM200EK, EL

Charging/lighting system	
Charging current	0.7A or more @ 3,000 rpm
	4A or less @ 8,000 rpm
Lighting voltage	11.3 volts or more @ 3,000 rpm
	18 volts or less @ 8,000 rpm
Lighting coil	
Resistance	0.34 ohms ±10%*
Wire connector colors	Yellow/red to black
Charging coil	
Resistance	0.4 ohms ±10%*
Wire connector colors	White to black
Ignition system	
Pickup coil	
Resistance	196 ohms ±10%*
Wire connector colors	White/red to white/green
Charging coil	
Resistance	381 ohms ±10%*
Wire connector colors	Brown to black
Ignition coil	
Primary	0.85 ohms ±20%*
Secondary	5.9K ohms ±20%*
* Test @ 68° F (20° C).	

Table 3 ELECTRICAL SPECIFICATIONS—YTM225 (ALL)

Charging/lighting system	
Charging current	
YTM225DXK, DXL, DXN	0.7A or more @ 3,000 rpm
	4A or less @ 8,000 rpm
All other models	1.8A or more 3,000 rpm
	4.5A or less @ 8,000 rpm
Lighting voltage	11.3 volts or more @ 3,000 rpm
	18 volts or less @ 8,000 rpm
Lighting coil	
Resistance	0.34 ohms ±10%*
Wire connector colors	Yellow to black
Charging coil	
Resistance	0.4 ohms ±10%*
Wire connector colors	White to black
Ignition system	
Pickup coil	
Resistance	196 ohms ±10%*
Wire connector colors	White/red to white/green
Charging coil	
Resistance	381 ohms ±10%*
Wire connector colors	Brown to black
Ignition coil	
Primary	0.85 ohms ±20%*
Secondary	5.9K ohms ±20%*

* Test @ 68° F (20° C).

Table 4 ELECTRICAL SPECIFICATIONS—YTM200ERN; YFM200

Charging/lighting system	
Charging current	
Day	1.8A or more @ 3,000 rpm
	4.5A or more @ 8,000 rpm
Night	0.7A or more @ 3,000 rpm
	1.7A or more @ 8,000 rpm
Lighting voltage	11.3 volts or more @ 3,000 rpm
	12.5-13.5 volts or less @ 8,000 rpm
Lighting coil	
Resistance	0.34 ohms ±10%*
Wire connector colors	
YFM200DXS	Yellow to black
All other models	Yellow/red to black
Charging coil	
Resistance	0.4 ohms ±10%*
Wire connector colors	White to black
Ignition system	
Pickup coil	
Resistance	196 ohms ±10%*
Wire connector colors	White/red to white/green
Charging coil	
Resistance	381 ohms ±10%*
Wire connector colors	Brown to black
Ignition coil	
Primary	0.85 ohms ±20%*
Secondary	5.9K ohms ±20%*

* Test @ 68° F (20° C).

Table 5 ELECTRIC STARTER SPECIFICATIONS

Armature coil resistance	0.023 ohms*
Brush length	10.5 mm (0.41 in.)
Wear limit	5.0 mm (0.20 in.)
Commutator diameter	23 mm (0.901 in.)
Wear limit	22 mm (0.866 in.)
Mica undercut	
YTM200EK, EL	1.8 mm (0.071 in).
All other models	0.55 mm (0.022 in.)
Cut-off relay resistance	75 ohms ±10% *
Starter relay resistance	3.43 ohms*

* @ 68° F (20° C).

Table 6 BULB SPECIFICATIONS

Headlight	45W
Taillight	
YTM225DRN, DRS; YFM200	7.5W
All other models	8W
Neutral indicator light	3.4W
Reverse indicator light	3.4W

7

CHAPTER EIGHT

FRONT SUSPENSION AND STEERING
(YTM 200 AND YTM 225)

This chapter describes repair and maintenance of the front wheel, forks and steering components.

Refer to **Table 1** for specifications. **Tables 1-3** are at the end of the chapter.

FRONT WHEEL

Removal/Installation

Refer to **Figure 1** for this procedure.

1. Park the vehicle on level ground and set the parking brake. Block the rear wheels so the vehicle will not roll in either direction.

2. Jack up the front of the vehicle with a small hydraulic jack or have assistants raise the front end and support the vehicle with large wood blocks. If a hydraulic jack is used, place a piece of wood between the jack and the engine crankcase if this location is used. Apply just enough pressure to take any weight off the front wheel.

3. Remove the cotter pin and axle nut from the left-hand side (A, **Figure 2**).

4. Completely unscrew the front brake cable adjusting nut (**Figure 3**). Withdraw the brake cable from the pivot pin in the brake arm.

5. Withdraw the axle (A, **Figure 4**) from the right-hand side.

6. Roll the wheel forward and remove the spacer (B, **Figure 4**).

7. Remove the brake panel from the wheel.

8. Place the spacer(s), washers and axle nuts on the axle to prevent their loss.

9. Installation is the reverse of these steps, noting the following:

    a. Align the boss on the outer fork tube with the locating slot on the brake panel. See B, **Figure 2**.

    b. Install the axle nut and tighten to specifications (**Table 2**). Install a new cotter pin and bend the end over completely.

    c. Adjust the front brake as described in Chapter Three.

FRONT HUB

Refer to **Figure 1** for this procedure.

Disassembly

1. Remove the front wheel as described in this chapter.

> *NOTE*
> *Do not remove the hub assembly from the tire/wheel assembly as it makes an ideal holding fixture.*

2. Remove the oil seals (**Figure 5**) from both sides of the wheel by prying the seal out with a large flat-tipped screwdriver.

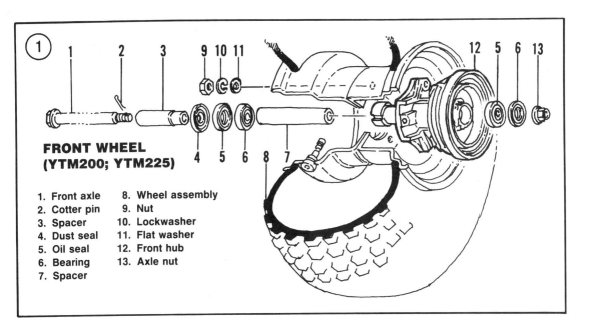

**FRONT WHEEL
(YTM200; YTM225)**

1. Front axle
2. Cotter pin
3. Spacer
4. Dust seal
5. Oil seal
6. Bearing
7. Spacer
8. Wheel assembly
9. Nut
10. Lockwasher
11. Flat washer
12. Front hub
13. Axle nut

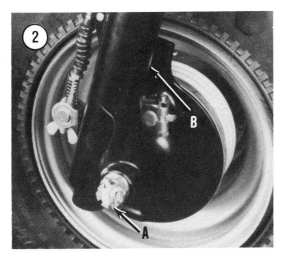

3. With the seals removed, turn each bearing by hand. The bearings should turn smoothly with no roughness or excessive noise. Check balls for evidence of wear, pitting or excessive heat (bluish tint). If the bearings are rough or appear worn, remove them as follows.

4. Determine which bearing you will remove first. Then apply heat with a propane torch to the hub assembly around the bearing. Wave the heat back and forth until the paint in the heated area begins to discolor slightly.

5. Turn the wheel over so that the heated hub area faces down.

6. Using a drift, pry the long spacer over slightly so that it can be struck with a metal rod to remove the bearing.

7. Place a drift on the long spacer and tap the spacer to drive the bearing out of the hub.

> *NOTE*
> *Tapping the bearing on its inner race destroys the bearing. Bearings removed by this method must be replaced.*

8. Heat the opposite bearing area as described in Step 4. Then turn the wheel assembly over and drive the opposite bearing out.

9. Remove the long spacer.

10. Deburr the center spacer as required, using a file or grinder. Then slide the spacer over the axle to make sure it slides freely.

11. To remove the hub from the wheel assembly, remove the mounting bolts (A, **Figure 6**) and remove the hub (B, **Figure 6**).

Inspection

1. Thoroughly clean the inside of the hub with solvent and dry with compressed air or a shop cloth.

2. If the bearings were not removed, clean non-sealed bearings in solvent. Then dry with compressed air, holding the inner race to prevent it from rotating. Do not clean sealed bearings.

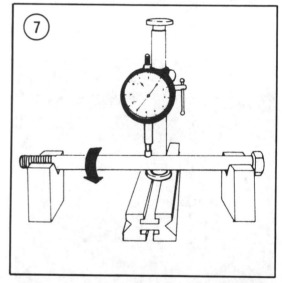

> *WARNING*
> *Never spin a bearing with the high-pressure air jet. This could damage the bearing or cause it to disintegrate, creating a severe safety hazard.*

> *NOTE*
> *Fully sealed bearings are available from good bearing specialty shops. Fully sealed bearings provide better protection from dirt and moisture that may get into the hub.*

3. A bent front axle will cause poor handling, vibration and premature wheel bearing wear. Check the axle for signs of fatigue, fractures and bends. Use V-blocks and a dial indicator as shown in **Figure 7**. If the runout is 0.5 mm (0.02 in.) or greater, the axle should be replaced.

4. Check the hub and wheel assembly for dents, cracks or other obvious signs of damage. Replace the hub and/or wheel if necessary.

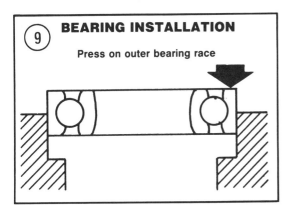

BEARING INSTALLATION

Press on outer bearing race

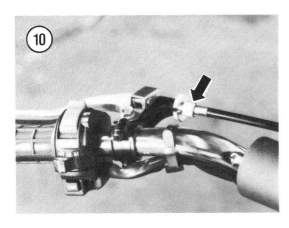

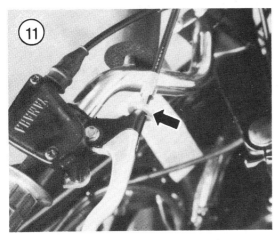

5. If so equipped, check the hole in the end of the axle where the cotter pin fits. Make sure there are no fractures or cracks leading out toward the end of the axle. If any are found, replace the axle immediately.

6. If the brake drum (**Figure 8**) appears worn or damaged, check it further as described in Chapter Eleven under *Front Brake*.

Assembly

1. If the old bearings were removed, install new bearings as follows:
  a. On non-sealed bearings, pack the bearings with a good quality bearing grease. Work the grease between the balls thoroughly. Turn the bearings by hand a couple of times to make sure the grease is distributed evenly inside the bearing.
  b. Pack the wheel hub and the center spacer with multipurpose grease.

CAUTION
*Install the wheel bearings with the sealed side facing out. During installation, tap the bearings squarely into place and tap on the outer race only. Use a socket (**Figure 9**) that matches the outer race diameter. Do not tap on the inner race or the bearing may be damaged. Be sure that the bearings are completely seated.*

  c. Apply heat with a propane torch to one end of the hub assembly around the bearing area. Wave the heat back and forth until the paint in the heated area begins to discolor slightly.
  d. Install the first bearing.
  e. Install the center spacer.
  f. Turn the hub over and install the opposite bearing in the same manner as the first.

2. Allow the hub to cool.

3. Apply a light coat of multipurpose grease to the grease seals and install one on each side of the hub.

4. Install the front wheel as described in this chapter.

HANDLEBAR

Removal

1. Park the vehicle on level ground. Block the wheels to prevent the vehicle from moving forward or backward. Release the parking brake.

2. Loosen the cable adjusters at the handlebar. See **Figure 10** (left-hand side) and **Figure 11** (right-hand side). Then disconnect the cable(s).

3. Loosen and remove the wire cable guides at the handlebar.

NOTE
In the following steps, be careful that the cables do not get crimped or damaged.

4. Remove the screws securing the left-hand handlebar switch assembly (**Figure 12**) and remove it from the handlebar.

5. Remove the throttle assembly clamp screws and remove the throttle assembly (**Figure 13**).

6. Remove the bolts and washers (**Figure 14**) securing the handlebar holders and remove the holders and the handlebar.

7. To maintain a good grip on the handlebar and to prevent it from slipping down, clean the knurled section of the handlebar with a wire brush. It should be kept rough so it will be held securely by the holders. The holders should also be kept clean and free of any metal that may have been gouged loose by handlebar slippage.

8. Examine the handlebar and replace it if bent.

WARNING
A bent handlebar should be replaced immediately as it can loosen in its clamps and cause an accident.

Installation

1. Position the handlebar on the lower holders. Install the upper handlebar holders with the bolts and washers (**Figure 14**).

2. Tighten the forward bolts first and then the rear bolts. Tighten all bolts to specifications (**Table 2**). Sit on the vehicle and check the height of the handlebar; reposition as required.

3. Install the throttle (**Figure 13**) and switch (**Figure 12**) assembly on the handlebar. Tighten the screws securely.

4. Attach the brake cables. See **Figure 10** and **Figure 11**. Adjust the cables as described in Chapter Three.

STEERING HEAD

The steering assembly supports the handlebar and front forks. Loose ball bearings in the upper and lower ends of the head pipe allow the steering stem to turn smoothly.

The steering stem assembly does not wear, but it can become bent or damaged.

All models use removable hydraulic forks. This procedure describes removal, installation and inspection of the steering head assembly.

Refer to **Figure 15** for this procedure.

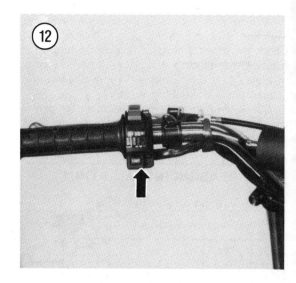

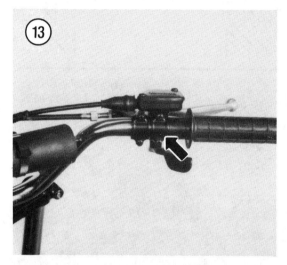

STEERING ASSEMBLY (YTM200; YTM225)

⑮

1. Steering bolt
2. Steering crown
3. Ring nut
4. Bearing cover
5. Bearing race
6. Ball bearings
7. Bearing race
8. Bearing race
9. Dust seal
10. Steering stem

Removal

1. Remove the front wheel as described in this chapter.

2. Remove the front fender.

3. Remove the front forks as described in this chapter.

4. Remove the handlebar assembly as described in this chapter.

5. Remove the screws securing the headlight to the front housing and remove the headlight assembly (**Figure 16**). Disconnect all electrical wires to the headlight assembly.

6. Remove the steering stem nut (A, **Figure 17**).

7. Remove the top steering crown (B, **Figure 17**).

8. Remove the steering adjusting nut (**Figure 18**). Use a large drift and hammer or use a universal

8

spanner wrench (**Figure 19**).

9. Remove the cover (**Figure 20**) and the bearing race (**Figure 20**).

> *NOTE*
> *Have an assistant hold a large pan under the steering stem while you carefully lower the steering stem.*

10. Lower the steering stem assembly down and out of the steering head. Remove the balls from the upper (**Figure 21**) and lower race. Do not intermix the balls because on some models, the upper and lower race balls are of different sizes. See **Table 1** for ball numbers and sizes.

Inspection

1. Clean the bearing races in the steering head, the steering stem races and the steel balls with solvent.
2. Check the welds around the steering head for cracks and fractures. If any are found, have them repaired by a competent frame shop or welding service.
3. Check the balls for pitting, scratches or discoloration indicating wear or corrosion. Replace them in sets if any are bad.
4. Check the races for pitting, galling and corrosion. If any of these conditions exist, replace the races as described in this chapter.
5. Check the steering stem for cracks and check its race for damage or wear. If this race or any race is damaged, the bearings should be replaced as a complete bearing set. Take the old races and bearings to your dealer to ensure accurate replacement.

Steering Head Bearing Races

The headset and steering stem bearing races are pressed into place. Because they are easily bent, do not remove them unless they are worn and require replacement.

Headset bearing race removal/installation

To remove the headset race, insert a hardwood stick or brass punch into the head tube (**Figure 22**) and carefully tap the race out from the inside. After it is started, tap around the race so that neither the race nor the head tube is damaged.

To install the headset race, tap it in slowly with a block of wood, a suitable size socket or piece of pipe (**Figure 23**). Make sure that the race is squarely seated in the headset race bore before tapping it into place. Tap the race in until it is flush with the steering head surface.

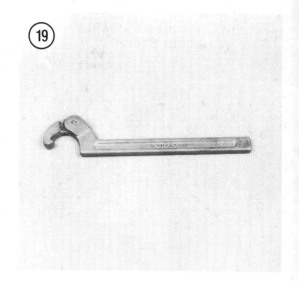

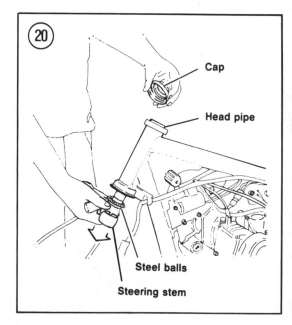

Cap

Head pipe

Steel balls

Steering stem

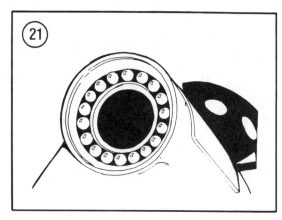

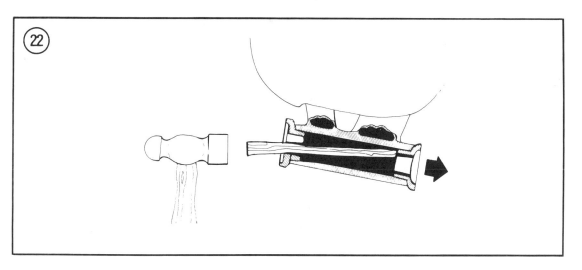

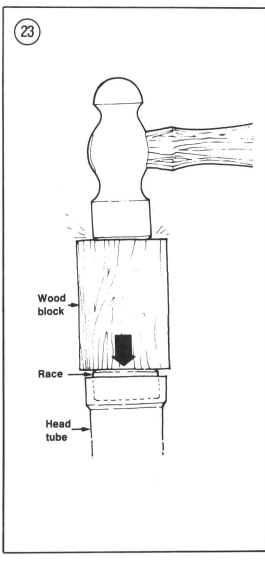

*Steering stem bearing race
and grease seal
removal/installation*

To remove the steering stem race, try twisting and pulling it up by hand. If it will not come off, carefully pry it up with a screwdriver; work around in a circle, prying a little at a time to remove it.

Slide the lower race over the steering stem with the bearing surface pointing up. Tap the race down with a piece of hardwood; work around in a circle so the race will not be bent or jam sideways. Make sure it is seated squarely and is all the way down.

Installation

1. Make sure the steering head and stem races are properly seated.
2. Apply a coat of cold grease to the upper bearing race cone and fit the correct number of balls around it. See **Table 1** and **Figure 21**.
3. Apply a coat of cold grease to the lower bearing race cone and fit the correct number of balls around it. See **Table 1**.
4. Install the steering stem assembly into the head tube and hold it firmly in place (**Figure 20**).
5. Install the upper race on top of the bearings.
6. Install the race cover (**Figure 20**).
7. Install the steering stem adjusting nut (**Figure 18**) and tighten it to approximately 38 N•m (27 ft.-lb.). Then back it off approximately 1/4 turn or as required to obtain proper steering stem play.

> *NOTE*
> *The adjusting nut should be just tight enough to remove both horizontal and vertical play, yet loose enough so that the assembly will turn to both lock positions under its own weight after an assist.*

8. Install the top fork crown (B, **Figure 17**) and steering stem bolts. Tighten the steering stem bolt to specifications. See **Table 2**.

9. Install the fork tubes as described in this chapter.

10. Attach the electrical wires to the headlight assembly.

11. Install the handlebar assembly as described in this chapter.

12. Install the front fender.

13. Install the front wheel as described in this chapter.

14. After a few hours of riding, the bearings have had a chance to seat; readjust the free play in the steering stem with the steering stem adjusting nut as described in Step 7.

Steering Stem Adjustment

If the steering head should become loose, adjust it as follows.

1. Raise the front of the vehicle so that the front wheel clears the ground.

> *WARNING*
> *Block the rear wheel to prevent the vehicle from sliding off the supports.*

2. Loosen the steering stem bolt (A, **Figure 17**).

3. Tighten the steering stem adjusting nut (**Figure 18**) to approximately 38 N•m (27 ft.-lb.). Then back it off approximately 1/4 turn or as required to obtain proper steering stem play.

> *NOTE*
> *The adjusting nut should be just tight enough to remove both horizontal and vertical play, yet loose enough so that the assembly will turn to both lock positions under its own weight after an assist.*

4. Tighten the steering stem bolt to specifications (**Table 2**).

5. Lower the vehicle's front wheel back onto the ground.

FRONT FORKS

This section describes removal, disassembly, inspection and installation of the front forks. Service procedures pertaining to the steering head are found under *Steering Head and Front Fork* in this chapter.

To simplify fork service and to prevent the mixing of parts, the legs should be removed, serviced and installed individually.

Removal/Installation

1. Remove the front wheel as described in this chapter.

> *NOTE*
> *Before removing the fork, measure and write down the distance from the top of the fork tube to the top of the upper fork crown. This is a factory dimension. Some models are installed with the top of the fork flush with the fork crown.*

2. Loosen the upper and lower fork crown bolts (**Figure 24**).

3. Slide the fork boot rubber hose (A, **Figure 25**) out from the center of the steering stem. See **Figure 26**.

4. Remove the fork tube (B, **Figure 25**). It may be necessary to slightly rotate the fork tube while pulling it down and out.

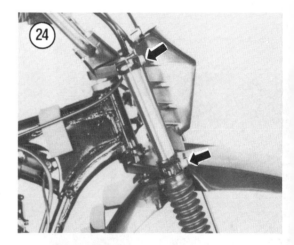

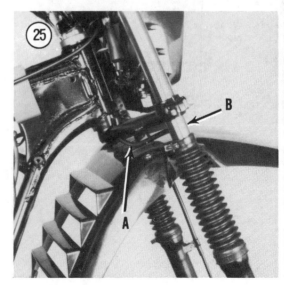

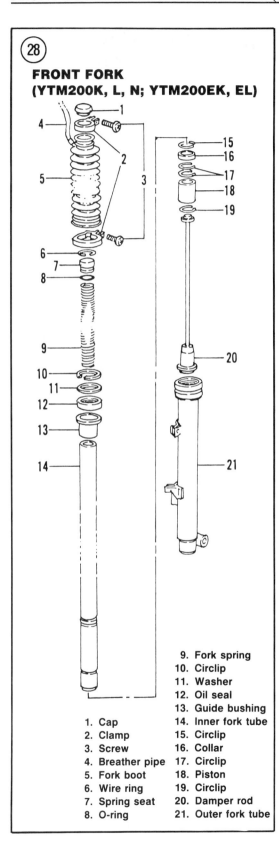

**FRONT FORK
(YTM200K, L, N; YTM200EK, EL)**

1. Cap
2. Clamp
3. Screw
4. Breather pipe
5. Fork boot
6. Wire ring
7. Spring seat
8. O-ring
9. Fork spring
10. Circlip
11. Washer
12. Oil seal
13. Guide bushing
14. Inner fork tube
15. Circlip
16. Collar
17. Circlip
18. Piston
19. Circlip
20. Damper rod
21. Outer fork tube

5. Install by reversing these removal steps, noting the following:

6. *YTM200K, L, N and YTM200EK and EL:* Install the fork tube so that the top of the fork tube is at the specified distance to the fork crown as shown in **Figure 27**:

   a. YTM200K, L, N: 10 mm (13/32 in.).

   b. YTM200EK and EL: 9 mm (11/32 in.).

7. Tighten the bolts to the torque values in **Table 2**.

8. When inserting the fork boot rubber hose (A, **Figure 25**) into the bottom of the steering stem, it will be easier if the 4 front fender bolts are first loosened.

9. Install the front wheel as described in this chapter.

Disassembly

The fork tube assemblies are shown in **Figures 28-30**.

   a. **Figure 28**: YTM200K, L, N, YTM200EK and EL.

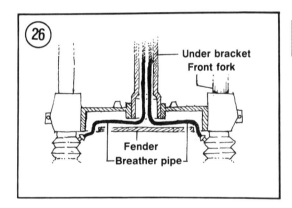

Under bracket
Front fork
Fender
Breather pipe

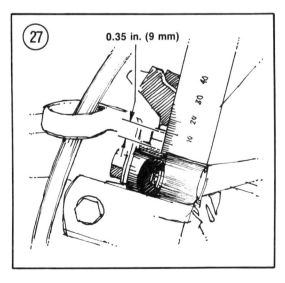

0.35 in. (9 mm)

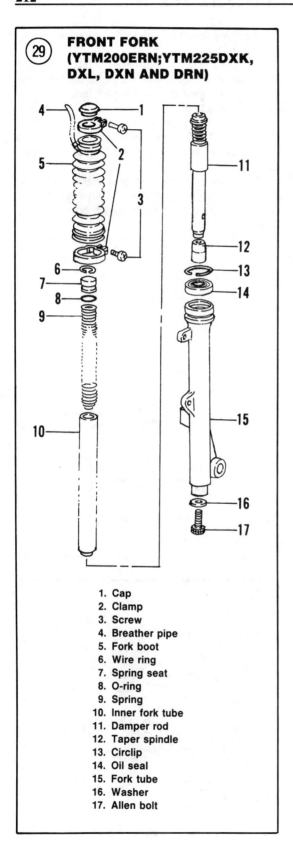

FRONT FORK (YTM200ERN;YTM225DXK, DXL, DXN AND DRN)

1. Cap
2. Clamp
3. Screw
4. Breather pipe
5. Fork boot
6. Wire ring
7. Spring seat
8. O-ring
9. Spring
10. Inner fork tube
11. Damper rod
12. Taper spindle
13. Circlip
14. Oil seal
15. Fork tube
16. Washer
17. Allen bolt

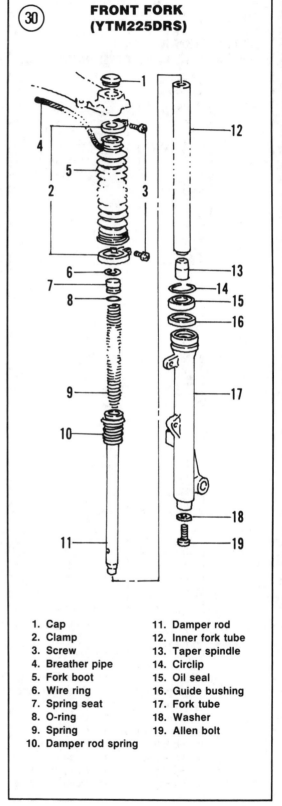

FRONT FORK (YTM225DRS)

1. Cap
2. Clamp
3. Screw
4. Breather pipe
5. Fork boot
6. Wire ring
7. Spring seat
8. O-ring
9. Spring
10. Damper rod spring

11. Damper rod
12. Inner fork tube
13. Taper spindle
14. Circlip
15. Oil seal
16. Guide bushing
17. Fork tube
18. Washer
19. Allen bolt

b. **Figure 29**: YTM200ERN; YTM225, DXK, DXL, DXN, DRN.

c. **Figure 30**: YTM225DRS.

Pay particular attention to the location and positioning of spacers, washers and springs to make sure they are assembled in the correct location.

YTM200ERN and YTM225

NOTE
*All models use a wire ring to secure the fork cap and spring. See **Figure 31**. It will be easier to remove the wire ring with the front fork and front tire installed on the vehicle.*

1. Remove the fork tube rubber cap (**Figure 32**).

WARNING
The fork is assembled with spring preload. Keep your face away from the fork end. The fork cap may spring out.

2. Remove the fork cap (**Figure 33**) by pushing the cap in and prying out the wire ring. See **Figure 34**.

NOTE
*A small screwdriver or scribe will be necessary to pry out the wire ring. See **Figure 35**.*

3. Remove the fork tube as described in this chapter.

4. Remove the fork spring (**Figure 36**).

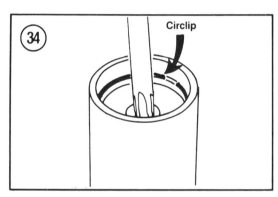

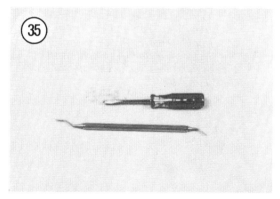

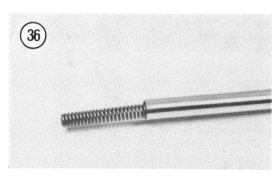

5. Pour the fork oil out and discard it. Pump the fork several times by hand to expel most of the remaining oil.

6. Slide the rubber boot off the fork tube (**Figure 37**).

7. Hold the upper fork tube in a vise with soft jaws (**Figure 38**).

> *NOTE*
> *When removing the Allen bolt in Step 8, make sure to use a metric Allen wrench or socket. This will insure a good "bite" on the bolt and reduce the chances of rounding out the bolt's Allen slot.*

8. Remove the Allen bolt and gasket from the bottom of the slider. See **Figure 39**.

> *NOTE*
> *The bolt has been secured with Loctite and can be difficult to remove; the damper rod will turn inside the slider. It can be removed with an air impact driver or you may be able to install the fork spring and fork cap and wire ring to add pressure to the damper rod and get it off. If these methods are not successful, you will have to keep the damper rod from turning with a special tool on the end of several socket extensions. Your Yamaha dealer has a special tool (**Figure 40**) that can be used. If you are unable to remove it, take the fork tubes to a dealer and have the bolts removed.*

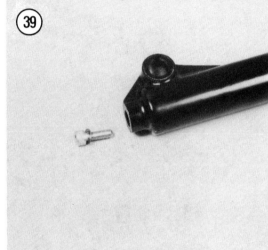

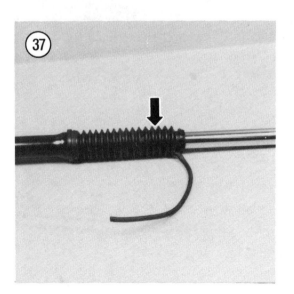

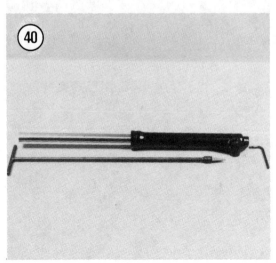

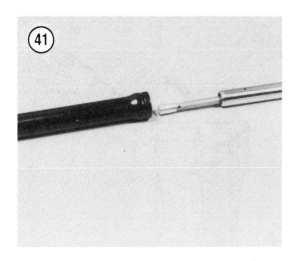

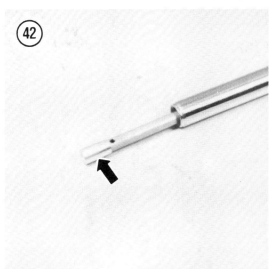

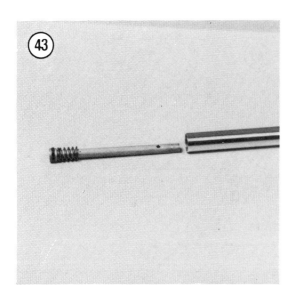

9. If the damper rod Allen bolt slot is rounded out, it will be impossible to remove the bolt with the Allen socket or wrench. If this condition is present, remove the Allen bolt as follows:

    a. Secure the fork tube in a vise with soft jaws (**Figure 38**).

    b. Select a drill bit with almost the same diameter as that of the Allen screw.

    c. Carefully drill the Allen screw head until the head is completely drilled off of the bolt. Work slowly and do not drill into the fork tube. Stop and check your progress often.

    d. When the bolt head is drilled off, pull the fork slider off of the fork tube.

    e. Unscrew the remaining portion of the bolt from the damper rod.

10. Pull the fork tube out of the slider (**Figure 41**).

11. Remove the oil lock piece (**Figure 42**) from the damper rod.

12. Remove the damper rod and spring (**Figure 43**) through the top of the fork tube.

13. Slide the rebound spring (**Figure 44**) off of the damper rod.

14. If oil has been leaking from the top of the slider, remove the oil seal as follows:

    a. Secure the slider in a vise with soft jaws.

    b. Remove the oil seal circlip (**Figure 45**).

8

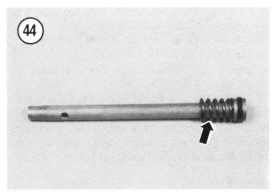

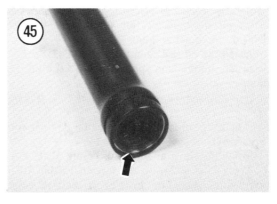

c. Place a rag onto one edge of the slider. Then use a screwdriver or pry bar and carefully pry the oil seal up and out of the slider (**Figure 46**). When prying the seal, start at one point and slowly work around the oil seal; pry the seal up evenly. Do not pry continuously at one point. Check often to make sure the screwdriver does not cut through the shop rag and damage the top of the slider.

Inspection

1. Thoroughly clean all parts in solvent and dry. Check the fork tube for signs of wear or scratches.
2. Check the damper rod for straightness. **Figure 47** shows one method. The rod should be replaced if the runout is 0.2 mm (0.008 in.) or greater.
3. Check the damper piston ring (**Figure 48**) for wear or damage.
4. Inspect the oil seals for scoring, nicks and loss of resiliency. Replace them if their condition is questionable.
5. Check the upper fork tube for straightness. If bent or severely scratched, it should be replaced.
6. Check the lower slider for dents or exterior damage that could cause the upper fork tube to hang up during riding conditions. Replace if necessary.
7. Measure the uncompressed length of the main fork spring. The standard spring length for all models is listed in **Table 1**. Replace the spring if shorter than the standard dimensions.
8. Inspect the O-ring in the fork cap (**Figure 49**). Replace the O-ring if necessary.
9. Replace the fork boot (**Figure 50**) if damaged.
10. Any parts that are worn or damaged should be replaced. Simply cleaning and reinstalling unserviceable components will not improve performance of the front suspension.

Assembly

1. Install a new oil seal by driving it into the slider with a large socket or piece of pipe. Make sure the driver fits the outer portion of the seal. Do not drive on the inner seal area.
2. Install the oil seal snap ring (**Figure 45**).
3. Install the rebound spring (**Figure 44**) onto the damper rod.
4. Insert the damper rod into the fork tube (**Figure 51**).
5. Install the oil lock piece onto the damper rod (**Figure 42**).
6. Install the slider as shown in **Figure 41**.
7. Apply Loctite 242 to the threads of the Allen bolt before installation. Install it in the fork slider

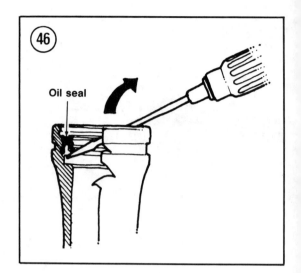

Oil seal

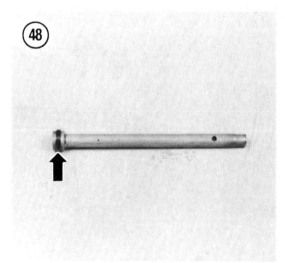

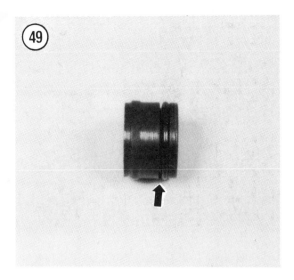

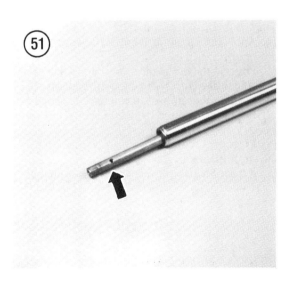

(**Figure 39**) and tighten it to specifications (**Table 2**). If necessary, use Yamaha tool shown during disassembly to prevent the damper rod from turning when tightening the bolt.

8. Install the fork boot (**Figure 37**) so that the hose faces to the top of the fork.

9. Install the fork tube onto the vehicle. Tighten the fork bolts to the specifications in **Table 2**.

10. Fill each fork with the specified viscosity and quantity of fork oil. Refer to **Table 1**.

NOTE
*The viscosity of the oil can be varied according to your own preference and to the type of riding terrain (lower viscosity for less damping and higher viscosity for more damping action). Always use the specified **amount** of oil.*

NOTE
To measure the correct amount of fluid, use a plastic baby bottle. These have measurements in fluid ounces (oz.) and cubic centimeters (cc) on the side.

11. Install the fork spring (**Figure 36**).

NOTE
An assistant will be required to help install the fork cap and wire ring.

12. Insert the fork cap in the fork tube and push it down with a drift. Then install a new wire ring, making sure it engages the ring in the fork tube. See **Figure 34**. Release tension against the drift and allow the fork cap to seat against the wire ring.

YTM200K, L, N; YTM200EK, EL

The fork tube (**Figure 28**) on these models requires a press and special tools for complete disassembly and reassembly. Thus it is recommended that the all service related to fork tube disassembly and reassembly be referred to a Yamaha dealer. Fork oil replacement is described in Chapter Three. Refer to Chapter Thirteen for suspension adjustment procedures.

TIRES

All models are equipped with low pressure tires designed specifically for off-road use only. Rapid tire wear will occur if the vehicle is ridden on paved surfaces. Due to their low pressure requirements, they should be inflated only with a hand-operated air pump instead of using an air compressor or the air available at service stations.

CAUTION
Do not overinflate the stock tires as they will be permanently distorted and damaged. If overinflated they will bulge out similar to an inner tube that is not within the constraints of a tire and they will not return to their original contour.

The rims used on these models are of the 1-piece type and require a special type of tool for tire changing. There are various models available from dealers and mail order houses. When purchasing a tire tool, get the type that exerts all of the applied pressure to a very small section of the tire bead at a time. Many aftermarket bead breakers spread out the applied pressure over a larger section of the tire bead and therefore are unable to break the bead loose from the rim.

NOTE
A tire tool that applies pressure to a small area and that can break all ATV tire/wheel assemblies is "The Original Bead Buster." See **Figure 52**. *This tool is available from Jenco Products, P.O. Box 610, Glide, Oregon 97443.*

CAUTION
Do not use conventional motorcycle tire irons *for tire removal as the tire sealing bead will be damaged when forced away from the rim flange.*

Tire Changing

1. Remove the valve stem cap and core and partially deflate the tire. Do not let all of the air out. Leave approximately 0.05-0.10 kg/cm2 (0.7-1.4 psi) of air pressure in the tire. This will help during the initial tire removal sequence.
2. Lubricate the tire bead and rim flanges with water.

CAUTION
If you are running aftermarket aluminum wheels, special care must be taken when changing tires to avoid scratches and gouges to the outer rim surface.

3. Position the wheel into the tire removal tool (**Figure 52**).
4. Slowly work the tire tool, making sure the tool is up against the rim, and break the tire bead away from the rim.

5. Using your hands, press down on the tire on either side of the tool and try to break the rest of the bead free from the rim.
6. If the rest of the tire bead cannot be broken loose, raise the tool, rotate the tire/rim assembly and repeat Step 4 and Step 5 until the entire bead is broken loose from the rim.
7. Remove the tire/rim assembly from the tool assembly.
8. Reinflate the tire to approximately 0.05-0.10 kg/cm2 (0.7-1.4 psi).
9. Turn the wheel over and repeat Steps 2-6 for the rim flange on the other side.
10. Remove the tire from the rim using tire irons and rim protectors (**Figure 53**).
11. Inspect the rim sealing surface of the rim. If the rim has been severely hit it will probably cause an air leak. Repair or replace any damaged rim.
12. Inspect the tire for cuts, tears, abrasions or any other defects.
13. Apply clean water to the rim flanges, tire rim beads and onto the outer rim. Make sure the rim flange is clean. Wipe with a lint-free cloth.
14. Apply tire mounting lubricant or water to both tire beads.
15. Position the tire so the arrow on the sidewall is pointing in the correct direction of rotation.
16. Position the rim with the outer side facing up.
17. Install the rim into the tire as shown in **Figure 54**.
18. Press the tire onto the rim with your hands as shown in **Figure 55**.
19. Repeat Step 18 for the other side of the tire.

CAUTION
Do not inflate the tire past the maximum inflation pressure of 0.7 kg/cm2 (10 psi).

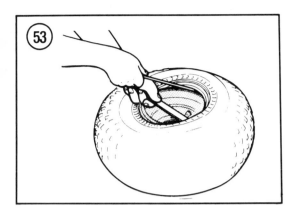

20. Inflate the tire to the recommended tire pressure; refer to **Table 3**.

21. Inspect the "rim line" of the tire in relation to the rim. It must be equally spaced from the rim all around the circumference (**Figure 56**). If the distance varies, the bead is not properly seated and the tire must be reinstalled correctly on the rim. Repeat Steps 15-21.

22. Check for air leaks and install the valve cap.

Cold Patch Repair

Refer to the manufacturer's instructions when using cold patch products.

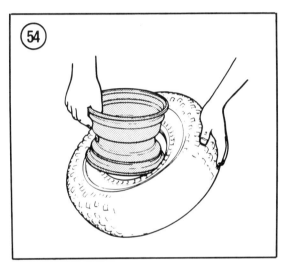

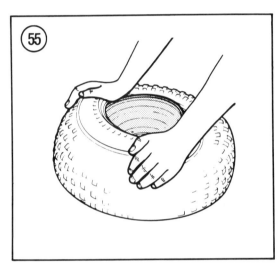

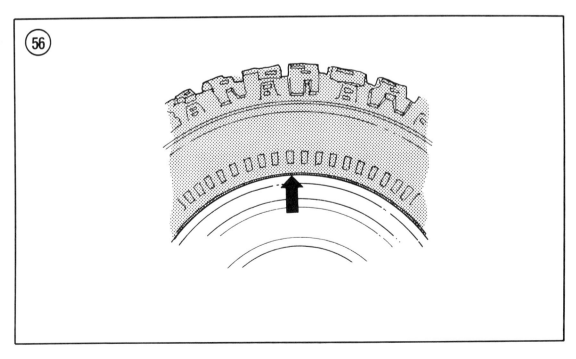

Table 1 STEERING SPECIFICATIONS—YTM200 AND YTM225

Steering
  Ball bearings
   Quantity (size)
    YTM200K, L, N; YTM200EK, EL; YTM225DXK, DXL, DXN
     Upper   22 (1/4 in.)
     Lower   19 (3/16 in.)
    YTM200ERN; YTM225DRN; YTM225DRN; YTM225DRS
     Upper and lower   19 (1/4 in.)
 Front fork spring free length limit
  YTM200K, L, N   395.1 mm (15.56 in.)
  YTM200EK, EL   395.1 mm (15.56 in.)
  YTM225DXK, DXL, DXN   501.1 mm (19.73 in.)
  YTM200ERN   395.1 mm (15.56 in.)
  YTM225DRN   501.1 mm (19.73 in.)
  YTM225DRS   526.6 mm (20.73 in.)
 Rim runout limit
  YTM200K, L, N; YTM200EK, EL;
  YTM200DXK, DXL, DXN;   2.0 mm (0.08 in.)
  YTM200ERN; YTM225   1.0 mm (0.04 in.)

Table 2 TIGHTENING TORQUES—YTM200 AND YTM225

	N·m	ft.-lb.
Front axle nut	50	36
Front wheel panel	45	32
Lower steering bracket and inner fork tube		
YTM225DRS	48	35
All other models	30	22
Steering stem and inner fork tube	20	14
Steering stem bolt	90	65
Steering shaft ring nut	38	27
Handlebar holder	20	14

Table 3 TIRE INFLATION PRESSURE

Tire size	Air pressure
YTM200 and YTM225 models	
22×11-8	
Recommended	0.15 kg/cm² (2.2 psi)
Maximum	0.7 kg/cm² (10 psi)
Minimum	0.12 kg/cm² (1.8 psi)
25×12-9	
Recommended	0.15 kg/cm² (2.2 psi)
Maximum	0.7 kg/cm² (10 psi)
Minimum	0.12 kg/cm² (1.8 psi)
YFM200 models	
YFM200N	
25×12-9 (front)	
and 22×11-8 (rear)	
Recommended	0.15 kg/cm² (2.2 psi)
Maximum	0.7 kg/cm² (10 psi)
Minimum	0.12 kg/cm² (1.8 psi)
YFM200DXS	
22×8-10 (front)	
and 22×11-8 (rear)	
Recommended	0.20 kg/cm² (2.8 psi)
Minimum	0.17 kg/cm² (2.4 psi)

8

FRONT SUSPENSION AND STEERING (YFM 200)

This chapter describes repair and maintenance of the front wheels, suspension and steering components for YFM200 models.

Tables 1-3 are located at the end of the chapter.

FRONT WHEEL

Removal/Installation

Refer to **Figure 1** for this procedure.

1. Park the vehicle on level ground and set the parking brake. Block the rear wheels so the vehicle will not roll in either direction.

2. Jack up the vehicle with a small hydraulic jack. Place the jack under the frame with a piece of wood between the jack and frame.

3. Remove the 4 nuts (**Figure 2**) securing the wheel to the hub and remove the wheel.

4. Installation is the reverse of these steps, noting the following.

5. Tighten the wheel nuts to the specifications in **Table 2** or **Table 3**.

Inspection

1. With the wheel mounted on the vehicle, check the vertical and lateral wheel runout with a dial indicator. The vertical and lateral runout limits are 2.0 mm (0.08 in.). If a dial indicator is not available, visually check side play as follows:

   a. Jack up the vehicle's front end.

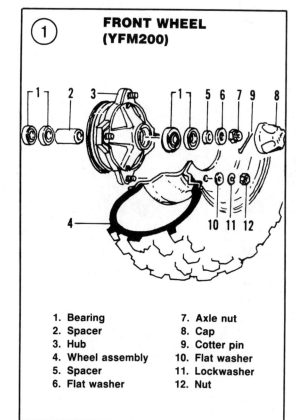

① FRONT WHEEL (YFM200)

1. Bearing	7. Axle nut
2. Spacer	8. Cap
3. Hub	9. Cotter pin
4. Wheel assembly	10. Flat washer
5. Spacer	11. Lockwasher
6. Flat washer	12. Nut

b. Push the wheel from side to side and detect the amount of play at the hub at the point shown in **Figure 3**.

2. If the runout is excessive, remove the wheel and inspect the wheel bearing as described under *Front Hubs* in this chapter. If the bearing is okay, it will be necessary to replace the wheel.

FRONT HUBS

Removal/Installation

This procedure describes removal of the front hub. If the front hub is being removed to service the wheel bearings and/or grease seals, it is not necessary to remove the tire/wheel assembly from the hub as described under *Front Wheel Removal* in this chapter. The tire/wheel assembly is an ideal holding fixture for the hub. All service can be performed with the tire/wheel installed on the hub.

1. Park the vehicle on level ground and set the parking brake. Block the rear wheels so the vehicle will roll in either direction.

2. Jack up the vehicle with a small hydraulic jack. Place the jack under the frame with a piece of wood between the jack and frame.

3. If necessary, remove the front wheel as described in this chapter.

4. Remove the wheel cap.

5. Remove the front axle cotter pin and axle nut (**Figure 4**).

6. Remove the front hub (**Figure 5**).

7. Installation is the reverse of these steps, noting the following.

8. Tighten the front hub nut to the specifications in **Table 2** or **Table 3**.

9

9. Secure the front axle nut with a new cotter pin and bend it over completely (**Figure 6**).

> *NOTE*
> *Always use a new cotter pin whenever possible. A reused cotter pin may break and fall out of the axle. Purchase extra cotter pins and store them in your tool box.*

Inspection

1. Thoroughly clean the inside of the hub with solvent and dry with compressed air or a shop cloth.

2. Rotate the bearings (**Figure 7**) by hand and check for roughness and radial play (some axial play is normal). The bearings should turn smoothly. Replace any bearing with tight spots or excessive play as described in this chapter.

3. If the bearings are not to be removed, clean non-sealed bearings (**Figure 7**) in solvent. Then dry with compressed air, holding the inner race to prevent it from rotating. Do not clean sealed bearings (**Figure 8**).

> *WARNING*
> *Never spin a bearing with the high-pressure air jet. This could damage the bearing or cause it to disintegrate, creating a severe safety hazard.*

4. A bent front axle (**Figure 9**) will cause poor handling, vibration and premature wheel bearing wear. Check the axle for signs of fatigue, fractures and bends. If necessary, replace it as described under *Steering Knuckle Removal/Installation* in this chapter.

5. Check the hole in the end of the axle where the cotter pin fits. Make sure there are no fractures or cracks leading out toward the end of the axle. If any are found replace the steering knuckle as described in this chapter.

6. Check the hub and wheel assembly for dents, cracks or other obvious signs of damage. Replace the hub and/or wheel if necessary.

7. If the brake drum (**Figure 8**) appears worn or damaged, check it further as described in Chapter Eleven under *Front Brake*.

Bearing Replacement

Hub bearings (**Figure 7**) should only be removed when they are worn or damaged as removal usually damages them. See **Figure 1**.

1. Remove the front wheel as described in this chapter.

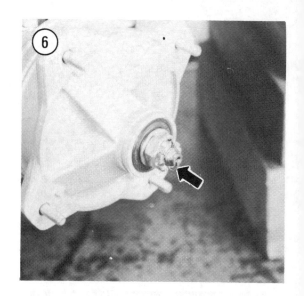

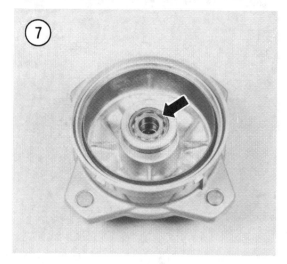

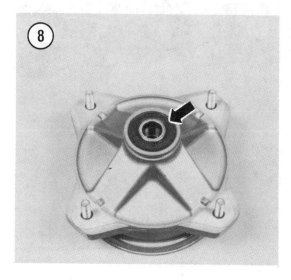

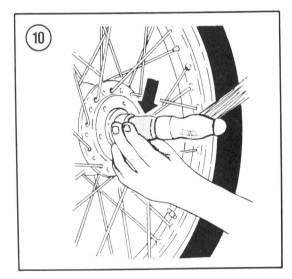

NOTE
Do not remove the hub assembly from the tire/wheel assembly as it makes an ideal holding fixture.

2. To remove the bearings perform the following:
   a. Insert a long driver into end side of the hub. Push the spacer to one side so that the drift can be applied to the inner race of the bearing.
   b. Tap the bearing out of the hub by working the perimeter of the bearing race.
   c. Remove the second bearing in the same manner.
   d. Remove the spacer.
   e. Tap out the opposite bearings.
3. Thoroughly clean all bearing cavities with solvent and a clean rag. Do not clean sealed bearings (**Figure 8**) in solvent.
4. Install new bearings as follows:
   a. On non-sealed bearings, pack the bearings with a good quality bearing grease. Work the grease between the balls thoroughly. Turn the

bearings by hand a couple of times to make sure the grease is distributed evenly inside the bearing.
   b. Pack the wheel hub and the center spacer with multipurpose grease.

CAUTION
*Install the wheel bearings with the sealed side facing out (**Figure 8**). During installation, tap the bearings squarely into place and tap on the outer race only. Use a socket (**Figure 10**) that matches the outer race diameter. Do not tap on the inner race or the bearing may be damaged. Be sure that the bearings are completely seated.*

   c. Apply heat with a propane torch to one end of the hub assembly around the bearing area. Wave the heat back and forth until the paint in the heated area begins to discolor slightly.
   d. Install the bearings for one side.
   e. Install the center spacer.
   f. Turn the hub over and install the opposite bearings in the same manner as the first.

STEERING

The steering assembly on YFM200N models consists of a steering shaft connected by a tie rod to a right and left steering knuckle (**Figure 11**). On YFM200DXS models, a lower arm and shock absorber have been added (**Figure 12**).

Always keep all steering components clean and well lubricated. The environment these machines are operated in (dirt, sand and water) is particularly harmful to steering components if they are not properly maintained. Proper maintenance can ensure a long service life; however, if neglected, the parts will wear quickly.

STEERING SHAFT

Removal/Lubrication/Installation

Refer to **Figure 11** or **Figure 12** for this procedure.
1. Remove the seat and front fender assembly.
2. Remove the fuel tank cover as described in Chapter Six.
3. Remove the engine guard from underneath the frame.
4. Remove the handlebar cover.
5. Remove the headlight bracket securing bolts and remove the bracket.

⑪   **STEERING ASSEMBLY**

1. Headlight bracket
2. Bolt
3. Bolt
4. Upper handlebar holder
5. Lower handlebar holder
6. Steering shaft
7. Steering guide
8. O-ring
9. Flat washer
10. Lockwasher
11. Nut
12. Circlip
13. Bolt
14. Lockwasher
15. Steering shaft holder
16. Cotter pin

17. Kingpin nut
18. Washer
19. Thrust cover
20. Bushing
21. Bushing
22. Steering knuckle
23. Grease fitting
24. Kingpin bolt
25. Nut
26. Tie rod joint
27. Nut
28. Tie rod
29. Washer
30. Nut
31. Tie rod joint nut

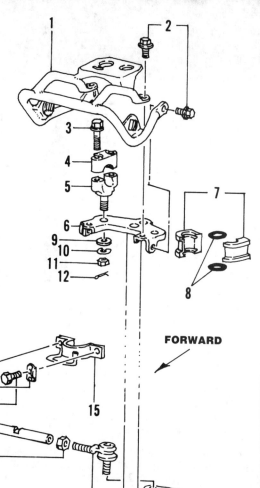

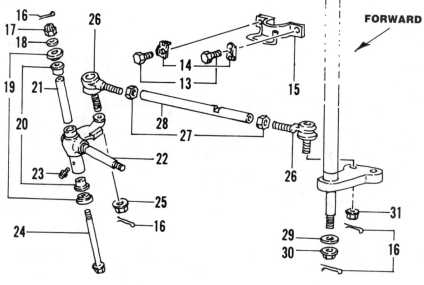

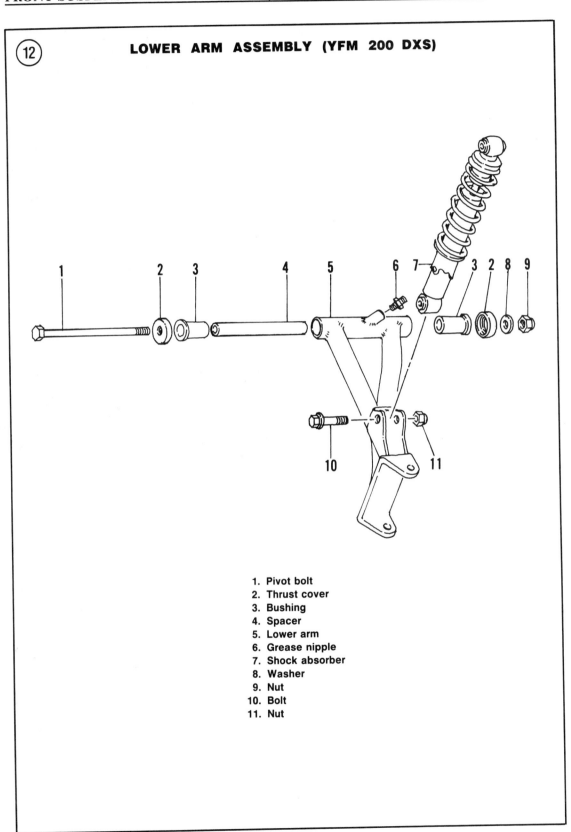

LOWER ARM ASSEMBLY (YFM 200 DXS)

1. Pivot bolt
2. Thrust cover
3. Bushing
4. Spacer
5. Lower arm
6. Grease nipple
7. Shock absorber
8. Washer
9. Nut
10. Bolt
11. Nut

6. Remove the handlebar as described in this chapter.

7. Flatten the steering shaft guide holder lockwasher tabs (**Figure 11**). Then remove the guide holder bolts.

8. Remove the guide holder (**Figure 11**) and O-rings (**Figure 11**).

9. Remove the left- and right-hand side tie rod-to-steering shaft cotter pins and nuts (**Figure 13**).

10. Detach the tie rods from the steering shaft.

11. Remove the cotter pin securing the steering shaft nut (**Figure 14**) and remove the nut and washer.

12. Lift the lower end of the steering shaft (**Figure 15**) out of the frame and carefully remove it.

13. Remove the steering shaft bushings (**Figure 11**).

14. Inspect the steering shaft as described in this chapter.

15. Installation is the reverse of these steps, noting the following.

16. Lubricate all bushings and O-rings with a waterproof grease such as boat trailer wheel bearing grease.

17. Tighten the steering shaft and tie rod nuts to the specifications in **Table 2** or **Table 3**.

18. Tighten the guide holder bolt to the specifications in **Table 2** or **Table 3**. Then bend the lockwasher tabs against the guide holder bolts to lock them.

19. Tighten the handlebar nut to the specifications in **Table 2** or **Table 3**.

NOTE
Refer to ***Handlebar Installation*** *to make sure all cables and wiring are routed correctly.*

20. Install new cotter pins.

Steering Shaft Inspection

1. Carefully inspect the entire steering shaft assembly (**Figure 11**), especially if the vehicle has been involved in a collision or spill. If the shaft is bent or twisted in any way it must be replaced. If a damaged shaft is installed in the machine, it will cause rapid wear on the bushings as well as place undue stress on other components in the frame and steering system.

2. Examine the lower bushings in the frame (**Figure 11**) for wear or for signs of galling due to lack of lubrication. Check bushing wear by installing the steering shaft into the bushing and checking free play. There should be no noticeable free play when the shaft is moved back and forth. Replace the bushings if necessary.

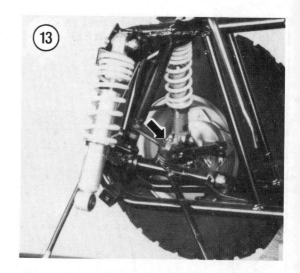

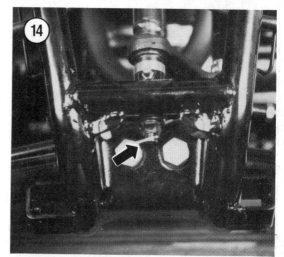

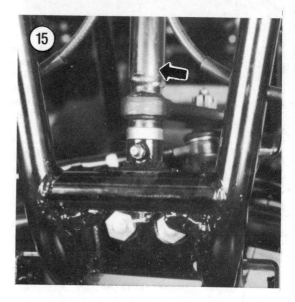

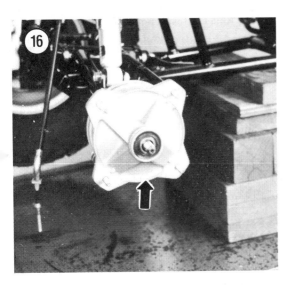

3. Check the steering shaft guides and O-rings for wear or damage. If the O-rings are damaged in any way, they should be replaced. A damaged O-ring will allow grit and moisture to enter the steering shaft guide.

4. Check the lower bushing guide holder (**Figure 11**) at the frame for damage or cracking. If the holder is damaged, have a Yamaha dealer or mchine shop repair the frame.

Steering Knuckle
Removal/Installation

The removal procedure is the same for either side. Refer to **Figure 11** for this procedure.

1. Remove one or both front wheels as described in this chapter.

2. Remove the front hub (**Figure 16**) if it was not removed with the wheel.

3. Remove the brake backing plate from the steering knuckle as described in Chapter Eleven.

4. Remove the cotter pin securing the tie rod nut (**Figure 17**).

5. Remove the nut and washers and lift the tie rod end out of the arm on the steering knuckle. If the tie rod end is difficult to remove, install the nut just enough to cover the threads on the end of the bolt and tap the tie rod end out of the steering knuckle with a soft-faced mallet.

> *CAUTION*
> *If the tie rod is difficult to remove from the steering knuckle, do not attempt to pry it out or damage to the seal on the tie rod end may result.*

6. Remove the cotter pin securing the kingpin nut (**Figure 18**).

7. Remove the nut securing the kingpin bolt and remove the kingpin bolt (**Figure 19**) and washer.

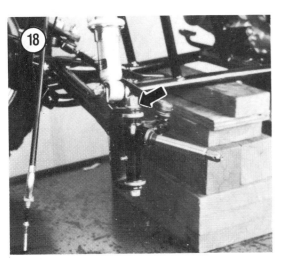

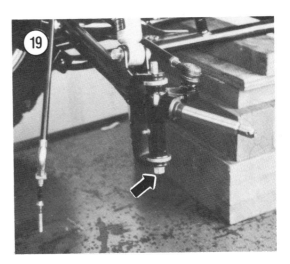

Slide the steering knuckle out of the frame (**Figure 20**). Take care not to drop the thrust covers on each end of the steering knuckle.

8. Perform *Steering Knuckle Inspection and Lubrication* in this chapter.

9. Installation is the reverse of these steps, noting the following.

10. Lightly grease the kingpin bolt before installing the bolt through the steering knuckle.

11. Tighten the nuts securing the tie rod end and the kingpin bolt to the torque values specified in **Table 2** or **Table 3**.

12. Use new cotter pins to secure the tie rod end and kingpin nuts. Bend both halves of the cotter pin to lock it.

13. Reinstall the brake backing plate as described in Chapter Eleven.

14. Install the front wheel as described in this chapter.

Steering Knuckle Inspection and Lubrication

Refer to **Figure 11** for this procedure.

1. Remove the steering knuckle as described in this chapter.

2. Remove the thrust covers from each end of the steering knuckle. Wipe the inside of each cover with a clean rag and carefully check it for damage or wear (**Figure 21**).

3. Remove the kingpin spacer (**Figure 22**) from the steering knuckle.

4. Clean the steering knuckle and spacer in clean solvent or wipe the parts with a clean rag.

5. Examine the kingpin spacer for signs of wear or corrosion caused by moisture. Replace the spacer if it is damaged or worn.

6. Slide the spacer into the steering knuckle. Try to move the spacer side-to-side in the bushing. The spacer should rotate freely but have no side-to-side

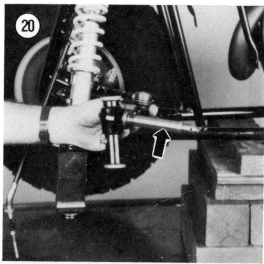

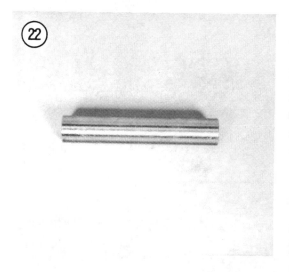

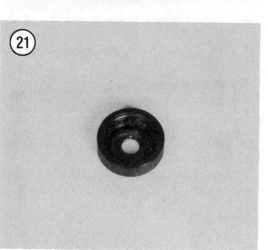

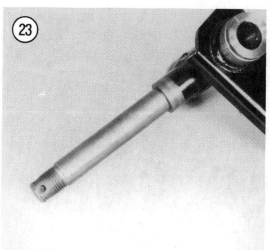

movement. Any side-to-side movement (more than just perceptible) is an indication that the steering knuckle bushings are worn.

7. Visually inspect the steering knuckle bushings for wear or damage. In most cases damage will be caused by lack of lubrication or entry of sand and dirt. If the bushings show any signs of damage or wear, have a Yamaha dealer or machine shop replace them.

8. Inspect the front axle (**Figure 23**) for signs of wear or damage. A hard spill or collision may cause a bend in the front axle. If the axle is damaged in any way, the steering knuckle must be replaced.

> *CAUTION*
> *If the vehicle is operated with a bent front axle, further damage to the wheel bearings and front hub will result.*

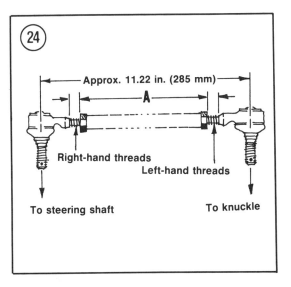

Approx. 11.22 in. (285 mm)

A

Right-hand threads

Left-hand threads

To steering shaft   To knuckle

9. Coat the inside of the steering knuckle bushings with a waterproof grease such as boat trailer wheel bearing grease. Apply a light film of grease to the spacer and install the spacer in the steering knuckle.

10. Apply a small quantity of grease to the inside lips of each thrust cover and install the covers over each end of the steering knuckle.

11. Install the steering knuckle as described in this chapter.

Tie Rod
Removal/Installation

Refer to **Figure 11** and **Figure 24** for this procedure.

1. Remove one or both front wheels as described in this chapter.

2. Remove the cotter pin securing the tie rod nut on each end. See **Figure 13** and **Figure 17**.

3. Remove the nut and washer from both ends and lift the tie rod end out of the steering knuckle and steering shaft. If either tie rod end is difficult to remove, install the nut just enough to cover the threads on the end of the bolt and tap the tie rod end out of the steering knuckle with a soft-faced mallet. The inner tie rod ends can be reached with a long drift through the bottom of the frame.

> *CAUTION*
> *If the tie rod is difficult to remove from the steering knuckle, do not attempt to pry it out or damage to the seal on the tie rod end may result.*

4. Ensure that the rubber boot over each tie rod swivel joint is in good condition (**Figure 25**). Replace the tie rod end if the rubber boot is damaged in any way. The swivel joints are permanently packed with grease. If the rubber boots are damaged, dirt and moisture can enter the swivel joints and destroy them. Tie rod ends can be replaced separately.

5. If tie rod ends are to be replaced, refer to **Figure 24** and perform the following:

    a. Carefully measure the overall length of the old tie rod assembly before removing the worn tie rod ends. **Figure 24** shows the approximate factory length setting.

    b. Loosen the locknuts securing the tie rod end to be replaced. The nuts securing the outside tie rod ends have left-hand threads (**Figure 24**).

    c. Unscrew the old tie rod end. Install the new tie rod end and turn it in or out until the overall length of the tie rod is the same as the old unit. Leave the locknuts securing each tie rod end loose at this time. They are tightened after the wheel alignment is adjusted.

6. Installation is the reverse of these steps, noting the following.

7. Make sure the tie rods are installed with the flat spot (**Figure 24**) toward the center of the machine.

8. Perform *Wheel Alignment* as described in this chapter.

9. Tighten the nuts securing the tie rods to the torque valves specified in **Table 2** or **Table 3**.

10. Install new cotter pins.

Wheel Alignment

Wheel alignment consists of centering the handlebars and adjusting the toe-in of both front wheels. The handlebars are centered when the tie rods are adjusted to equal lengths on both sides. Toe-in of the front wheels is obtained by adjusting the tie rods until the distance between the front tires at the front is less than the distance between the front tires at the rear.

1. Park the vehicle on level ground with the handlebars straight ahead.

2. Set the tire pressure on all tires. See Chapter Three.

3. Use a stick with 2 marking points or a ruler in front of the machine and carefully measure the distance between the center of both front tires (**Figure 26**). Mark the tires with a piece of chalk at these points. Write down the measurement.

4. Move the vehicle so that the front tires rotate exactly 180°. Measure the distance between the center of both front tires at the points marked in Step 3. Write down the measurement.

5. Subtract the measurement in Step 3 from Step 4 as shown in **Figure 27**. Toe-in is correct if the difference is 0-5 mm (0-0.2 in.).

6. Refer to **Figure 28**. If the measurement is not correct, loosen the locknuts (A) securing each tie rod. Use a wrench on the flat portion of the tie rods (B) and slowly adjust one or both tie rods until the measurement is correct. Recheck each measurement after each adjustment. Turn the tie rods only a small amount each time. It takes very little adjustment of the tie rods to move each tire a large amount.

7. When the adjustments are correct, hold each tie rod in place and tighten the locknuts securing each tie rod end. Install new cotter pins.

Lower Arm Removal/Installation (YFM200DXS)

Both lower arm assemblies are the same. Refer to **Figure 12** for this procedure.

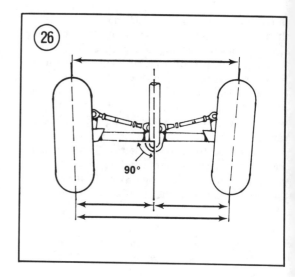

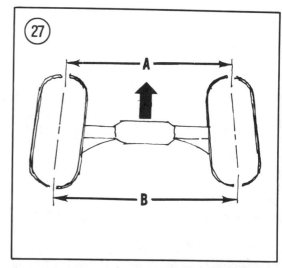

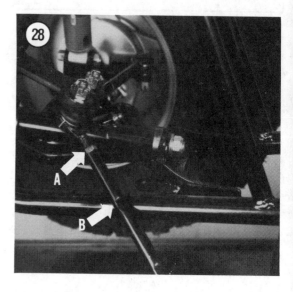

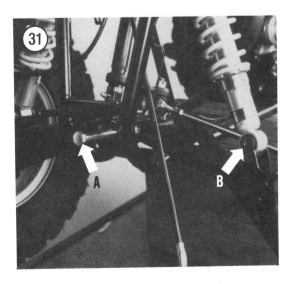

1. Remove the steering knuckle (A, **Figure 29**) at the lower arm as described in this chapter.

2. Remove the lower shock absorber bolt (B, **Figure 29**) and disconnect the shock from the lower arm.

3. Remove the lower arm pivot bolt nut (**Figure 30**).

4. Remove the pivot bolt (A, **Figure 31**) and remove the lower arm (B, **Figure 31**). Take care not to drop the dust seals on each end of the lower arm pivot area.

5. Perform *Lower Arm Inspection.*

6. Installation is the reverse of these steps, noting the following.

7. Lightly grease the lower arm pivot bolt before installing the bolt through the lower arm.

8. Tighten the lower arm nuts to the specifications in **Table 3**.

Lower Arm Inspection

Refer to **Figure 12** for this procedure.

1. Remove the lower arm as described in this chapter.

2. Remove the thrust covers from each end of the lower arm (**Figure 32**). Wipe the inside of each cover with a clean rag and carefully check it for damage or wear (**Figure 21**).

3. Remove the spacer (**Figure 33**) from the lower arm.

9

4. Clean the lower arm and spacer in clean solvent or wipe the parts clean with a clean rag.

5. Examine the lower arm oil seals for wear or damage. Replace them by prying them out with a small screwdriver.

6. Examine the spacer for signs of wear or corrosion caused by moisture. Replace the spacer if it is damaged or worn.

7. Slide the spacer into the lower arm. Try to move the spacer side-to-side in the bushing. The spacer should rotate freely but have no side-to-side movement. Any side-to-side movement (more than just perceptible) is an indication that the lower arm bushings are worn.

8. Visually inspect the lower arm bushings for wear or damage. In most cases damage will be caused by lack of lubrication or entry of sand and dirt. If the bushings show any signs of damage or wear, have a Yamaha dealer or machine shop replace them.

9. Check the lower arm for bending, cracks or other damage. Replace it if necessary.

> *CAUTION*
> *If the vehicle is operated with a bent lower arm, further damage to the wheel bearings and front hub will result.*

10. If removed, install new oil seals by driving them into the lower arm with a suitable size socket or piece of pipe placed on the outside of each seal.

11. Coat the inside of the bushings with a waterproof grease such as boat trailer wheel bearing grease. Apply a light film of grease to the

spacer and install the spacer in the steering knuckle.

12. Apply a small quantity of grease to the inside lips of each thrust cover and install the covers over each end of the lower arm (**Figure 32**).

13. Install the lower arm as described in this chapter.

HANDLEBAR

Removal/Installation

Refer to Chapter Eight under *Handlebar* for complete procedures.

FRONT SHOCK ABSORBERS (YFM200DXS)

Removal/Installation

1. Jack the vehicle front end up. Set the parking brake and block the rear wheels.

2. Remove the front wheels as described in this chapter.

3. Remove the upper and lower shock absorber bolts (**Figure 34**) and remove the shock.

4. Installation is the reverse of these steps, noting the following.

5. Install the shock bolts so that the bolt head faces to the front of the vehicle (**Figure 35**).

6. Tighten the shock bolts to the specifications in **Table 3**.

Table 1 STEERING SPECIFICATIONS

Toe-in	
YFM200N	0-5 mm (0-0.2 in.)
YFM200DXS	0-10 mm (0-0.4 in.)

Table 2 TIGHTENING TORQUES—YFM200N

	N·m	ft.-lb.
Front axle nut	85	61
Front wheel nut	28	20
Knuckle shaft bolt	30	22
Tie-rod end to steering shaft nut	45	32
Tie-rod end to knuckle nut	40	29
Tie-rod locknut	39	22
Steering shaft nut	30	22
Steering shaft holder bolt	23	17
Handlebar		
Upper holder bolt	20	14
Lower holder nut	30	22

Table 3 TIGHTENING TORQUES—YFM200DXS

	N·m	ft.-lb.
Steering knuckle nut	85	61
Front wheel panel and hub nut	28	20
Steering knuckle and lower arm bolt	35	25
Tie rod nut		
At steering knuckle	40	29
At steering shaft	40	29
Tie rod locknut	30	22
Steering shaft and frame nut	30	22
Steering shaft holder and frame bolt	23	17
Steering shaft and lower handlebar nut	30	22
Lower arm and frame nut	68	49
Shock absorber nut (upper and lower)	45	32

9

CHAPTER TEN

REAR SUSPENSION AND FINAL DRIVE

This chapter contains repair and replacement procedures for the rear wheels, rear hub, rear suspension and final drive components. **Tables 1-6** are at the end of the chapter.

REAR WHEEL

Removal/Installation

1. Park the vehicle on level ground and set the parking brake. Block the front wheel so the vehicle will not roll in either direction.
2. Jack up the rear of the vehicle with a small hydraulic jack. Place wood blocks under the engine; release jack pressure and securely support the vehicle on the wood blocks.
3. Remove the wheel nuts securing the wheel to the hub and remove the wheel. See **Figure 1**.
4. If necessary, remove the hub as follows:
   a. Remove the rear axle cotter pin and axle nut (**Figure 2**).
   b. Slide the hub (**Figure 3**) off of the axle.

> *NOTE*
> *If necessary the hub can be removed with the rear wheel. To do so, remove the rear axle cotter pin and axle nut and slide the wheel assembly off of the axle (**Figure 4**).*

5. Install by reversing these removal steps. Tighten the wheel nuts to specifications. See **Tables 2-6**.
6. If necessary, install a new cotter pin and bend it over completely. Never reuse an old cotter pin as it may break and fall out.

REAR AXLE (CHAIN DRIVE)

Refer to **Figure 5** for procedures in this section.

Removal

1. Park the vehicle on level ground. Block the front wheel.
2. Remove the seat and fenders.
3. Remove both rear wheels as described in this chapter.
4. Remove the cotter pin and castellated nut securing the left-hand rear hub (**Figure 2**). Remove the lockwasher and slide the hub (**Figure 3**) off the axle. Remove the right-hand hub in the same manner.
5. Remove the sprocket cover from the left-hand side.
6. Remove the brake caliper and brake disc as described in Chapter Eleven.

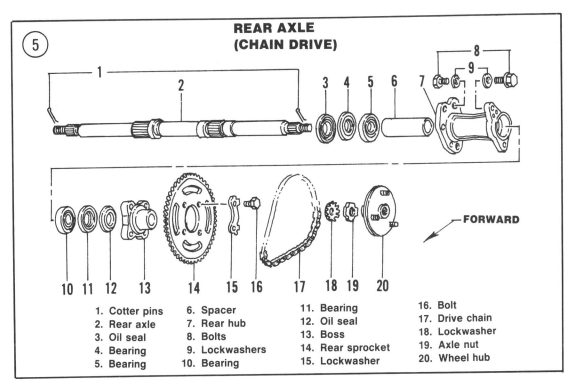

**REAR AXLE
(CHAIN DRIVE)**

FORWARD

1. Cotter pins	6. Spacer	11. Bearing	16. Bolt
2. Rear axle	7. Rear hub	12. Oil seal	17. Drive chain
3. Oil seal	8. Bolts	13. Boss	18. Lockwasher
4. Bearing	9. Lockwashers	14. Rear sprocket	19. Axle nut
5. Bearing	10. Bearing	15. Lockwasher	20. Wheel hub

10

7. Loosen the chain adjuster (**Figure 6**) to obtain as much drive chain slack as possible.

8. Remove the bolts (**Figure 7**) securing the driven sprocket to the sprocket boss and pull the sprocket and chain off the boss (**Figure 8**). Slide the drive chain off both sprockets and remove the driver sprocket.

9. Pry back the lockwasher clips (**Figure 9**) and remove the ringnut securing the sprocket boss. The ringnut can be loosened with a spanner wrench (**Figure 10**) or with a punch and hammer (**Figure 11**). Remove and discard the lockwasher.

> *CAUTION*
> *Do not heat the ringnut in order to remove it, as the heat would remove the temper from the axle. If you are unable to remove the ringnut, have a mechanic do it for you.*

10. Slide the sprocket boss (**Figure 12**) off the axle.

> *NOTE*
> *Mark the axle's left or right side before removing it. The axle should be installed so that it operates in its original installed position.*

11. Pull the axle out of the bearing holder from the right-hand side.

Inspection

1. Inspect the hub splines and the threads on the hub nut studs. See **Figure 13**. Replace the hub if necessary.

2. Inspect the sprocket boss splines. Replace the boss if necessary. The dust seal should be replaced if worn or damaged.

3. Inspect the axle for signs of fatigue, fractures or damage. Inspect all splines for wear or damage.

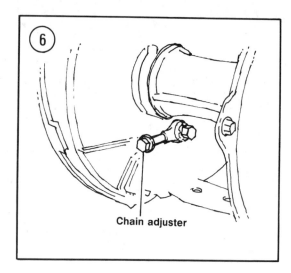

Chain adjuster

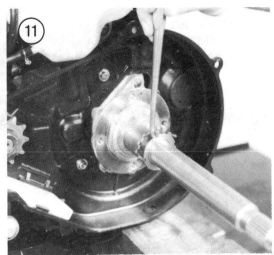

4. Check the axle bearing surfaces for wear or scoring marks. Replace the axle if damage or wear is apparent.

5. Check the hole at each end of the axle where the cotter pin fits in. Make sure there are no fractures or cracks leading out toward the end of the axle. If any are found, replace the axle.

6. Check the axle runout. Use V-blocks and a dial indicator as shown in **Figure 14**. If the runout is 1.5 mm (0.06 in.) or greater the axle must be replaced.

7. Inspect the drive chain and the driven sprocket as described in this chapter.

8. Inspect the brake components as described in Chapter Eleven.

Installation

1. Grease all splines and bearing surfaces on the axle.

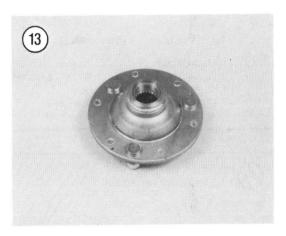

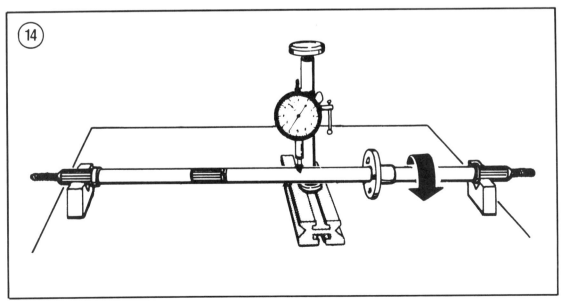

10

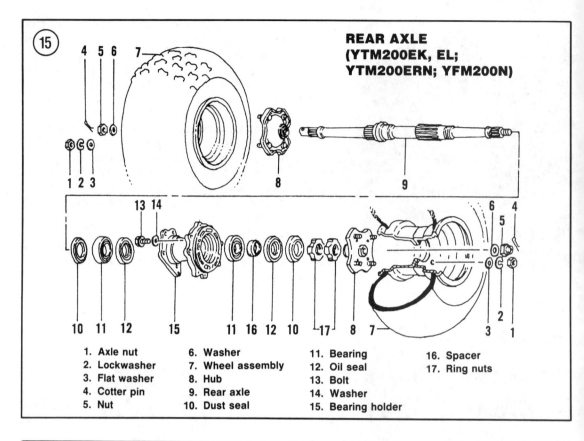

**REAR AXLE
(YTM200EK, EL;
YTM200ERN; YFM200N)**

1. Axle nut	6. Washer	11. Bearing	16. Spacer
2. Lockwasher	7. Wheel assembly	12. Oil seal	17. Ring nuts
3. Flat washer	8. Hub	13. Bolt	
4. Cotter pin	9. Rear axle	14. Washer	
5. Nut	10. Dust seal	15. Bearing holder	

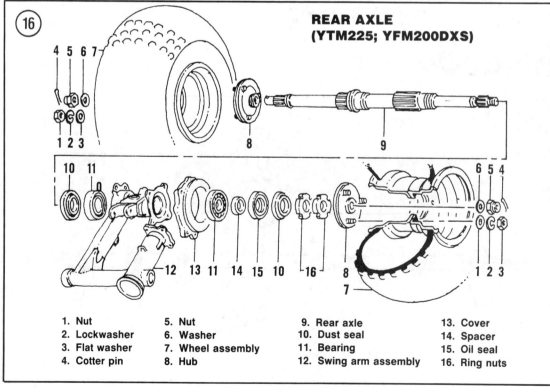

**REAR AXLE
(YTM225; YFM200DXS)**

1. Nut	5. Nut	9. Rear axle	13. Cover
2. Lockwasher	6. Washer	10. Dust seal	14. Spacer
3. Flat washer	7. Wheel assembly	11. Bearing	15. Oil seal
4. Cotter pin	8. Hub	12. Swing arm assembly	16. Ring nuts

2. Install the axle. Approximately line up the bearing surfaces on the axle with the bearings in the bearing holder.

3. Grease the dust seal on the backside of the sprocket boss. Then slide the boss onto the axle and seat it against the left-hand bearing.

4. Slide the driven sprocket over the axle. Attach the drive chain to the front and rear sprockets and fit the driven sprocket onto the driven sprocket boss (**Figure 8**). Turn the axle by hand to align the holes in the boss with the sprocket holes. Install the sprocket bolts with lockwashers and tighten securely.

5. Install the brake disc and caliper as described in Chapter Eleven.

6. Install the lockwasher and ringnut onto the left-hand side of the axle. Using a spanner wrench, tighten it to specifications in **Table 2**.

7. Bend over the lockwasher lock tabs to lock the ringnut.

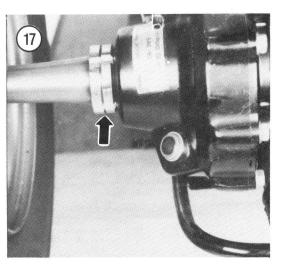

NOTE
Make sure when installing the ringnut and washer to replace any damaged or worn part before tightening to specification.

8. Clean out the left-hand side cover. Remove any accumulation of drive chain lubricant, sand, gravel and other trail dirt. Then install the side covers.

9. Apply a light coat of multipurpose grease to the axle splines.

10. Install both wheel hubs and wheels as described in this chapter.

11. Adjust the drive chain as described in Chapter Three.

12. Adjust the rear brake as described in Chapter Three.

REAR AXLE
(SHAFT DRIVE)

Refer to **Figure 15** or **Figure 16** for this procedure.

Removal

1. Park the vehicle on level ground. Block the front wheel.

2. Remove the seat and fenders.

3. Remove both rear wheels as described in this chapter.

4. Remove the cotter pin and castellated nut securing the left-hand rear hub (**Figure 2**). Remove the lockwasher and slide the hub (**Figure 3**) off the axle. Remove the right-hand hub in the same manner.

5. Remove the trailer hitch.

6. Remove the rear axle ring nuts (**Figure 17**) from the left-hand side. The ringnuts can be loosened with a spanner wrench (**Figure 10**) or with a punch and hammer (**Figure 11**).

CAUTION
Do not heat the ringnut in order to remove it as the heat would remove the temper from the axle. If you are unable to remove the ringnut, have a professional mechanic do it for you.

7. Remove the rear brake caliper as described in Chapter Eleven.

NOTE
Mark the axle's left or right side before removing it in Step 8. The axle should be installed so that it operates in its original installed position.

8. Tap the axle out of the bearing holder from the right-hand side. See **Figure 18**.

Inspection

1. Inspect the axle for signs of fatigue, fractures or damage. Inspect all splines for wear or damage.
2. Check the axle bearing surfaces for wear or scoring marks. Replace the axle if damage or wear is apparent.
3. Check the hole at each end of the axle where the cotter pin fits in. Make sure there are no fractures or cracks leading out toward the end of the axle. If any are found, replace the axle.
4. Check the axle runout. Use V-blocks and a dial indicator as shown in **Figure 14**. If the runout is 1.5 mm (0.06 in.) or greater the axle must be replaced.
5. Inspect the brake components as described in Chapter Eleven.

Installation

1. Grease all splines and bearing surfaces on the axle.
2. Install the axle. Approximately line up the bearing surfaces on the axle with the bearings in the bearing holder. **Figure 19** shows the axle installed.
3. Install the rear brake caliper as described in Chapter Eleven.
4. Adjust the rear brake as described in Chapter Three.
5. Apply the parking brake.
6. Install the inner ringnut and tighten it to specifications (**Tables 3-6**).
7. Apply Loctite to the outer ringnut and install it onto the axle. Hold the inner ringnut with a wrench to prevent it from turning. Then tighten the outer ringnut to specifications (**Tables 3-6**).
8. Install both wheel hubs (**Figure 3**).
9. Install the washer and castellated nut on each side of the axle. Tighten to specifications in **Tables 3-6** (**Figure 2**).
10. Install a *new* cotter pin and bend it over completely (**Figure 2**). Never reuse an old cotter pin as it may break and fall out.
11. Install the rear wheels as described in this chapter.
12. Install the trailer hitch.
13. Install the fenders and seat.

DRIVE CHAIN
(YTM200K, L, AND N)

Removal/Installation

Refer to **Figure 5** for this procedure.
1. Park the vehicle on level ground. Block the front wheel.
2. Remove the seat and fenders.

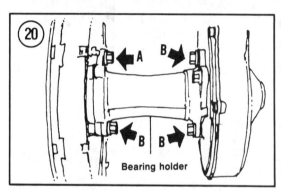

Bearing holder

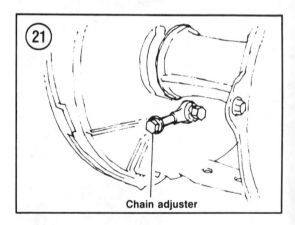

Chain adjuster

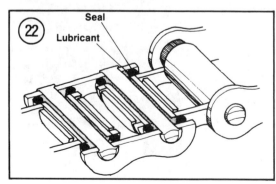

Seal
Lubricant

3. Remove the left-hand wheel as described in this chapter.

4. Remove the the drive sprocket cover.

5. Loosen the rear wheel hub bolts (**Figure 20**). Then referring to **Figure 21**, turn the chain adjuster bolt to loosen the drive chain as much as possible.

6. With the drive chain loosened all the way, attempt to work it off of the rear sprocket (**Figure 22**). Do not try to force the chain off. If the chain will not come off, perform Step 7.

7. Remove the drive chain as follows:

  a. Remove the bolts securing the driven sprocket to the sprocket boss and pull the sprocket and chain off the boss (**Figure 8**).

  b. Slide the drive chain off both sprockets and remove from the axle.

8. Installation is the reverse of these steps, noting the following.

9. Attach the drive chain to the front and rear sprockets and fit the driven sprocket onto the driven sprocket boss. Turn the axle by hand to align the holes in the boss with the sprocket holes. Install the sprocket bolts with lockwashers and tighten securely. Bend over the lockwasher tabs to lock the sprocket bolts.

10. Clean out the drive chain side cover. Remove any accumulation of drive chain lubricant, sand, gravel and other trail dirt.

11. Install the drive chain side cover.

12. Install the rear wheel as described in this chapter.

13. Adjust the drive chain as described in Chapter Three.

14. Adjust the rear brake as described in Chapter Three.

Cleaning/Inspection/Lubrication

1. Remove the drive chain as described in this chapter.

NOTE
*Special care must be observed when servicing and cleaning the drive chain on all models. The drive chain has small rubber O-rings fitted between the side plates (**Figure 23**). The O-rings can be damaged by steam cleaning and high-pressure car washes. Clean the drive chain with kerosene (do not use any other solvent) and wipe it dry.*

2. Immerse the chain in a pan of kerosene and allow it to soak for about half an hour. Move it around and flex it during this period so that the dirt

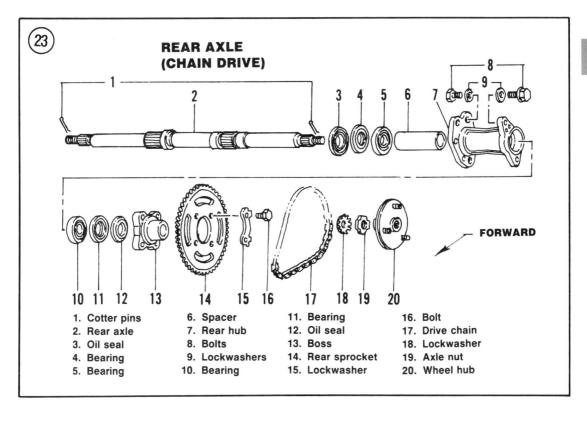

23 **REAR AXLE (CHAIN DRIVE)**

FORWARD

1. Cotter pins	6. Spacer	11. Bearing	16. Bolt
2. Rear axle	7. Rear hub	12. Oil seal	17. Drive chain
3. Oil seal	8. Bolts	13. Boss	18. Lockwasher
4. Bearing	9. Lockwashers	14. Rear sprocket	19. Axle nut
5. Bearing	10. Bearing	15. Lockwasher	20. Wheel hub

10

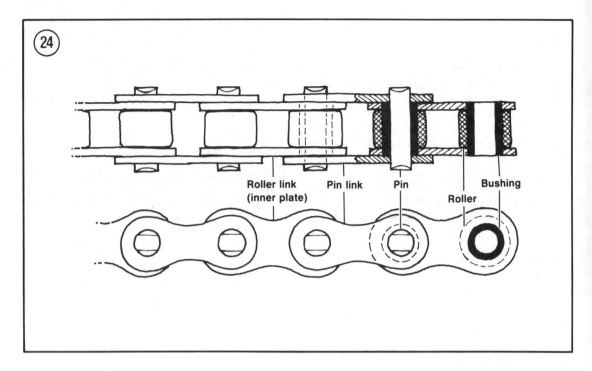

Roller link (inner plate)   Pin link   Pin   Bushing   Roller

between the links, pins and rollers (**Figure 24**) may work its way out.

3. Scrub the rollers and side plates with a stiff brush and rinse away loosened dirt. Rinse it a couple of times to make sure all dirt and grit are washed out. Hang up the chain and allow it to drip dry.

4. After cleaning the chain, examine it carefully for wear or damage. If any signs are visible, replace the chain.

> *NOTE*
> *Always check both sprockets every time the chain is removed. If any wear is visible on the teeth, replace the sprockets and chain (**Figure 25**). Never install a new chain over worn sprockets or a worn chain over new sprockets.*

5. The chain on these models should be lubricated only with SAE 20W-50 weight motor oil. Do not use any other type of lubricant as it may damage the O-rings.

6. Reinstall the chain as described in this chapter.

DRIVEN SPROCKET (CHAIN DRIVE)

Removal/Inspection/Installation

1. Remove the driven sprocket as described under *Rear Axle Removal* in this chapter.

2. Inspect the teeth on the sprocket. If the teeth are visibly worn, replace the sprocket.

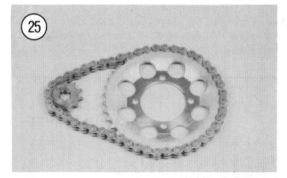

NOTE
If the driven sprocket is worn or damaged and must be replaced, also inspect the drive chain and drive sprocket for damage. Never replace just one of these 3 components without a thorough inspection of all the rest. If one is replaced, the other 2 should also be replaced or the new component will wear out prematurely.

3. Install the driven sprocket as described under *Rear Axle Installation* in this chapter.

TIRE CHANGING AND TIRE REPAIRS

Service the rear tire in the same manner as the front tire. See Chapter Eight.

REAR SHOCK ABSORBER (YTM225 AND YFM200DXS)

Adjustment

Refer to Chapter Three for complete shock adjustment procedures.

Removal

1. Park the vehicle on level ground. Block the front wheel.

2. Remove the seat and fender assembly.

3. Remove the rear wheels as described in this chapter.

4. Remove the cotter pin from the lower shock absorber pivot bolt (**Figure 26**). Then remove the washers and pivot pin.

5. Lift the shock up slightly and remove the thrust covers from both sides of the shock (**Figure 27**).

6. Remove the upper shock absorber mounting bolt (**Figure 28**).

7. Lift the rear of the shock away from the swing arm. Then remove it through the rear of the frame (**Figure 29**), making sure not to damage the shock body.

8. Remove the 2 upper shock bushings (**Figure 30**).

9. Installation is the reverse of these steps, noting the following.

10

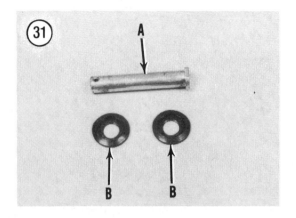

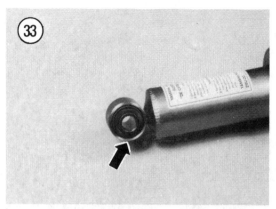

10. Apply a coat of molybdenum disulfide grease to the upper bushings (**Figure 30**) and to the lower pivot bolt (A, **Figure 31**).

11. Make sure the 2 thrust covers (**Figure 27**) are installed in the lower shock bushings.

12. Install the upper bolt from the right-hand side (**Figure 28**).

13. Install the lower shock pivot shaft from the left-hand side.

14. Install a new pivot shaft cotter pin (**Figure 26**).

Inspection

> *WARNING*
> *The shock absorber body contains highly compressed nitrogen gas. Do not tamper with or attempt to open the damper unit. Do not place it near an open flame or other extreme heat. Do not dispose of the shock assembly yourself. Take it to a dealer where it can be deactivated and disposed of properly. Do not store a worn or damaged shock assembly.*

Service by the home mechanic is limited to removal and installation of the shock and adjustment (Chapter Three). Under no circumstances should you attempt to disassemble the shock absorber unit due to the high internal pressure of the nitrogen. See the warning label on the reservoir (**Figure 32**).

1. Check the upper and lower shock bushings (**Figure 33**) for wear or damage. If the bushings are worn, it is necessary to replace the shock absorber.

2. Check the shock body for dents, oil leakage or other damage. Make sure the damper rod is straight.

> *NOTE*
> *The shock cannot be rebuilt; it must be replaced as a unit.*

3. Check the thrust covers (B, **Figure 31**) for wear or damage. Replace them if necessary.

SWING ARM
(YTM225 AND YFM200DXS)

Removal/Installation

Refer to **Figure 34** for this procedure.

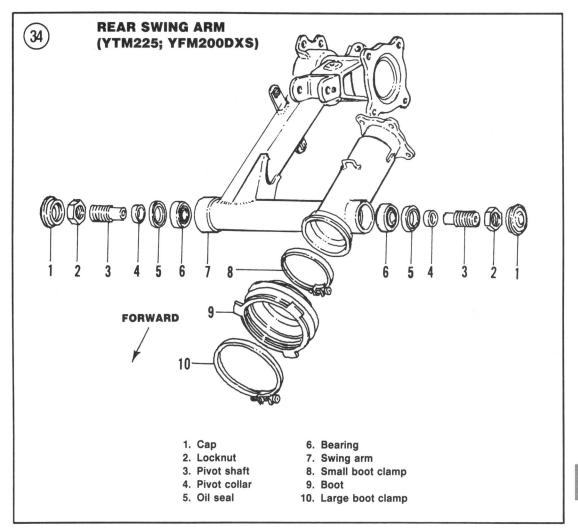

(34) **REAR SWING ARM
(YTM225; YFM200DXS)**

1   2   3   4   5   6   7   8   6   5   4   3   2   1

FORWARD

9

10

1. Cap
2. Locknut
3. Pivot shaft
4. Pivot collar
5. Oil seal
6. Bearing
7. Swing arm
8. Small boot clamp
9. Boot
10. Large boot clamp

10

(36)

1. Park the vehicle on level ground. Block the front wheel.

2. Remove the seat and fender.

3. Remove the rear axle as described in this chapter.

4. Remove the shock absorber as described in this chapter.

5. Grasp the rear end of the swing arm and try to move it from side to side in a horizontal arc. There should be no noticeable side play. If play is evident and the pivot bolt is tightened correctly, the bearings or pivot collars should be replaced.

6. Remove the final gear and drive shaft assemblies from the swing arm as described in this chapter.

7. Remove the pivot shaft caps (**Figure 35**) from the left and right sides.

8. Remove the locknut and pivot shafts from both sides. See **Figure 36**.

9. Pull back on the swing arm and remove the swing arm from the frame.

10. Inspect the swing arm as described in this chapter.

11. Installation is the reverse of these steps, noting the following.

12. Apply wheel bearing grease to the pivot shafts before installation.

13. Align the swing arm in the frame and install the left- and right-hand pivot shafts finger-tight only.

14. Tighten the left-hand pivot shaft (**Figure 37**) to 6 N•m (4.3 ft.-lb.).

15. Install the left-hand pivot shaft locknut. Then while holding the left-hand pivot shaft with an Allen wrench to prevent the shaft from turning, tighten the locknut to 100 N•m (72 ft.-lb).

16. Tighten the right-hand pivot shaft (**Figure 36**) to 6 N•m (4.3 ft.-lb.).

17. Install the right-hand pivot shaft locknut. Then while holding the right-hand pivot shaft with an Allen wrench to prevent the shaft from turning, tighten the locknut to 100 N•m (72 ft.-lb.).

18. Lift the swing arm up and down by hand to make sure the bearings are not binding. Loosen and retighten the swing arm pivot shafts and locknuts if necessary.

19. Install the pivot shaft caps (**Figure 35**).

20. Install the drive shaft and final gear assemblies as described in this chapter.

21. Install the rear axle as described in this chapter.

22. Tighten all remaining nuts and bolts to the specifications in **Table 4** and **Table 6**.

Disassembly/Inspection/Assembly

Refer to **Figure 34** for this procedure.

1. Remove the swing arm as described in this chapter.

2. Remove the pivot collar (4, **Figure 34**) and seal (5, **Figure 34**) from both pivot points.

3. Remove the tapered bearings from each side.

4. Clean all parts in solvent and dry thoroughly.

5. Yamaha does not provide service limit dimensions for the pivot collars. Inspect the inside and outside of all pivot collars for wear, abrasion or cracks. Remove rust from the pivot collars with a wire wheel chucked in a drill press or hand drill. Replace parts if necessary.

NOTE
*If the swing arm pivot collars are replaced, the bearings (6, **Figure 34**) at each end must be replaced at the same time.*

6. Wipe off any excess grease from the bearing races within each swing arm pivot area. Turn each bearing with your fingers; make sure they rotate smoothly. Check the rollers for evidence of wear, pitting or color change (reddish tint) indicating lack of lubrication.

NOTE
Always replace both bearings even though only one may be worn.

7. Replace the bearing races as follows:
  a. Purchase the new bearings. Place the new bearing races in a freezer. This will allow the races to shrink slightly for installation. Reinstall the roller bearings into their box until installation.
  b. Using a blind bearing puller, remove both bearing races.
  c. Clean the bearing race cavity in the swing arm of all dirt and grease.
  d. Secure the swing arm in a vise with soft jaws.
  e. Locate a socket or piece of pipe with an outside diameter of approximately 39.5 mm.
  f. Remove one of the bearing races from the freezer. Then align the race with the bearing area facing up and drive the race squarely into the swing arm until it bottoms on the bearing stop. A change in sound will let you know when the bearing has bottomed.
  g. Repeat Step f for the opposite bearing race.

8. Thoroughly grease the new tapered roller bearings and install them into the bearing races in the swing arm.

9. Install the new swing arm bearing seals by tapping them into the swing arm with a suitable size socket or piece of metal (solid) placed over the seal.

> *NOTE*
> *If you are using a socket to install the grease seals, place the bottom side of the socket against the seal. This will place a large amount of surface area over the seal to prevent damage. Use a brass hammer when driving the socket to prevent socket damage.*

10. Before installing the pivot collars, coat them with a good quality axle grease. Insert the pivot collars.

FINAL DRIVE UNIT AND DRIVE SHAFT

Removal

1. Drain the final drive unit oil as described in Chapter Three.
2. Remove the rear axle as described in this chapter.
3. Remove the nuts and washers securing the final drive/drive shaft unit to the swing arm or frame.
4. Pull the final drive unit and drive shaft straight back until it is disengaged from the splines on the universal joint.
5. Installation is the reverse of these steps, noting the following.
   a. Apply a light coat of molybdenum disulfide grease to the splines of the drive shaft and to the ring gear in the final drive unit.
   b. Tighten all nuts and bolts to the specifications in **Tables 3-6**.

Disassembly/Inspection/Reassembly

The final drive unit requires a considerable number of special Yamaha tools for disassembly and assembly. The price of all these tools could be more than the cost of most repairs to the final drive unit. Refer all service and adjustment to a Yamaha dealer.

REAR AXLE BEARING HOLDER

The rear axle bearing holder is attached to the frame at the rear or is an integral part of the swing arm. The bearing holder contains the rear axle bearings and grease seals. It is also part of the rear brake. If the axle bearings require replacement, it is best to leave the bearing holder attached in the frame or the swing arm on the vehicle, since the frame acts as a holding fixture.

Removal/Installation

Refer to **Figure 5**, **Figure 15** or **Figure 16** for this procedure.
1. Remove the rear axle as described in this chapter.
2. *Final drive models:* Remove the final drive unit as described in this chapter.
3. *Swing arm models:* The bearing holder on these models is an integral part of the swing arm. If necessary, remove the swing arm as described in this chapter.
4. Remove the bearing holder bolts, lockwashers and washers.
5. Pull the bearing holder out of the frame.
6. Install by reversing these removal steps, noting the following.
7. Tighten the bearing holder bolts to the specifications in **Tables 1-3**.
8. Adjust the brakes and drive chain (if equipped) as described in Chapter Three.

Bearing Removal

1. Remove the oil seal from each side of the bearing. Pry the seal out with a large screwdriver.
2. Thoroughly clean the inside of the bearing holder with solvent and dry with compressed air or a shop cloth.
3. Check the bearings carefully for any signs of damage. Turn the bearings by hand to make sure they operate without wear or damage. Check balls for evidence of wear, pitting or excessive heat (bluish tint). Replace bearings if necessary; always replace as a complete set.
4. To remove the left- and right-hand bearings and center spacer, insert a soft aluminum or brass drift into one side of the hub. Push the center spacer (if used) over to one side and place the drift on the inner race of the opposite bearing. Tap the bearing out of the hub with a hammer, working around the perimeter of the inner race.

> *NOTE*
> *Tapping the bearing on its inner race destroys the bearing. Bearings removed by this method must be replaced.*

5. Remove that bearing and the center spacer.
6. Repeat Step 4 for the opposite bearing.

Bearing Installation

1. On non-sealed bearings, pack the bearings with a good quality bearing grease. Work the grease between the balls thoroughly. Turn the bearings by

hand a couple of times to make sure the grease is distributed evenly inside the bearing.

2. Pack the bearing holder and the center spacer with multipurpose grease.

CAUTION
Install the bearings with the sealed side facing out. During installation, tap the bearings squarely into place and tap on the outer race only. Use a socket that matches the outer race diameter. Do

not tap on the inner race or the bearing may be damaged. Be sure that the bearings are completely seated.

3. Install the left-hand bearing.

4. Install the center spacer (if used) and the right-hand bearing.

5. Apply a light coat of multipurpose grease to the grease seals and install one on each side of the bearing holder.

6. Install the rear axle as described in this chapter.

Table 1 REAR SUSPENSION SPECIFICATIONS—YTM200 AND YTM225

Drive chain size (number of links)	
YTM200K, L, N	DID520 (60)
Rear shock spring	
Free length	
YTM225DXK, DXL	201 mm (7.91 in.)
YTM225DRN, DRS	201 mm (7.91 in.)
Installed length	
YTM225DXK, DXL	196 mm (7.72 in.)
YTM225DRN, DRS	196 mm (7.72 in.)

Table 2 TIGHTENING TORQUES—YTM200K, L, N

	N•m	ft.-lb.
Rear axle shaft		
Nut	130	94
Ring nut	140	100
Sprocket nut	45	32
Rear hub and frame		
Left-upper bolt	60	43
All other bolts	45	32

Table 3 TIGHTENING TORQUES—YTM200EK, EL; YTM200ERN

	N•m	ft.-lb.
Rear axle		
Ring nuts	100	72
Hex nuts		
Nut flush with axle	210	150
Nut not flush with axle	145	105
Rear hub and frame bolts	50	36
Final gear housing and frame bolt		
YTM200EK, EL	45	32
Rear wheel hub and final gear		
housing bolt	23	17

Table 4 TIGHTENING TORQUES—
YTM225DXK, DXL, DXN; YTM225DRN; YTM225DRS

	N·m	ft.-lb.
Rear axle shaft		
YTM225DRS	100	72
All other models		
Hex nut	130	94
Ring nut	100	72
Final gear housing and swing arm nut	23	17
Bearing retainer	100	72
Ring gear bearing housing and final gear housing bolt		
M8	23	17
M10	45	32
Rear wheel hub and final gear housing bolt	45	32
Pivot shaft		
Screw	6	4.3
Locknut	100	72
Shock absorber bolt	25	18

Table 5 TIGHTENING TORQUES—YFM200N

	N·m	ft.-lb.
Rear axle nut	100	72
Rear wheel nut	45	32
Rear wheel hub bolt	50	36
Final gear to housing stay bolt	50	36
Housing stay to frame bolt	50	36
Rear wheel hub and final gear housing bolt		
M8	23	17
M10	23	17

10

Table 6 TIGHTENING TORQUES—YFM200DXS

	N·m	ft.-lb.
Rear axle nut	120	85
Rear axle ring nut	See text	
Rear wheel panel and wheel collar bolt	43	31
Caliper and rear arm nut	50	36
Bearing housing and swing arm bolt	45	32
Rear gear housing and swing arm bolt	23	17
Rear shock bolt	25	18
Pivot shaft	See text	

CHAPTER ELEVEN

BRAKES

All models are equipped with front single-leading shoe drum brakes (**Figure 1**) and rear mechanical disc brakes.

All models are equipped with a parking brake. This uses the rear brake and is activated by a lever (**Figure 2**) on the left-hand side of the handlebar. By pulling the brake lever on all the way and then flipping the lock into position, the rear brake will be held on.

Lever and pedal free play must be maintained on both brakes to minimize brake drag and premature brake wear and maximize braking effectiveness. Refer to Chapter Three for complete adjustment procedures.

All brake cables must be inspected and replaced periodically as they will stretch with use until they can no longer be properly adjusted.

Table 1 and **Table 2** list brake specifications and tightening torques. **Table 1** and **Table 2** are at the end of the chapter.

FRONT DRUM BRAKE

Disassembly

Refer to **Figure 3** (YTM200 and YTM225) or **Figure 4** (YFM200DXS) for this procedure.
1A. *YTM200 and YTM225:* Perform the following:

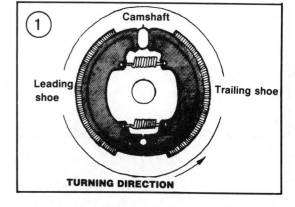

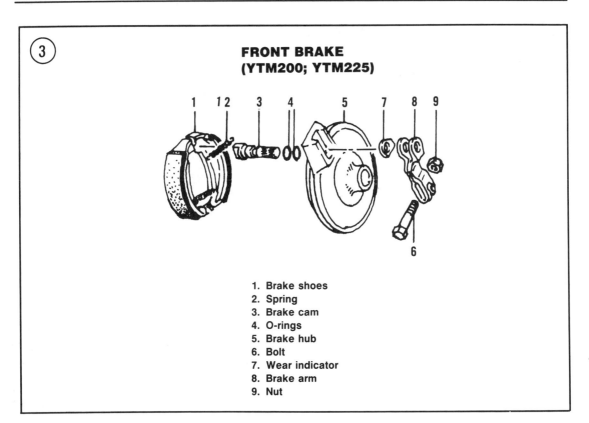

**FRONT BRAKE
(YTM200; YTM225)**

1. Brake shoes
2. Spring
3. Brake cam
4. O-rings
5. Brake hub
6. Bolt
7. Wear indicator
8. Brake arm
9. Nut

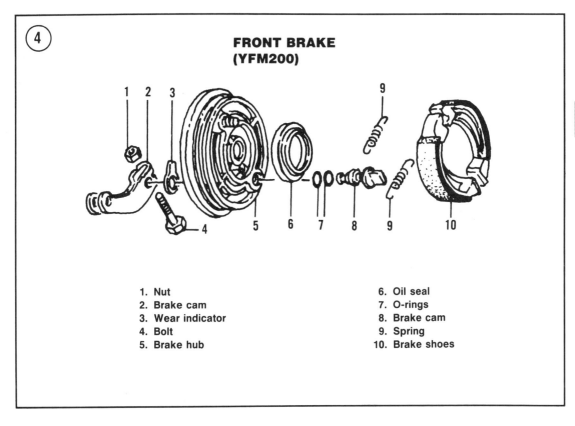

**FRONT BRAKE
(YFM200)**

1. Nut
2. Brake cam
3. Wear indicator
4. Bolt
5. Brake hub
6. Oil seal
7. O-rings
8. Brake cam
9. Spring
10. Brake shoes

11

a. Loosen the front brake wingnut (**Figure 5**) and remove it.

b. Remove the cable guide .

c. Remove the spring (**Figure 3**).

d. Remove the front wheel (Chapter Eight).

e. Pull the brake assembly straight out of the brake drum. See **Figure 6**.

1B. *YFM200DXS:* Perform the following:

a. Remove the front wheel and hub.

b. Loosen the front brake wingnut (**Figure 7**) and remove it.

c. Remove the cable guide (A, **Figure 8**) and lower spring (B, **Figure 8**).

d. Remove the upper washer and spring (**Figure 9**).

e. Remove the circlip (**Figure 10**) and remove the brake cable (**Figure 11**) from the backing plate.

f. Remove the backing plate (**Figure 12**).

g. If necessary, repeat for the opposite side.

2. Mark the shoes (**Figure 13**) as either left or right so they may be reinstalled in the same position.

> *NOTE*
> *Before removing the brake shoe assembly in Step 3, place a clean shop rag on the linings to protect them from oil and grease during removal.*

3. Remove the brake shoe assembly, including the return springs, from the backing plate as shown in **Figure 14**.

4. Remove the return springs (**Figure 15**) and separate the shoes.

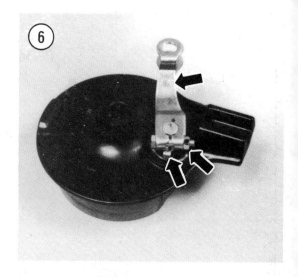

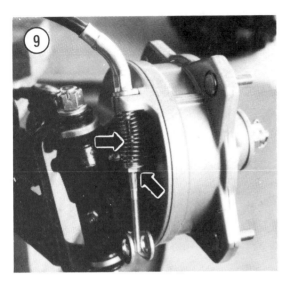

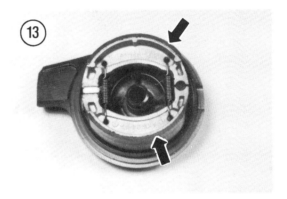

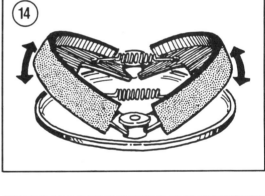

11

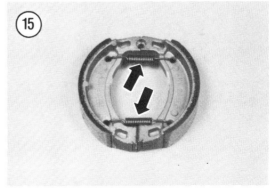

5. Refer to **Figure 16**. Loosen the bolt (A) securing the brake lever to the cam. Remove the lever (B) and wear indicator (C). Remove the camshaft (**Figure 17**) from the opposite side.

Inspection

1. Thoroughly clean and dry all parts except the linings.

2. Check the contact surface of the drum for scoring. See A, **Figure 18** or A, **Figure 19**. If there are grooves deep enough to snag a fingernail, the drum should be replaced and new shoes fitted. This type of wear can be avoided to a great extent if the brakes are disassembled and thoroughly cleaned after riding the vehicle in water, mud or deep sand.

3. If oil or grease is on the drum surface, clean it off with a clean rag soaked in lacquer thinner—do not use any solvent that may leave an oil residue.

> *NOTE*
> *Check the front wheel hub bearing oil seal B, **Figure 18** or B, **Figure 19** for signs of leakage or damage. If the seal is leaking, replace it as described in Chapter Eight or Chapter Nine under **Front Hub**. Grease leakage from this seal can work its way onto the brake shoes, causing brake fade.*

4. Use vernier calipers (**Figure 20**) and measure the brake drum inside diameter. The drum should be replaced if the diameter it too large (**Table 1**).

5. Use vernier calipers (**Figure 21**) and measure the thickness of each brake shoe lining. They should be replaced if lining thickness is less than specified (**Table 1**).

> *NOTE*
> *In Step 5, measure the thickness of the brake shoe lining only. Do not include the shoe's aluminum casting.*

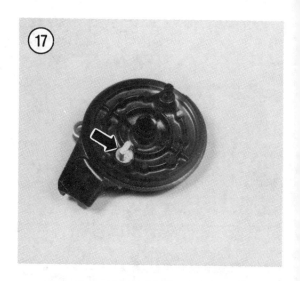

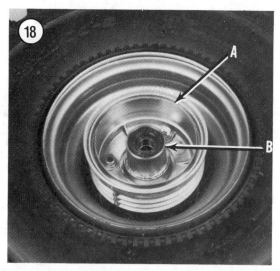

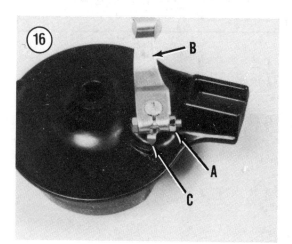

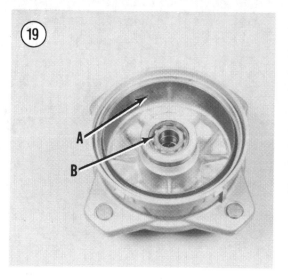

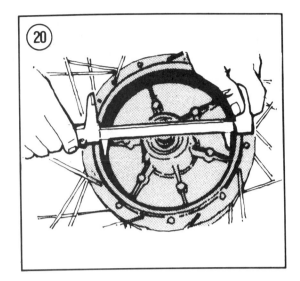

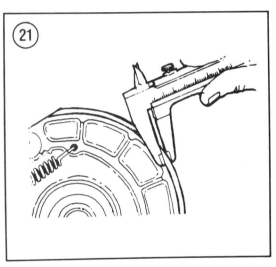

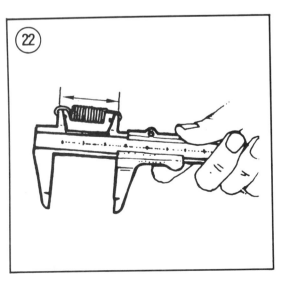

6. Inspect the linings for embedded foreign material. Dirt can be removed with a stiff wire brush. Check for traces of oil or grease. If the linings are contaminated, they must be replaced as a set.

7. Inspect the cam lobe and pivot pin area of the shaft for wear and corrosion. Minor roughness can be removed with fine emery cloth.

8. Check the brake shoe return springs for wear or distortion with vernier calipers (**Figure 22**). Refer to **Table 1** for specifications. If they are stretched, they will not fully retract the brake shoes from the drum, resulting in a power-robbing drag on the drums and premature wear of the linings. Replace as necessary and always replace as a pair.

9. *YFM200:* Check the brake backing plate seal (**Figure 23**) for wear or damage. Replace if necessary.

Assembly

1. Assemble the brake by reversing the disassembly steps, noting the following.

2. Grease the camshaft and anchor posts with a light coat of molybdenum disulfide grease; avoid getting any grease on the brake plate where the linings come in contact with it.

3. Hold the brake shoes in a "V" formation with the return springs attached (**Figure 14**) and snap them in place on the brake backing plate. Make sure they are firmly seated on it and that the springs are positioned correctly. See **Figure 15**.

4. When installing the brake arm onto the brake camshaft, align the punch marks on the brake lever and housing and tighten the bolt securely.

5. Insert the brake panel assembly into the brake drum.

11

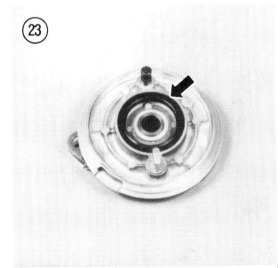

6. Install the front wheel as described in Chapter Eight or Chapter Nine.

7. Adjust the rear brake as described in Chapter Three.

REAR DISC BRAKE

This section describes service for the rear brake pads, brake caliper and brake disc.

Removal/Disassembly

1. Remove the right rear wheel as described in Chapter Ten.

2. Release the parking brake.

3. Remove the cotter pin and castellated nut securing the right-hand rear hub (**Figure 24**). Remove the lockwasher and slide the hub (**Figure 25**) off the axle.

4. Disconnect the 2 brake cables, guides and springs at the brake arm (**Figure 26**).

5. Remove the 2 nuts (A, **Figure 27**) and remove the brake cable guide (B, **Figure 27**).

6. Remove the remaining nut and remove the brake arm (**Figure 28**).

7. Slide the outer brake cover (**Figure 29**) away from the brake and off the axle.

8. Remove the outer brake pad (**Figure 30**).

9. Remove the outer brake caliper half (**Figure 31**).

10. Remove the 2 inner brake caliper bolts (**Figure 32**) and remove the inner brake caliper half (**Figure 33**) and brake pad (**Figure 34**).

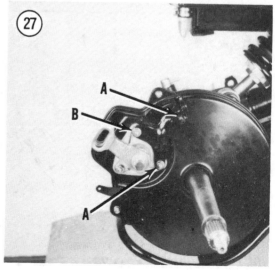

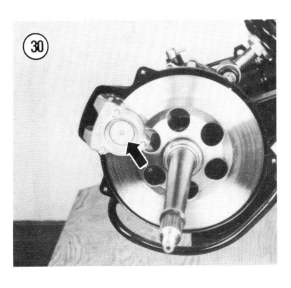

11

11. Slide the brake disc (**Figure 35**) off of the axle.
12. Remove the inner brake cover screws and slide the cover (**Figure 36**) off of the axle.

Inspection

1. Thoroughly clean and dry all parts except the brake pads.
2. Inspect the brake disc splines (**Figure 37**). Then measure the thickness around the disc at several locations with vernier calipers (**Figure 38**). The disc must be replaced if the thickness at any point is less than minimum (**Table 1**).
3. Referring to **Figure 39**, work the brake arm back and forth and check its operation. It should operate smoothly and with no binding or hesitation. Replace worn parts as necessary.
4. Check the brake arm push pad (**Figure 40**). It should show no signs of dirt, rust or damage. Clean or replace the pad as required.
5. Check the brake pad's friction surfaces (**Figure 41**) for oil or dirt buildup. Dirt can be removed with fine grade sandpaper but oil- or grease-contaminated pads must be replaced as a set.
6. Use vernier calipers and measure the thickness of the brake pads as shown in **Figure 42**. They should be replaced as a set if any one pad is worn to the service limit (**Table 1**).

> *NOTE*
> *When measuring the brake pads in Step 7, measure the pad lining material only. Do not include the pad backing plate.*

7. Inspect the inner brake caliper bore (**Figure 43**) for wear or damage. Also check the studs for thread damage. Replace the caliper if necessary.

Assembly/Installation

1. Install the inner brake cover (**Figure 36**) and secure with it with the screws.
2. Install the brake disc (**Figure 35**) partway onto the axle.
3. Install the inner brake pad (**Figure 34**) into the inner caliper half. Then align the cutout in the caliper with the brake disc (**Figure 33**) and install the caliper half over the brake disc. Align the caliper with the brake cover.
4. Insert the 2 brake caliper bolts through the cover and insert into the brake caliper (**Figure 32**). Do not tighten the bolts at this time.
5. Install the outer brake cover (**Figure 29**) and screws.

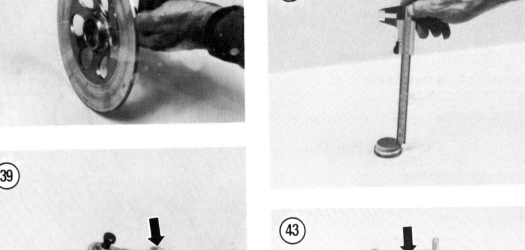

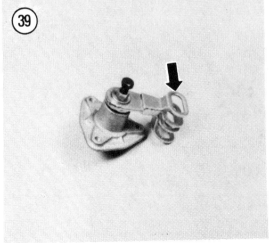

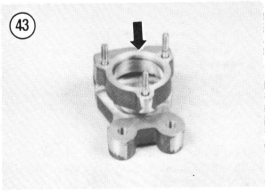

11

6. Install the outer brake pad into the outer caliper half and install the brake arm assembly (**Figure 28**). Install the lower nut (**Figure 28**) with the washer.

7. Install the brake cable guide (B, **Figure 27**) and the 2 nuts (A, **Figure 27**).

8. Tighten the 2 inner brake caliper bolts (**Figure 32**) to the specifications in **Table 2**. Tighten the outer brake caliper nuts securely.

9. Attach the brake cables, guides and springs (**Figure 26**).

10. Adjust the brakes as described in Chapter Three.

11. Install the rear hub and wheel as described in Chapter Ten.

BRAKE CABLES

Brake cable adjustment should be checked periodically as the cable stretches with use and increases brake lever free play. Free play is the distance that the brake lever travels between the released position and the point when the brake linings come in contact with the drum or disc.

If the brake adjustment as described in Chapter Three can no longer be achieved, the cable (or brake shoes or pads) must be replaced.

> *WARNING*
> *Improperly installed brake cables can cause loss of brake or brake lockup. If you are unsure as to how a cable is correctly routed or installed, ask your Yamaha dealer.*

Front Brake Cable Replacement (YTM200 and YTM225)

1. Park the vehicle on level ground. Block the wheels.

2. At the brake assembly, completely unscrew the adjusting wingnut (A, **Figure 44**).

3. Pull the brake cable out of the pivot pin in the brake lever.

4. Remove the cable guide screws. See B, **Figure 44** and **Figure 45**.

> *NOTE*
> *Before removing any cable, make a drawing (or take a Polaroid picture) of the cable routing through the frame. It is very easy to forget once it has been removed. Replace it exactly as it was, avoiding any sharp turns.*

5. Loosen the knurled locknut securing the cable adjuster on the handlebar lever (**Figure 46**). Screw in the adjuster as far as possible to provide maximum cable slack.

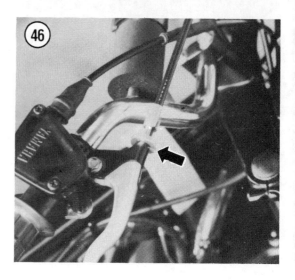

6. Disconnect the cable from the adjuster.

7. Pull the cable through the cable guides (**Figure 47**) and remove the cable.

8. Install by reversing these removal steps, noting the following:

  a. Lubricate the new cable as described in Chapter Three.

  b. Adjust the brake as described in Chapter Three.

  c. Make sure the cable is routed with no kinks or sharp bends.

Front Brake Cable Replacement (YFM200)

The brake cable assembly on these models is composed of 3 separate cables. The top cable connected to the left-hand brake lever connects to a junction box at the front of the vehicle. From the junction box, left- and right-hand cables are routed to their respective brake assemblies at the front wheels. The top cable is attached to the 2 lower cables by a slide mechanism. When the front brake lever is applied, the top cable pulls evenly on the slide mechanism to activate the 2 lower cables.

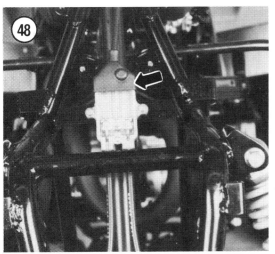

NOTE
Prior to removing any cable, make a drawing (or take a Polaroid picture) of the cable routing through the frame. It is very easy to forget once it has been removed. Replace it exactly as it was, avoiding any sharp turns.

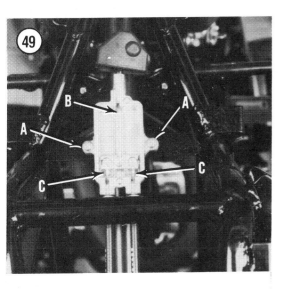

Top cable

1. Park the vehicle on level ground. Block the wheels.

2. Remove the front fender.

3. Loosen the knurled locknut securing the cable adjuster on the handlebar lever (**Figure 46**). Screw in the adjuster as far as possible to provide maximum cable slack.

4. Disconnect the cable at the adjuster.

5. At the junction box, perform the following:

  a. Slide the rubber cover up (**Figure 48**).

  b. Remove the cover screws (A, **Figure 49**) and remove the cover.

  c. Lift the top cable up and disconnect the cable end from the junction box slide mechanism (B, **Figure 49**).

11

6. Remove the upper brake cable (**Figure 50**).

7. Installation is the reverse of these steps, noting the following.

8. Lubricate the new cable as described in Chapter Three.

9. Make sure the cable is routed correctly with no sharp bends. See **Figure 50** and **Figure 51**.

10. Make sure the upper cable is securely connected to the junction box.

11. Tighten the junction box cover screws securely. Then pull the cover over the box (**Figure 48**).

12. Adjust the brake as described in Chapter Three.

Lower cables

1. Park the vehicle on level ground and block the rear wheels.

2. Perform the following:
   a. Loosen the front brake wingnut (**Figure 52**) and remove it.
   b. Remove the cable guide (A, **Figure 53**) and lower spring (B, **Figure 53**).
   c. Remove the upper washer and spring (**Figure 54**).
   d. Remove the circlip (**Figure 55**) and remove the brake cable (**Figure 56**) from the backing plate.

3. At the junction box, perform the following:
   a. Slide the rubber cover up (**Figure 48**).
   b. Remove the cover screws (A, **Figure 49**) and remove the cover.
   c. Lift the bottom cables up and disconnect them from the junction block slide mechanism (C, **Figure 49**).

4. Remove the lower brake cables (**Figure 57**).

5. Installation is the reverse of these steps, noting the following.

6. Lubricate the new cables as described in Chapter Three.

7. Make sure the cables are routed correctly with no sharp bends. See **Figure 57** and **Figure 58**.

8. Make sure the lower cables are securely connected to the junction box slide mechanism.

9. Tighten the junction box cover screws securely. Then pull the cover over the box (**Figure 48**).

10. Adjust the brake as described in Chapter Three.

Rear Brake Cable Replacement

The rear brake is operated by the left-hand brake lever and the right-hand rear brake pedal. Both assemblies use individual cables.

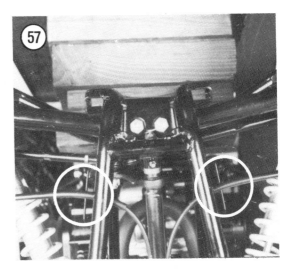

11

Hand brake lever cable

1. Park the vehicle on level ground and block the wheels so the vehicle will not roll in either direction.
2. Remove the seat and fenders.
3. Remove the fuel tank as described in Chapter Six.
4. Release the parking brake if set.
5. Loosen the knurled locknut securing the cable adjuster on the handlebar lever (**Figure 59**). Screw the adjuster in as far as possible to provide maximum cable slack.
6. Loosen the rear brake adjuster wingnut (A, **Figure 60**). Then remove the wingnut, cable guide and spring.
7. Disconnect the brake cable from the rear brake arm.
8. Pull the cable through the handlebar (**Figure 61**) and towards the rear of the vehicle. Then disconnect the cable from the cable guides. See **Figure 62** and **Figure 63**.
9. Remove the brake cable.

10. Installation is the reverse of these steps, noting the following.
11. Lubricate the new cable as described in Chapter Three.
12. Adjust the brake as described in Chapter Three.

Brake pedal cable

1. Loosen the rear brake adjuster wingnut (B, **Figure 60**). Then remove the wingnut, cable guide and spring.
2. Disconnect the brake cable from the rear brake arm.
3. Remove the rear cable return spring (C, **Figure 60**).
4. At the brake pedal, disconnect the return spring (A, **Figure 64**) and brake cable (B, **Figure 64**).
5. Remove the brake cable.
6. Installation is the reverse of these steps, noting the following.
7. Lubricate the new cable as described in Chapter Three.
8. Adjust the brake as described in Chapter Three.

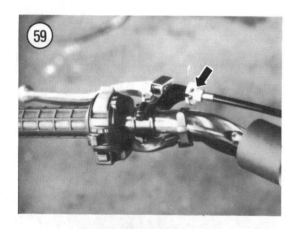

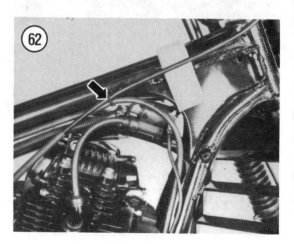

Table 1 BRAKE SPECIFICATIONS

Front drum brake	
Drum inside diameter	110 mm (4.33 in.
Wear limit	111 mm (4.37 in.)
Lining thickness	4.0 mm (0.16 in.)
Wear limit	2.0 mm (0.08 in.)
Brake shoe spring free length	34.5 mm (1.36 in.)
Rear disc brake	
Brake disc	
Outside diameter	224 mm (8.82 in.)
Thickness	4 mm (0.16 in.)
Wear limit	3.0 mm (0.12 in.)
Brake pad thickness	8.0 mm (0.31 in.)
Wear limit	
YTM225DRS	2.0 mm (0.079 in.)
All other models	1.5 mm (0.06 in.)

Table 2 BRAKE TIGHTENING TORQUES

	N·m	ft.-lb.
Rear brake caliper body bolt	45-50	32-36
Rear brake caliper nut	9	6.5
Brake pad adjuster locknut	16	11

11

INDEX

12

12

YFM200 DXS

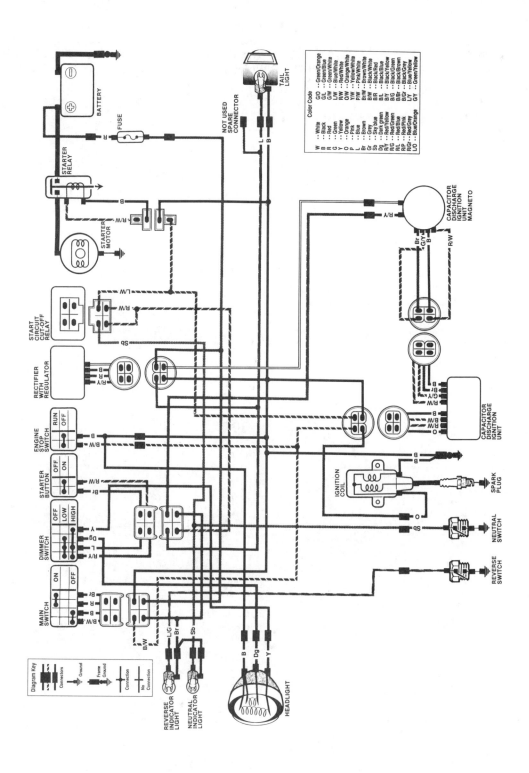

YTM225 ERN

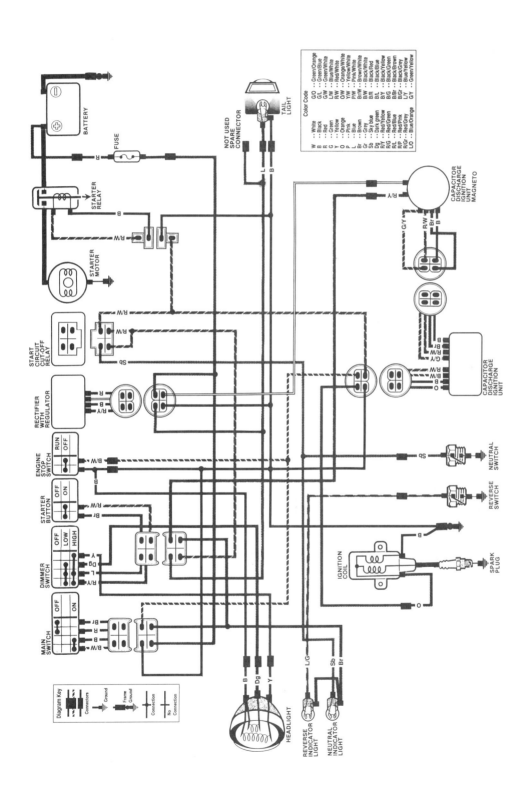

YTM200 K, L, N

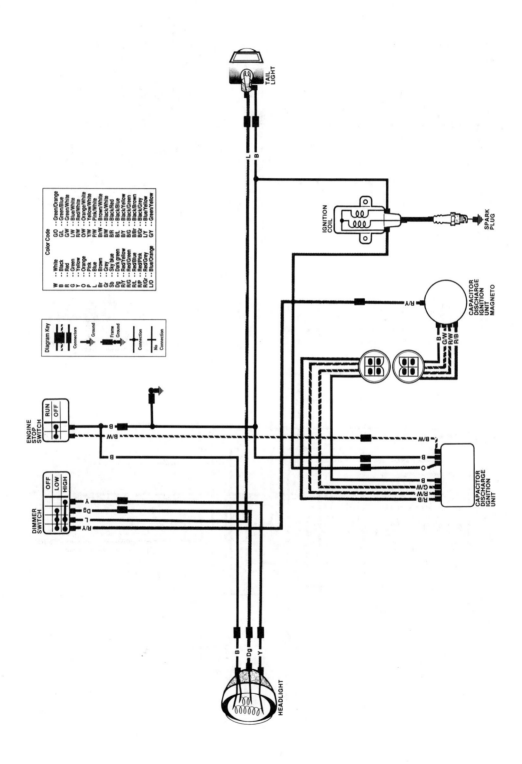

YTM200 EK, EL

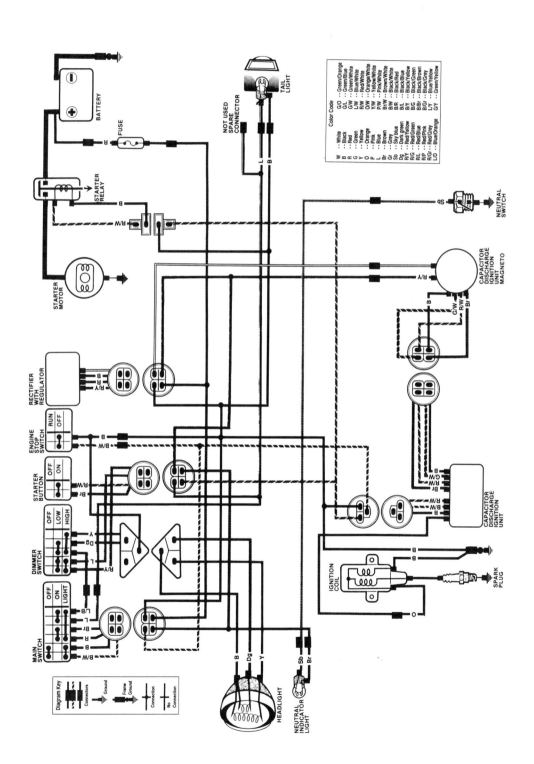

YTM225 DRN, DRS

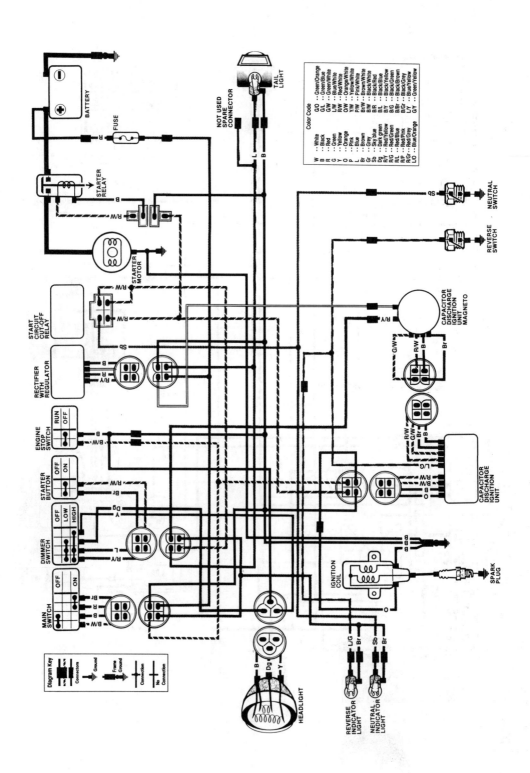

YTM225 DXK, DXL, DXN

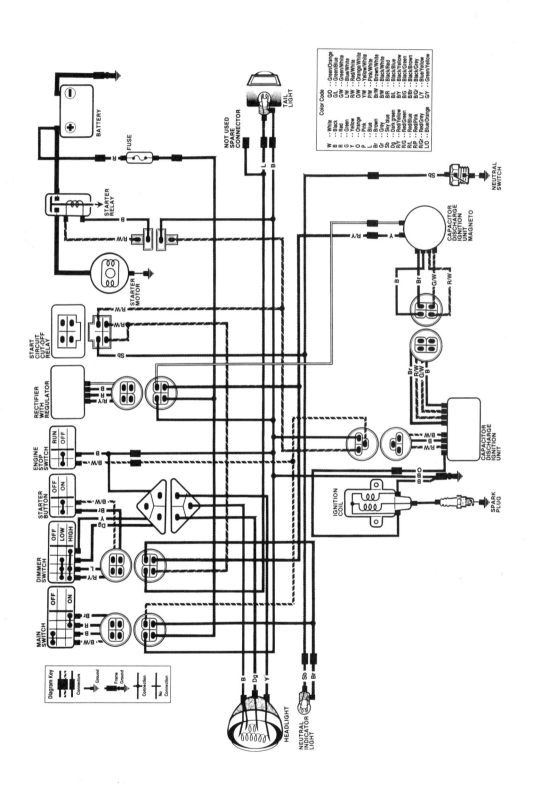

YTM225 ERN

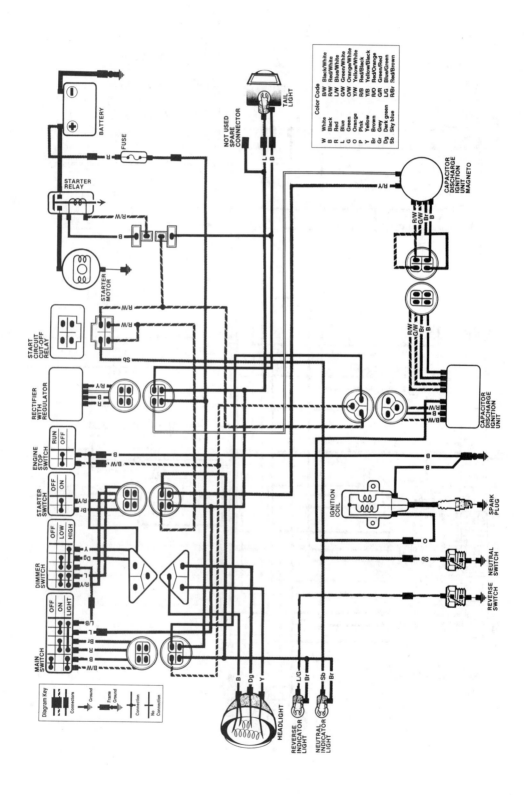

MAINTENANCE LOG

Date	Miles	Type of Service

BMW

M308	500 & 600 CC twins, 55-69
M502	BMW R-Series, 70-94
M500	BMW K-Series, 85-95
M503	R-850 & R-1100, 93-98

HARLEY-DAVIDSON

M419	Sportsters, 59-85
M428	Sportster Evolution, 86-90
M429-3	Sportster Evolution, 91-02
M418	Panheads, 48-65
M420	Shovelheads, 66-84
M421	FX/FL Softail Big-Twin Evolution, 84-94
M422	FLT/FXR Big-Twin Evolution, 84-94
M424	Dyna Glide, 91-95
M425	Dyna Glide Twin Cam, 99-01
M430	FLH/FLT 1999-2002

HONDA

ATVs

M316	Odyssey FL250, 77-84
M311	ATC, TRX & Fourtrax 70-125, 70-87
M433	Fourtrax 90 ATV, 93-00
M326	ATC185 & 200, 80-86
M347	ATC200X & Fourtrax 200SX, 86-88
M455	ATC250 & Fourtrax 200/250, 84-87
M342	ATC250R, 81-84
M348	TRX250R/Fourtrax 250R & ATC250R, 85-89
M456	TRX250X 1987-1988, 91-92; TRX300EX 93-96
M446	TRX250 Recon 1997-02
M346-3	TRX300/Fourtrax 300 & TRX300FW/Fourtrax 4x4, 88-00
M459	Fourtrax Foreman 95-98
M454	TRX400EX 1999-02

Singles

M310-13	50-110cc OHC Singles, 65-99
M315	100-350cc OHC, 69-82
M317	Elsinore, 125-250cc, 73-80
M442	CR60-125R Pro-Link, 81-88
M431-2	CR80R, 89-95, CR125R, 89-91
M435	CR80, 96-02
M457-2	CR125R & CR250R, 92-97
M443	CR250R-500R Pro-Link, 81-87
M432	CR250R & CR500R, 88-96
M437	CR250R, 97-01
M312-12	XL/XR75-100, 75-02
M318	XL/XR/TLR 125-200, 79-87
M328-2	XL/XR250, 78-00; XL/XR350R 83-85; XR200R, 84-85; XR250L, 91-96
M320	XR400R, 96-00
M339-6	XL/XR 500-650, 79-02

Twins

M321	125-200cc, 64-77
M322	250-350cc, 64-74
M323	250-360cc Twins, 74-77
M324-4	Rebel 250 & Twinstar, 78-87; Nighthawk 250, 91-97; Rebel 250, 96-97
M334	400-450cc, 78-87
M333	450 & 500cc, 65-76
M335	CX & GL500/650 Twins, 78-83
M344	VT500, 83-88
M313	VT700 & 750, 83-87
M460	VT1100C2 A.C.E. Shadow, 95-97
M440	Shadow 1100cc V-Twin, 85-96

Fours

M332	350-550cc 71-78
M345	CB550 & 650, 83-85
M336	CB650, 79-82
M341	CB750 SOHC, 69-78
M337	CB750 DOHC, 79-82
M436	CB750 Nighthawk, 91-93 & 95-99
M325	CB900, 1000 & 1100, 80-83
M439	Hurricane 600, 87-90
M441-2	CBR600, 91-98
M434	CBR900RR Fireblade, 93-98
M329	500cc V-Fours, 84-86
M438	Honda VFR800, 98-00
M349	700-1000 Interceptor, 83-85
M458-2	VFR700F-750F, 86-97
M327	700-1100cc V-Fours, 82-88
M340	GL1000 & 1100, 75-83
M504	GL1200, 84-87

Sixes

M505	GL1500 Gold Wing, 88-92
M506	GL1500 Gold Wing, 93-95
M462	GL1500C Valkyrie, 97-00

KAWASAKI

ATVs

M465	KLF220 Bayou, 88-95
M466-2	KLF300 Bayou, 86-98
M467	KLF400 Bayou, 93-99
M470	KEF300 Lakota, 95-99
M385	KSF250 Mojave, 87-00

Singles

M350-9	Rotary Valve 80-350cc, 66-01
M444	KX60-80, 83-90
M351	KDX200, 83-88
M447	KX125 & KX250, 82-91 KX500, 83-93
M472	KX125, 92-98
M473	KX250, 92-98

Twins

M355	KZ400, KZ/Z440, EN450 & EN500, 74-95
M360	EX500/GPZ500S, 87-93
M356-2	700-750 Vulcan, 85-01
M354	VN800 Vulcan 95-98
M357	VN1500 Vulcan 87-98
M471	VN1500 Vulcan Classic, 96-98

Fours

M449	KZ500/550 & ZX550, 79-85
M450	KZ, Z & ZX750, 80-85
M358	KZ650, 77-83
M359	900-1000cc Fours, 73-80
M451	1000 & 1100cc Fours, 81-85
M452-3	ZX500 & 600 Ninja, 85-97
M453-3	Ninja ZX900-1100 84-01
M468	ZX6 Ninja, 90-97
M469	ZX7 Ninja, 91-98
M453	900-1100 Ninja, 84-93

POLARIS

ATVs

M496	Polaris ATV, 85-95
M362	Polaris Magnum ATV, 96-98
M363	Scrambler 500, 4X4 97-00
M365	Sportsman/Xplorer, 96-00

SUZUKI

ATVs

M381	ALT/LT 125 & 185, 83-87
M475	LT230 & LT250, 85-90
M380	LT250R Quad Racer, 85-88
M343	LTF500F Quadrunner, 98-00
M483	Suzuki King Quad/ Quad Runner 250, 87-95

Singles

M371	RM50-400 Twin Shock, 75-81
M369	125-400cc 64-81
M379	RM125-500 Single Shock, 81-88
M476	DR250-350, 90-94
M384	LS650 Savage Single, 86-88
M386	RM80-250, 89-95

Twins

M372	GS400-450 Twins, 77-87
M481-3	VS700-800 Intruder, 85-02
M482	VS1400 Intruder, 87-98
M484-2	GS500E Twins, 89-00

Triple

M368	380-750cc, 72-77

Fours

M373	GS550, 77-86
M364	GS650, 81-83
M370	GS750 Fours, 77-82
M376	GS850-1100 Shaft Drive, 79-84
M378	GS1100 Chain Drive, 80-81
M383-3	Katana 600, 88-96 GSX-R750-1100, 86-87
M331	GSX-R600, 97-00
M478-2	GSX-R750, 88-92 GSX750F Katana, 89-96
M485	GSX-R750, 96-99
M338	GSF600 Bandit, 95-00

YAMAHA

ATVs

M394	YTM/YFM200 & 225, 83-86
M487-3	YFM350 Warrior, 87-02
M486-3	YFZ350 Banshee, 87-02
M488-3	Blaster ATV, 88-01
M489-2	Timberwolf ATV, 89-00
M490-2	YFM350 Moto-4 & Big Bear, 87-98
M493	YFM400FW Kodiak, 93-98

Singles

M492-2	PW50 & PW80, BW80 Big Wheel 80, 81-02
M410	80-175 Piston Port, 68-76
M415	250-400cc Piston Port, 68-76
M412	DT & MX 100-400, 77-83
M414	IT125-490, 76-86
M393	YZ50-80 Monoshock, 78-90
M413	YZ100-490 Monoshock, 76-84
M390	YZ125-250, 85-87 YZ490, 85-90
M391	YZ125-250, 88-93 WR250Z, 91-93
M497	YZ125, 94-99
M498	YZ250, 94-98 and WR250Z, 94-97
M491	YZ400F, YZ426F & WR400F, 98-00
M417	XT125-250, 80-84
M480-2	XT/TT 350, 85-96
M405	XT500 & TT500, 76-81
M416	XT/TT 600, 83-89

Twins

M403	650cc, 70-82
M395-9	XV535-1100 Virago, 81-99
M495	XVS650 V-Star, 98-00

Triple

M404	XS750 & 850, 77-81

Fours

M387	XJ550, XJ600 & FJ600, 81-92
M494	XJ600 Seca II, 92-98
M388	YX600 Radian & FZ600, 86-90
M396	FZR600, 89-93
M392	FZ700-750 & Fazer, 85-87
M411	XS1100 Fours, 78-81
M397	FJ1100 & 1200, 84-93

VINTAGE MOTORCYCLES

Clymer® Collection Series

M330	Vintage British Street Bikes, BSA, 500 & 650cc Unit Twins; Norton, 750 & 850cc Commandos; Triumph, 500-750cc Twins
M300	Vintage Dirt Bikes, V. 1 Bultaco, 125-370cc Singles; Montesa, 123-360cc Singles; Ossa, 125-250cc Singles
M301	Vintage Dirt Bikes, V. 2 CZ, 125-400cc Singles; Husqvarna, 125-450cc Singles; Maico, 250-501cc Singles; Hodaka, 90-125cc Singles
M305	Vintage Japanese Street Bikes Honda, 250 & 305cc Twins; Kawasaki, 250-750cc Triples; Kawasaki, 900 & 1000cc Fours